the Bar

Student Guide

SECOND EDITION

Ann Bulleid, Pam Rabone,
Caroline Ritchie, Tim Roberts

First published in 1993 by:
Stanley Thornes (Publishers) Ltd
Ellenborough House
Wellington Street
CHELTENHAM GL50 1YW
England

Second edition 1996

96 97 98 99 00 / 10 9 8 7 6 5 4 3 2 1

A catalogue record for this book
is available from the British Library.

ISBN 0 7487 2592 X

Acknowledgements

The authors and publishers gratefully acknowledge the help and advice of the following people in the preparation of this book: Jeffrey T. Clarke, Iain R. Loe, P.J. Ogie, John Shaw, Gerry Shurman, Jim Slavin and Keith Thomas.

Cover photograph courtesy of Bass Taverns Ltd.

Typeset by Columns Design Ltd, Reading
Printed and bound in Great Britain by Scotprint Ltd, Musselburgh

Contents

UNIT NG1

Maintain a safe and secure working environment

This unit covers:
ELEMENT 1: **Maintain personal health and hygiene**
ELEMENT 2: **Carry out procedures in the event of a fire**
ELEMENT 3: **Maintain a safe environment for customers, staff and visitors**
ELEMENT 4: **Maintain a secure environment for customers, staff and visitors**

ELEMENT 1: **Maintain personal health and hygiene**

What you need to do

- Ensure that you wear clean, smart and appropriate clothing, footwear and headgear.
- Ensure your hair is neat and tidy, and worn in line with operational requirements.
- Wear jewellery in line with operational requirements.
- Carry out your work in line with hygiene practices.
- Ensure cuts, grazes and wounds and any illness and infections are reported promptly to the appropriate person.
- Work in an organised and efficient manner in line with appropriate organisational procedures and legal requirements.

What you need to know

- Why it is important to comply with health and safety legislation.
- Where and from whom information on current health and safety legislation can be obtained.
- What general hygiene practices must be adhered to in your own working environment.
- Why correct headgear and footwear must be worn at all times.
- Why and to whom illness and infections should be reported.
- Why it is important to maintain good personal hygiene.

INTRODUCTION

When dealing with customers the image you project can say a lot about the way the company operates. People are more likely to use a bar if they have confidence in the way the staff take care of their appearance and follow good hygiene practice when dealing with food and drink.

Besides looking good, everyone involved in the service of food and drink has a duty under the Food Hygiene Regulations to protect the food from risk of infection through careful storage and handling. You will find this covered in more detail in Units 2ND11, 2ND22, 1ND1.

As someone involved in the service of food and drink there are a number of points you need to be aware of, about the way you dress, your habits and your cleanliness that can greatly help to reduce any risk of food poisoning to yourself, your colleagues and your customers, and will increase customers' confidence in their visit to the operation in which you work.

Take care of your appearance and look clean and tidy

In food areas in particular there are legal requirements laid down which influence all aspects of the way you work.

FOOD HYGIENE REGULATIONS

The Food Hygiene Regulations, particularly those related to people involved in the preparation and service of food and drink, have identified the main risk areas and included them in the appropriate legislation known as the *Food Hygiene (General) Regulations 1970*.

This legislation has been amended and updated by the *Food Safety Act 1990*. The features contained within the 1970 regulations are retained within this new Act and have been amended, where necessary, to reflect the tighter regulations contained within the new Act. The new Food Safety Act came about as a response to genuine public concern about the risks associated with food preparation and production and the increase in the number of incidents of food-related illnesses.

The Food Safety Act has been developed to take account and to impact on every stage of the food chain from its source to its presentation and consumption by the customer. This means there needs to be even more care and attention when dealing with the service of food and drink. The Act has increased the scope and impact of penalties and includes the following main provisions:

● it is now an offence to supply food that fails to comply with food safety requirements
● powers of enforcement, including detention and seizure of food, are strengthened
● training in basic food hygiene is required for all food handlers
● registration is required of all food premises
● Environmental Health Officers are empowered to issue emergency Prohibition Notices to force caterers to stop using the food premises or equipment immediately.

MEMORY JOGGER

What are the main provisions of the Food Safety Act 1990?

Complying with legislation

The impact on an establishment which contravenes hygiene regulations can be significant and could lead to a loss or even closure of the business. As an employee working within an establishment, you have a responsibility to comply with the regulations, to carry out your work to the standards expected and to ensure you attend any training in basic food handling you are required to.

Environmental Health Officers (EHOs) are responsible for enforcing the regulations and have a number of powers which include:
● being able to enter food premises to investigate possible offences
● inspecting food and, where necessary, detaining suspect food or seizing it to be condemned
● asking for information and gaining assistance.

EHOs also have the power to issue Improvement Notices if they feel there is a potential risk to the public. They may also, where it is felt there has been a breach of the legislation, impose a Prohibition Order which closes all or part of the premises.

The Food Safety Act has increased the maximum penalties available to the courts and these include:
● up to two years imprisonment for offenders or the imposition of unlimited fines (in Crown Courts)
● up to £2000 per offence and a prison sentence of up to six months (through a Magistrates Court) – up to a maximum of £20 000.

There are also penalties for obstructing an Enforcement Officer.

Complying with the legislation is important as the fines may not just relate to an employer, but can also affect an employee who contravenes and fails to demonstrate hygienic working practices.

Finding out about current legislation

When you are working in an establishment, you should be able to find out about the food hygiene legislation through your manager or supervisor. There should be information and copies of the legislation available on the premises in which you work, so it is important you find out where this is kept and make use of it. You will also find out further information through the training sessions your manager or supervisor will organise for you.

The library is a good source of information on this subject, as well as keeping up to date through trade magazines, newspapers, etc. You will also find the local Environmental Health Office will be able to supply information should you need it.

Do this

✔

1 Find out where the establishment displays food hygiene information.
2 Look out for new hygiene information related to your work in magazines and newspapers.

Your responsibilities under the hygiene regulations

The responsibilities of food handlers are clearly detailed in the legislation and have formed the basis for the guidelines you will follow if you are involved in the preparation or the service of food and drink.

It is stated that food handlers must:
● protect food from risk of infection

- wear suitable protective clothing
- wash hands after visiting the toilet
- not smoke, spit or take snuff in food rooms
- cover cuts or wounds with clean washable dressing
- report illness or contact with illness.

Much of the guidance for those involved in the service of food and drink in the bar is aimed at reducing the risk of bacterial food poisoning. By protecting the food from people through the wearing of a uniform or protective clothing and by ensuring that staff follow some basic guidelines for good personal hygiene, the risks are greatly reduced.

Bacteria such as Staphylococcus is naturally found on the human body, particularly in the ears, nose, throat and on the hands.

Other bacteria can be carried in the intestines and can contaminate food through poor personal hygiene, for example, using the toilet and not washing your hands afterwards.

Some bacteria, such as Salmonella, can be transferred from one source to another through clothes, dirty hands and equipment.

The number of reported cases of food poisoning has been increasing in recent years and many of the outbreaks can be traced to people as the main cause of the spread of infection.

SOURCES OF FOOD POISONING

If you are involved in the service of food and drink in the bar it is important to be aware of the most common sources of infection so that you can take practical measures to prevent poisoning outbreaks.

Chemical contamination can occur through accidents in the bar

There are three main sources of food poisoning:
- through naturally occurring poisons in, for example, poisonous plants such as toadstools, deadly nightshade
- through chemical or metal contamination, such as pesticides, cleaning fluids, mercury, lead, copper. Food poisoning from this source can be caused through the chemical being inadvertently spilt into the food or drink
- through bacteria germs, such as Salmonella, Staphylococcus, Clostridium perfringens. These are naturally present all around us and can easily contaminate food if you do not have good personal hygiene. Bacteria are microscopic and invisible to the naked eye, so it is difficult to know when you may be carrying bacteria which may cause food poisoning.

Bacterial food poisoning is by far the most common source of illness in humans.

PERSONAL HYGIENE

If you are involved in the service of food in the bar and you follow some basic principles of good personal hygiene, you can contribute to reducing the risk of infecting or cross-contaminating food and causing problems for your customers, colleagues and your employer.

Most of these principles are common sense and have a place in our daily life, but they need to be emphasised to ensure that you comply with your responsibilities under the food hygiene legislation.

The points are in no particular order of importance as each one is essential to you in demonstrating good hygiene practice at work.

Clean hands

Bacteria (germs) on your hands can be one of the main methods of spreading infection. Germs are easily transmitted by touching, say, some dirty bottles, then picking up plates on which to serve food. This moves the bacteria from one place to the other and could result in cross-contamination.

Or it may be that you have visited the toilet, returned to work without washing and now have bacteria on your hands. If you then return to the bar to, say, make sandwiches, bacteria present on your hands can be easily transmitted to the food while you are preparing it. By washing your hands in hot soapy water after visiting the toilet you will be greatly reducing the risk of infection.

So, when involved in serving food and drink in the bar, it is important to bear the following points in mind.

Washing your hands regularly prevents germs from contaminating food

Keep your hands clean
Wash your hands as often as necessary, but particularly:
- before starting work
- before handling food
- when moving between jobs
- after visiting the toilet
- after touching your nose, hair or ears
- after coughing and sneezing
- after smoking.

You will probably be aware that you are not allowed to smoke behind the bar, in storage areas or in food preparation areas. Some companies have gone as far as to ban smoking in their bars altogether. This rule about smoking is to improve the atmosphere of the pub, or eating area for the customers, and to reduce the risk of contamination. When smoking you can easily transmit germs from your mouth to your hands and then to items of food or equipment you may be handling. Ash may also be dropped into food and drink, making it unpleasant for the customer.

Use disposable tissues in food areas
Bacteria are present in ears, nose and throat, so it is very easy to transfer them to your hands by sneezing without using a tissue, coughing, spitting or picking your ears or nose. DON'T DO IT. If you need to use a tissue, use disposable ones and wash your hands immediately afterwards. Try to use a tissue away from service areas to avoid your customers' attention.

Keep fingernails short, free from polish and use a nail brush to clean them
Bacteria can gather under nails and spread when your hands touch food.

This is why it is a legal requirement that all hand wash-basins in food and bar areas are equipped with nailbrushes as well as soap and disposable paper towels or hot air dryers.

It is also a good idea to avoid wearing nail polish, even clear polish as it can hide the presence of bacteria under nails. Nail polish can also chip, fall into or onto food thereby contaminating it.

Wear only plain rings or jewellery
This will, of course, depend upon the particular operational standards where you work. Some establishments will limit their staff to wearing plain rings and very little jewellery, whereas others are more flexible and allow a more ornate style.

The amount of jewellery allowed can be influenced by the style of the operation and the type of customers who frequent the bar.

If you are involved in preparing or serving food it is important to remember that ornate jewellery can harbour bacteria and cause infection. Food particles can also damage the stones, or cause them to become loose and fall out. Rings can also be a safety hazard as they can become hot and burn you or you may trap them in equipment.

Do this

✔

1 Find out the standards for wearing jewellery within your own establishment.
2 Check the wash-basins are correctly stocked and used only for hand-washing.

Keep hair away from food and drink

Food and drink can become very unappetising and offputting to the customer if a stray hair has been allowed to fall into it. Apart from being unsightly, hairs also carry bacteria and can infect food.

If you are involved in serving food, and you often need to be in areas where the food is prepared, you may be required to wear head covering to reduce the risk of loose hair falling into food.

So you should:
● wear a head covering if required
● keep hair clean by washing it regularly.

This will reduce the risk of bacteria accumulating on hair and will improve your general appearance.

Do not comb or brush hair anywhere near food or drink
You are always encouraged to look smart and professional while on duty. Brushing or combing hair behind the bar, or in front of customers can appear unprofessional and be offputting to them. It can also result in stray hairs finding their way into food or drink. Always ensure you groom yourself in an appropriate area and away from customers.

Keep hair, moustaches and beards neat and tidy
This will reduce risks from bacteria carried on hair.

Different establishments vary the standards they set for the personal appearance of the staff employed. These standards will depend on the theme of the bar, the house style, the uniform worn (if any) and the type of customers attracted.

Trim and tidy hair gives your customers the right impression, and reflects your own professionalism and pride in your work.

If you are involved in serving food, you are required to comply with food hygiene legislation. Long hair must be tied back or up, as well as kept away from your eyes. This style can help prevent you from touching or playing with your hair when serving customers.

Essential knowledge

Correct clothing, footwear and headgear should be worn to:
● maintain a clean and professional appearance
● avoid the risk of contamination of food from hair
● ensure personal freshness and eliminate the risk of body odour
● prevent accidents from clothes/jewellery coming into contact with equipment
● ensure your comfort.

GENERAL HEALTH

People involved in the service of food and drink should be in good general health. Healthy looking staff can do a great deal to increase customers' confidence in the food and drink they consume. Healthy staff will also minimise the risk of infection, which, if serious, can lead to lost trade and damaged reputation.

When dealing with the general public and handling food and drink you have a responsibility to be aware of some of the dangers there may be.

- Do not work if you have any symptoms linked to food poisoning, or have been in contact with someone who has, for example, vomiting, diarrhoea, stomach pains and infections.
- Report your symptoms to your supervisor.
- Wash and shower daily to reduce body odour and risks from bacteria.
- Working behind a bar can often be a very hot activity. Customers will soon notice if you sweat too much and have strong body odour. This can make them and you very uncomfortable, especially if you are in close proximity, for example, when clearing tables, and may mean they choose not to return to the pub.
- Cover cuts or bruises with clean waterproof dressings. Open sores or cuts can harbour germs and can look, to a customer or colleague, very unpleasant. If you are required to help with food preparation in the lead up to the bar opening you will find that waterproof plasters in the first aid kit in a food preparation area are blue, so that they can be seen if they fall into the food.
- Avoid working with food when wounds are infected and unsightly and likely to cause danger to customers.
- Avoid bad habits such as:
  - licking fingers when opening bags or picking up paper
  - picking, scratching or touching your nose
  - scratching your head or spots
  - tasting food, or picking at food returned to the preparation area
  - eating food such as crisps behind the bar
  - coughing or sneezing over food
  - smoking
  - using hand wash-basins for washing food or utensils.

All of these habits can cause bacteria to spread and must be avoided at all times. They are also unpleasant for your customers and colleagues to see.

MEMORY JOGGER

What should food handlers do when working with food to ensure they comply with food hygiene regulations?

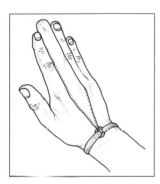

A covered finger

The food hygiene legislation requires you to report any sickness

Staff Sickness Notice

If you develop any illness involving vomiting or diarrhoea, or have come into contact with anyone with these symptoms, you must report it to your Department Manager before commencing work.

Other illnesses you must report to your Manager include: abdominal pain, skin rashes, fever, septic skin, lesions or discharges from your ear, nose or throat.

Essential knowledge	Illness and infections should be reported:
	● to avoid contagion of disease with other staff members
	● to avoid contamination of food and drink
	● so that appropriate action may be taken to alert appropriate staff.

Case study	*One day, when you are working a lunch shift in the bar you notice a colleague has been quieter than usual and seems a little under the weather. She has been preparing sandwiches for lunch as usual but has mentioned to you she has been feeling sick and has had a bout of diarrhoea.*
	1 What is the potential risk to your customers in this situation?
	2 What would you advise your colleague to do?
	3 What action would you take in this situation?

PROTECTIVE CLOTHING

Many operations today require their staff to wear a uniform, or some form of protective clothing, such as an apron or a tabard. This is often a good idea as it can help project a particular image or style which complements the operation.

Uniforms also help project a much more professional image and increase customers' confidence in the operation.

Uniforms, or any other form of protective clothing, can also be of benefit to you, reducing the wear and tear on your own clothes and perhaps minimising costs of buying new clothes for the job.

If you are provided with a uniform to wear, you may find it will be your responsibility to ensure you wear it, keep it clean and in good repair.

There are a few guidelines to follow.
● Wear protective clothing when in a food preparation area. This can prevent the risk of transmitting to food bacteria which have been carried in on outdoor clothing. Everyday clothing can easily be contaminated by contact with pets, dirt and other people.
● Keep your uniform in good condition, with no tears or missing buttons. Damaged protective clothing can look unsightly and be a danger to you if you catch it on equipment, or edges of the bar counter.
● Keep your uniform clean and change it daily. The uniform is often light coloured and washable as food stains and dirt harbour bacteria. Avoid using aprons and glass cloths for drying your hands as this can lead to cross-contamination.
● Do not wear protective clothing outside work, for example, to travel to and from work, as this can eliminate its effectiveness in protecting food from contamination.
● It is a good idea to wear different shoes for indoors and outdoors to reduce risks of infection. Alternating the shoes you wear ensures foot odour is kept to a minimum, helps reduce the strain on your feet and protects them.
● Do not wear worn or open shoes in case of spillages or items such as barrels or bottles being dropped onto your feet. Open shoes offer little support if you slip on a wet floor, or trip. Low heeled, closed shoes give you the most protection and help you move quickly and efficiently about your place of work. Ensure your shoes are always clean and comfortable.
● Depending upon the style of the uniform, always ensure the socks, stockings or tights you wear are clean and complement the uniform to project a professional and hygienic appearance.

MEMORY JOGGER

Why is it important to ensure food handlers are wearing the correct protective clothing, footwear and headgear?

GENERAL APPEARANCE

When serving food and drink in the bar, you will be the focus of attention for your customers. They will be looking to you to provide the level of service and professionalism projected by the company image. It will be this that will have attracted them into the bar in the first place. You represent your company to your customers, so it is essential that you reflect this in the way you deal with your customers and in the image you present. Your appearance will say a lot about you and the service the customer should expect.

Whether or not you have a uniform to wear, ensure your overall appearance is professional and hygienic by:
● making sure your make-up is not overdone and distracting the customers. Too much make-up as well as too little can affect the overall impression you create
● avoiding wearing heavy perfumes and aftershave as it may be unpleasant to the customers. Strong perfume or aftershave can be transferred to glasses and crockery, tainting the food or drink
● wearing deodorant to protect against perspiration and odours
● not carrying excess items in your pockets, such as pens, tissues, or money as this can look untidy and unprofessional.

Remember to:
● check your appearance in a mirror before starting duty and take pride in your appearance and that of your uniform
● follow good personal hygiene practice at all times whether in front of customers or not by:
  – keeping yourself clean, washing your hair and body regularly
  – wearing a clean uniform or protective clothing at all times and keeping it in good repair
  – washing your hands regularly especially after visiting the toilet, touching your hair or face, smoking, bottling up, or preparing food
  – using only disposable tissues when sneezing or blowing your nose – and disposing of them!
  – keeping all cuts and wounds covered with clean waterproof dressing.

Follow these basic practices, and enhance the service you provide as well as minimise any risks from food poisoning there may be to your customers, yourself and your colleagues.

Do this

1 Find out what the correct uniform standard is for your job.
2 Examine the uniform or protective clothing you have and check it is clean and in good repair.
3 Check yourself against the points we have listed to see if you comply with personal hygiene requirements.

What have you learned

1 Why is it important to comply with health and safety legislation?
2 Why is it important to wear correct clothing, footwear and headgear at all times?
3 Why should you report illness and infections?
4 Why is it necessary to wear protective clothing if you are involved in preparing and serving food and drink?
5 Give five examples of good personal hygiene practice you must follow at work.
6 List four ways cross-contamination by bacteria could occur behind the bar.
7 Where can you obtain information on current health and safety legislation?

ELEMENT 2: Carry out procedures in the event of a fire

What you need to do

- In the event of a fire, raise the alarm immediately.
- Use fire fighting equipment correctly and in line with manufacturers' instructions and organisational procedures.
- Adhere to all safety and emergency notices.

- Reach the nominated assembly point.
- Work in an organised and efficient manner in line with appropriate organisational procedures and legal requirements.

What you need to know

- What the possible causes of fire are in the working environment.
- What preventative actions can be taken to minimise the risk of fire.
- What establishment procedures should be followed in the event of a fire.
- Where alarms are located and how to activate them.

- Why a fire should never be approached unless it is safe to do so.
- Why it is important to comply with health and safety legislation.
- Where and from whom information on current health and safety legislation can be obtained.

INTRODUCTION

Fires occur regularly on premises where staff are working and customers or visitors are present. Many, fortunately, are quite small and can be dealt with quickly. Others lead to tragic loss of life, personal injury and destruction of property.

Some of these fires could have been prevented with a little forethought, care and organisation. The commonest causes are misuse of electrical or heating equipment, and carelessly discarded cigarette-ends. People are often the link needed to start a fire: by acting negligently, perhaps by leaving rubbish in a dark corner; or by being lazy and taking shortcuts in work methods.

FIRE LEGISLATION

The Fire Precautions Act 1971 requires companies to comply with certain legal conditions, such as:
- providing a suitable means of escape, which is unlocked, unobstructed, working and available whenever people are in the building
- ensuring suitable fire fighting equipment is properly maintained and readily available
- meeting the necessary requirements for a fire certificate. On larger premises, owners are required to have a fire certificate which regulates the means of escape and markings of fire exits. These premises must also have properly maintained fire alarms and employees must be made aware of the means of escape and the routine to follow in the event of a fire
- posting relevant emergency signs around the area giving people guidance on what to do and where to go in the event of a fire.

CAUSES OF FIRE

Fire can break out wherever there is a combination of fuel, heat and oxygen. As part of your responsibility in ensuring the safety of yourself, colleagues and customers you need to be aware of some of the most common causes of fire. These are:

MEMORY JOGGER

What are the main causes of fire in the working environment?

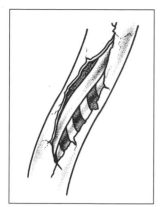

Damaged wiring

- *rubbish*. Fires love rubbish. Accumulations of cartons, packing materials and other combustible waste products are all potential flashpoints
- *electricity*. Although you cannot see it, the current running through your electric wiring is a source of heat and, if a fault develops in the wiring, that heat can easily become excessive and start a fire. Neglect and misuse of wiring and electrical appliances are the leading causes of fires in business premises
- *smoking*. The discarded cigarette-end is still one of the most frequent fire starters. Disposing of waste correctly will help reduce fires from this source, but even so, remember that wherever cigarettes and matches are used there is a chance of a fire starting
- *flammable goods*. If items such as paint, adhesives, oil or chemicals are stored or used on your premises they should be kept in a separate store room and well away from any source of heat. Aerosols, gas cartridges and cylinders, if exposed to heat, can explode and start fires
- *heaters*. Portable heaters, such as the sort used in bars to supplement the general heating, can be the cause of a fire if goods come into close contact with them or if they are accidentally knocked over. Never place books, papers or clothes over convector or storage heaters, as this can cause them to overheat and can result in a fire.

PREVENTING FIRES

Being alert to the potential hazard of fire can help prevent emergencies. Potential fire hazards exist in every area of the workplace, so regular preventative checks are essential as part of your everyday working practice.

- As far as possible, switch off and unplug all electrical equipment when it is not being used. Some equipment may be designed to be permanently connected to the mains (e.g. video recorders with digital clocks); always check the manufacturer's instructions.
- If new equipment has been installed, ensure that you are trained in its use and follow the manufacturer's instructions. If you are involved in carrying out maintenance on the equipment follow the schedule properly.
- Electrical equipment is covered by British Safety Standards, so look for plugs that conform to BS1363 and fuses that conform to BS1362.
- Ensure there are sufficient ashtrays available for smokers to use.
- Inspect all public rooms, kitchens, staff rooms and store rooms to ensure all discarded smoking equipment is collected in lidded metals bins and not mixed with other waste.
- As often as possible, look behind cushions and down the sides of seats to check a cigarette-end has not been dropped by mistake. You could check for this whenever you are tidying an area and when customers have left.
- Ensure rooms and corridors are free of waste and rubbish, especially in areas where litter tends to collect, such as in corners and underneath stairwells.
- Place all accumulated waste in appropriate receptacles, away from the main building.
- Check that all external stairways and means of escape are kept clear.
- Make sure that fire doors and smoke stop doors on escape routes are regularly maintained. These doors are designed to withstand heat and to reduce the risks from smoke. They must not be wedged open or prevented from working properly in the event of a fire.

FIRE HAZARDS IN THE BAR

In a bar there are additional hazards that you should be aware of. Note the following points:

- Electrical equipment (e.g. bottle coolers) with faulty controls or thermostats can overheat, ignite and cause a fire. All cooling equipment must be maintained and kept free from build-up of grease or dirt. Check that in-line coolers, bottle

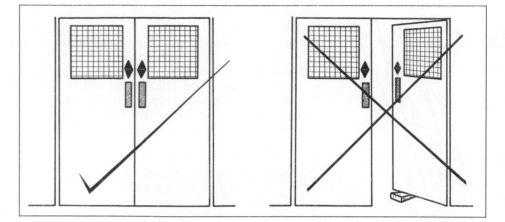

*Fire doors used correctly
(left) and incorrectly (right)*

coolers, etc. are cleaned and maintained regularly. Check non-essential electrical equipment is turned off and unplugged after service/session, e.g. gaming machines, tape recorders.

● Many customers in bars may smoke whilst consuming beverages. Staff must be particularly aware of the potential fire risk. All customer areas including toilets must be regularly checked as often as possible for discarded smoking debris. Build-up in ashtrays should be constantly disposed of in lidded metal bins.

● Spirituous liquor is a potential fire risk. All liquor before use must be stored in a safe secure area away from any potential heat source or naked flame.

● Any CO_2 cylinders in cellars must be properly secured and free from damage.

● If candles are used in the bar, care must be taken to ensure they are kept away from flammable material.

● If there is an open fire in the bar, customers, visitors and staff must be protected from the flames by a fireguard.

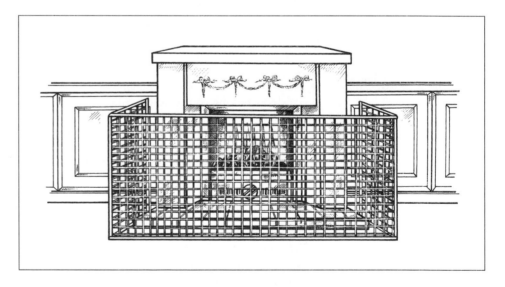

*Pub fire with fireguard
around it*

FIRE SAFETY CONDITIONS

The following conditions must always be met within a working area.

● Fire doors should not be hooked or wedged open (see illustration above). Check that they close automatically when released. Fire stop doors held by magnets need to be closed from 11 p.m.–7 a.m.

● Fire extinguishers should be available, full and not damaged.

● Fire exit doors should be easy to use and secure.

- Emergency lighting should be maintained and visible at all times. Make sure that the lights are not obscured by screens, drapes, clothing, etc.
- Signs and fire notices giving details of exit routes must be available in all areas and kept in good condition.
- Alarm points should be readily accessible and free from obstruction.
- Fire sprinklers and smoke detectors must be kept clear of obstruction for at least 24 inches in all directions.
- Fire exit doors and routes must be kept clear at all times and in a good state of repair.

Do this ✔

1. Carry out a full survey of your own work area and identify any potential fire hazards. List the hazards under the following categories: combustible material, flammable liquids, flammable gases, electrical hazards.
2. Discuss the potential dangers with your colleagues and agree ways of minimising the risk.
3. Revise your own working methods to minimise fire risks.

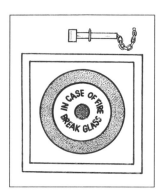

A break glass alarm

DISCOVERING A FIRE

If you discover a fire, follow the procedure given below:
1. sound the alarm immediately
2. call the fire brigade
3. evacuate the area
4. assemble in the designated safe area for roll call.

Sounding the alarm

The function of the alarm is to warn every person in the building that an emergency has arisen and that fire evacuation procedures may need to be put into action. Most alarms are known as *break glass* alarms, and, as the name suggests, you have to break the glass to make the alarm sound.

Calling the fire brigade

The responsibility for calling the fire brigade falls to different people in different establishments. Often it is a supervisor or manager who will be expected to deal with the call. Make sure that you know who is responsible for this in your establishment.

When calling the fire brigade, be ready with the following information:
- your establishment's address
- your establishment's telephone number
- the precise location of the fire.

You may like to write down the necessary information about the establishment and keep it near the telephone in case of an emergency. If you do have to make an emergency phone call, make sure that you listen for the address to be repeated back to you before replacing the telephone receiver.

Evacuating the area and assembling outside

It is essential for everyone to be able to escape from danger. If you do not have specific duties to carry out in the evacuation procedures you should leave the premises immediately on hearing the alarm.

When evacuating the premises:
- switch off equipment and machinery
- close windows and doors behind you
- follow marked escape routes
- remain calm, do not run
- assist others in their escape
- go immediately to an allocated assembly point
- do not return for belongings, no matter how valuable.

You and all of your colleagues should be instructed on what to do if fire breaks out. Customers and visitors should also be made aware of what to do in the event of a fire and should be made familiar with the means of escape provided. This is usually done by means of notices in all public areas and rooms. If the bar is frequented by foreign customers, notices should be printed in the most appropriate languages.

FIGHTING FIRES

Fighting fires can be a dangerous activity, and is generally to be discouraged. Personal safety and safe evacuation must always be your primary concern. If a fire does break out, it should only be tackled in its very early stages and before it has started to spread.

Before you tackle a fire:
- evacuate everyone and follow the emergency procedure to alert the fire brigade. Tell someone that you are attempting to tackle the fire
- always put your own and other people's safety first; never risk injury to fight fires. Always make sure you can escape if you need to and remember that smoke can kill. Remember the rule: *if in doubt, get out*
- never let a fire get between you and the way out. If you have any doubt about whether the extinguisher is suitable for the fire, do not use it; leave immediately
- remember that fire extinguishers are only for 'first aid' fire fighting. Never attempt to tackle the fire if it is beginning to spread or if the room is filling with smoke
- if you cannot put out the fire, or your extinguisher runs out, leave immediately, closing doors and windows as you go.

Fire fighting equipment

Types
On-premise fire fighting equipment is designed to be used for small fires only and is very specific to the type of fire. Hand extinguishers are designed to be easy to use, but can require practice and training in how to use them.

All fire fighting equipment is designed to remove one of the three factors needed for a fire: heat, oxygen or flammable material. Fire extinguishers are filled with one of the following:
- *water*. This type of extinguisher provides a powerful and efficient means of putting out fires involving wood, paper and fabric
- *dry powder*. These extinguishers can be used to put out wood, paper, fabric and flammable liquid fires, but are more generally used for fires involving electrical equipment
- *foam*. The pre-mix foam extinguishers use a combination of water and aqueous film, and are effective for extinguishing paper, wood, fabric and flammable liquid fires
- *carbon dioxide*. These extinguishers are not commonly in use, but can be used in situations where there is electronic equipment.

MEMORY JOGGER

What are the different types of on-site fire fighting equipment and the types of fire they can help control?

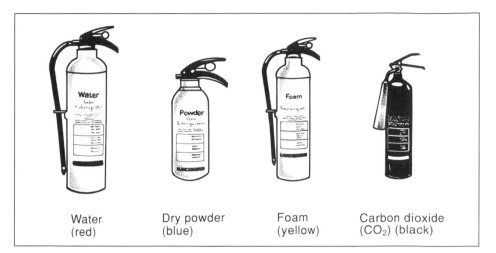

Fire extinguishers

Water
(red)

Dry powder
(blue)

Foam
(yellow)

Carbon dioxide
(CO_2) (black)

- A fire extinguisher must be wall-mounted on wall brackets (unless it is designed specifically to be floor standing) and should not be used as a door stop.
- When a fire extinguisher is discharged, it must be replenished as soon as possible, and at least within 24 hours.
- Every establishment should have a scale drawing indicating the location of fire fighting equipment.

Fire blankets are also used to extinguish fires. These are made from a variety of materials: some are made of woven fibreglass while others have a fibreglass base and are coated with silicone rubber on both sides. A fire blanket is generally housed in a wall-mounted plastic pack with a quick-pull front opening. It can be used to put a barrier between the user and the fire, and it removes the oxygen that a fire needs to burn.

How to use a fire blanket

An establishment may also have fire hoses which are linked to the water supply. These can be used in the same situations as the red, water-based extinguishers and are usually activated by the action of removing the hose from its mounting.

Maintaining equipment
Fire fighting equipment is essential in areas where there is a potential risk from fires. It is essential that equipment is:

- *maintained regularly and kept in good condition.* The fire brigade or your supplier will carry out annual checks and note on the extinguisher when the check was carried out
- *kept clear from obstruction at all times.* The equipment must be visible and readily available. Obstructions can prevent easy access and may result in unnecessary damage to the equipment
- *available in all areas of work.* Different types of extinguishers are needed for different fires, so the most suitable extinguisher should be available in the area. Guidance can be sought from the fire brigade or equipment suppliers
- *used by trained operators.* Fire extinguishers can be quite noisy and powerful and can startle you if you have not used one before. It is important that you know the best way of utilising the extinguisher to tackle a fire in the most effective way.

COMPLYING WITH FIRE LEGISLATION

The fire legislation has been developed to ensure premises and working practices are safe for employees, customers and visitors. As mentioned in the introduction, failure to observe the regulations can lead to damage to property and, in more serious situations, loss of life. The legislation has been developed for everyone's safety and everyone has a role in ensuring they do not ignore fire notices, information provided about fire exits and ensure they take part in fire evacuations and fire drills when necessary.

Finding out about the fire legislation

In your work area there will be notices and information posted around the building. Details about the fire regulations will also be kept on-site for you, your manager or your supervisor to refer to.

The local fire station will have a nominated fire officer to give advice and guidance to establishments on how well they are complying with the regulations and to identify any improvements in the evacuation drill that may be needed. The local fire officer will also give advice, support and, where appropriate, assist in the training of staff within the business.

Do this ✔

1. Find out where your nearest fire exits are located and the route you need to follow to reach your nominated assembly point.
2. Identify the fire extinguishers available in your area and learn how to use them.
3. Look out for potential fire hazards in your area and remove or report them immediately.
3. Take part in practice fire drills in your establishment and learn to recognise the type of sound made by the alarm in your building.

Case study

You are carrying out a security check of your establishment and you notice that two of the fire extinguishers have been removed from their wall brackets and that the fire exit near the delivery area is blocked with old cardboard boxes.
1. *What would be your main concern if you found these problems?*
2. *What immediate action would you take?*
3. *What would be the longer term action that could be taken to prevent this happening again?*

1 What are the possible causes of fire in the working environment?
2 What should you do first on discovering a fire?
3 What type of extinguisher would you use for putting out:
   (a) an electrical fire?
   (b) a fire in a deep fat fryer?
   (c) a fire in a store room where chemicals are stored?
4 List four points you need to remember when evacuating your work area if the fire alarm sounds.
5 Why is it important to comply with your responsibilities under the fire regulations?
6 How does a fire blanket work in preventing a fire from spreading?
7 Why should fire escapes and exits be kept free from rubbish and doors unlocked when people are on the premises?

ELEMENT 3: Maintain a safe environment for customers, staff and visitors

What you need to do

- Identify and promptly rectify hazards and potential hazards to the safety of customers, staff and visitors.
- Make customers, staff and visitors aware of hazards and potential hazards in line with operational requirements.
- Take cautionary measures to warn customers, staff and visitors of hazards and potential hazards.
- Report promptly to the appropriate person accidents, damage and non-rectifiable hazards.
- Work in an organised and efficient manner in line with appropriate organisational procedures and legal requirements.

What you need to know

- What cautionary measures can be taken to warn customers, staff and visitors of potential hazards.
- What the potential hazards are within your own working environment.
- Why suspicious items and packages must not be approached or tampered with.
- Where first aid equipment and the accident register are located.
- Which person in the working environment is responsible for first aid.
- Why it is important to use correct lifting techniques.
- Why it is important to comply with health and safety legislation.
- Where and from whom information on current health and safety legislation can be obtained.
- What the employee's responsibility is in relation to health and safety legislation.

INTRODUCTION

The safety of everyone who works or visits an establishment should be foremost in the minds of everyone. As a main part of any employee's work, he or she has to carry out procedures and comply with regulations which have been designed to encourage good working practices and to reduce the risks of injury to themselves and others. These regulations are also designed to make the working environment more comfortable and safe to work in.

HEALTH AND SAFETY LEGISLATION

The *Health and Safety at Work Act 1974* (HASAWA) states that the responsibility of employees and employers is to take a 'general duty of care', and places emphasis on the need for preventative measures to be enacted and managed. The Act encouraged the constant re-evaluation of systems and processes to prevent accidents and reduce risks to everyone in the establishment.

The Health and Safety at Work Act 1974 is an 'enabling' Act in that it imposes a general duty of care, but has the flexibility to be adapted to suit future needs. Relevant regulations passed under the 1974 Act so far include:
● Health and Safety (First Aid) Regulations, 1981
● Reporting of Injuries, Diseases and Dangerous Occurrences Regulations, 1985 (RIDDOR)
● Control of Substances Hazardous to Health Regulations, 1988 (COSHH).

Under the Health and Safety at Work Act 1974, there are certain responsibilities both employers and employees must comply with. Those given below are ones you should be particularly aware of.

Employers' responsibilities

Employers must, as far as reasonably practicable:
● provide and maintain plants and systems of work that are safe and without risks to health
● make arrangements to ensure safety and the absence of risks to health in connection with the use, handling, storage and transport of articles and substances
● provide such information, instruction, training and supervision as will ensure the health and safety of employees
● maintain any place of work under their control in a safe condition without risks to health and provide at least statutory welfare facilities and arrangements.

These duties also extend to include customers and others visiting the premises.

Employees' responsibilities

As an employee you also have responsibilities and must:
● take reasonable care of your own health and safety
● take reasonable care for the health and safety of other people who may be affected by what you do or neglect to do at work
● cooperate with the establishment in the steps it takes to meet its legal duties
● report any physical conditions or systems which you consider unsafe or potentially unsafe to a supervisor.

These responsibilities have been drawn up for the benefit of everyone in the workplace, to ensure that the risk of accident or injury to anyone is minimised through promotion of a thoughtful and considerate approach to work practices.

Many working days can be lost through accidents, which more often than not are caused through carelessness and thoughtlessness. As a result, the business suffers reduced productivity and, in serious cases, considerable trading time if forced to close while the premises are made safe.

Under the HASAWA, Health and Safety inspectors (often under the umbrella of the Environmental Health Office) have the authority to place prohibition notices on premises if they persistently fail to meet the standards set by law. This might occur if there were a physical problem in the building or in equipment, or an outbreak of food poisoning caused by poor hygiene practice.

Whatever the cause, it is important that you and your colleagues have a positive and active approach to maintaining the safety of the environment in which you operate.

The Health and Safety Executive (HSE) has the responsibility of advising on safety matters and of enforcing the HASAWA if the obligations of this Act are not met. This is one reason why serious accidents must always be reported to the Executive.

MEMORY JOGGER

What are employees' responsibilities under the Health and Safety Act of 1974?

In the case of hotel and catering establishments, local authorities appoint their own inspectors: Environmental Health Officers (EHOs) who work with companies and colleges on matters associated with health and safety.

Health and Safety Inspectors

These appointed representatives have a number of powers under the Act which include:
- being able to enter premises at reasonable times
- testing, measuring, photographing and examining as they see fit
- taking samples or dismantling equipment
- viewing Health and Safety records, accident books, etc.
- serving Improvement Notices requiring action within a period of not less than 21 days
- prosecuting *any* person contravening a statutory provision (penalty is a maximum fine of £5000 and/or term of imprisonment up to two years).

HAZARDS

Hazard spotting

Much of the Health and Safety legislation is aimed at preventing accidents from happening and ensuring the environment is free from risk and safe for everyone within it. A *hazard* is defined as something with the potential to cause harm. A *risk* can be expressed as the likelihood of that harm actually arising.

Some of the most common accidents in the workplace are caused through basic mistakes, such as someone not cleaning up a spillage, or a cable left trailing across a walkway.

By being aware of the potential danger of hazards, you will be able to contribute effectively to the safety of the area in which you work. The guidelines given here show areas in which you can start contributing towards maintaining a safe environment.

Cautionary measures

- When you spot a potential hazard, remove it immediately (if you can) and report the situation to your supervisor. Most organisations have a standard Health and Safety Report Form stating action to be taken and follow-up procedures.
  If you are unable to remove the hazard, as in the case of a doorway blocked by a delivery of goods, monitor the situation and if it appears the goods will not be moved quickly, report the problem to your supervisor.
  By taking immediate action over a potential hazard you will be contributing to your own well-being and that of your colleagues. Some hazards, however, may be due to poor working practices or faulty building design and they will need a different approach and more time to solve.
- You may also need to place signs, such as 'Caution wet floor' to warn others of the potential hazard they are approaching. In some cases you may even need to cordon off an area while you deal with, or make arrangements to deal with, the hazard.
- Other cautionary measures will include ensuring you keep potentially dangerous items such as chemicals under lock and key, or out of reach of others.
- Take note of all signs warning of dangers or potential hazards, especially those associated with:
  - use of machinery
  - hazardous chemicals
  - cleaning fluids.

In some instances, you may need to draw others' attention to the signs.

Essential knowledge	Preventative action should always be taken quickly when a hazard is spotted, in order to: ● prevent injury to staff and customers ● prevent damage to buildings and equipment ● comply with the law.

Damaged stair carpeting

Safety points to remember
- Be constantly aware of obstacles on the floor or in corridors and remove them, returning them to their rightful place.
- Watch out for damaged floor coverings or torn carpets: it is very easy to catch your heel and trip over a carpet edge.
- Make sure electrical cables or wires never run across walkways. Always keep them behind you when you are working to reduce the risk of damage to them.
- Clean up spillages as soon as they occur. If grease is spilt, use salt or sand to absorb the spillage before cleaning the area.
- If cleaning up spillages on non-porous floors, use wet floor signs to warn people of the danger.
- Never handle electrical plugs with wet hands. Water conducts electricity: this can cause death.
- Never use equipment that appears faulty or damaged. You are increasing the risk to yourself by doing so. Report the problem immediately and ensure the equipment is repaired.
- Use a step ladder to reach to the top of shelves. Never stand on piles of cases or boxes.
- If lifting a load, make sure it is not too heavy or awkward for you to move on your own. If you need help, ask. Back injuries are one of the most common reasons for people having to take time off from work – this is of particular importance when changing casks or kegs of beer, or moving cases of liquor.

Hazards in the bar

In the bar area there are some special hazards to be aware of. The following points show how these can be kept to a minimum.
- When using a knife (e.g. cutting lemons) always use the correct knife for the job you are doing. Use of incorrect knives can lead to accidents. Always leave a knife with its blade flat: if you leave the blade uppermost it would be very easy for you or a colleague to put a hand down on top of the blade and cut the palm of the hand. Never leave a knife immersed in water.
- If walking while carrying knives, always point the blade towards the floor, away from your body. If you were to trip or fall you might end up stabbing someone or injuring yourself.
- When polishing glasses always ensure you completely wrap the glass cloth around the glass to avoid cutting yourself in case the glass breaks.
- Always inspect glassware and bottles for damage. Staff and customers may cut themselves if served with damaged or chipped glasses. Where chipped bottles are used particles may fall into the beverage when pouring.

Much of the health and safety legislation focuses on people having a thoughtful and common-sense approach to their work and the safety of others. Many of the accidents which happen on premises, whether they be to staff, customers or visitors, occur as a direct result of someone not doing the right thing at the right time.

Hazardous substances

The *Control of Substances Hazardous to Health Regulations 1988* (COSHH) form part of the Health and Safety Regulations and lay down the essential requirements and a step-by-step approach to protecting people exposed to them. In the bar, the most likely exposure to chemicals is through the use of cleaning and associated chemicals.

The COSHH regulations set out the measures employers and employees have to take. Failure to comply with COSHH constitutes an offence and is subject to penalties under the Health and Safety at Work Act 1974.

Substances hazardous to health include:
- those labelled as dangerous (e.g. toxic, corrosive)
- those where exposure over a long time is thought dangerous (e.g. pesticides)
- harmful micro-organisms
- substantial concentration of dust of any kind
- any material, mixture or compound used at work, or arising from work activities, which can harm people's health.

In the bar, hazardous substances may include bleach, ammonia, chlorine, detergents, methylated spirits, solvents, and pipe cleaning fluid.

COSHH requires an employer to:
- assess the risk to health arising and state the precautions needed
- introduce appropriate measures to prevent or control the risk
- ensure the control measures are used
- where necessary, monitor the exposure of employees
- to inform and instruct employees on a regular basis.

COSHH requires an employee to:
- know what risks there are in using certain substances
- understand how these risks are controlled
- take the necessary precautions.

Storage of hazardous substances
When storing hazardous substances, it is important that:
- they are stored in a locked room
- they are clearly labelled in a securely capped container
- there are First Aid instructions and methods of summoning assistance
- there is a system of work related to their use.

Reporting hazards

Under the HASAWA, every company must have a procedure in place for employees to report potential hazards they have identified. In some companies there may be *Safety Representatives* whose role is to bring the hazard to the supervisor's attention. The Safety Representative may be part of a *Health and Safety Committee* which will meet regularly to deal with matters of safety and to ensure appropriate action is taken.

Your department may have a standard *Hazard Report Form* which you would complete to help you and your supervisor deal with the hazard through a formalised procedure. You may also be involved in carrying out regular safety audits in your department aimed at ensuring that planned preventative work is implemented.

Under the Health and Safety at Work Act it is your responsibility to be aware of potential hazards and to take the necessary action to prevent them from becoming actual hazards.

Do this

1 Carry out a hazard spotting tour of your area noting any actions needed and highlighting potential dangers.
2 Find out how you are required to report health and safety hazards in your place of work.
3 Examine the equipment you use in your department. Is the wiring in good condition? When was the equipment last serviced? Discuss any problems found with your supervisor.

DEALING WITH SUSPICIOUS ITEMS

In any area of work there may be times when an unattended item, package or bag raises suspicion. This could lead to an emergency and, if not handled correctly, may result in danger or injury to people in the area.

Because of the 'chance' or transient nature of custom, bars are a prime target for terrorists. It is important to treat any suspicious item seriously. Be aware of the danger it potentially contains and be prepared to inform people of your suspicions quickly and calmly.

A suspicious package which is not dealt with immediately may result in serious injury to people in the area or serious damage to the building. It is an essential part of your daily work to keep alert to dangers from suspect packages and follow procedures laid down for dealing with such a problem.

<table>
<tr><td>

MEMORY JOGGER

What are the actions to take if you discover a suspicious item in or around your area of work?

</td></tr>
</table>

Recognising a suspicious item or package

It is difficult to give precise guidance about where you may discover a suspicious package, or what size or shape it might be. Either of the types of package listed might raise your suspicions.

- Something that has been left unattended for some time, such as a briefcase next to a chair, or a suitcase left in a reception area.
- Something that looks out of place, like a man's holdall in the ladies' cloakroom, or a full carrier bag near a rubbish bin.

In fact, anything that sticks out in your mind as somewhat unusual.

A full carrier bag left next to an empty rubbish bin might be enough to arouse suspicion

On discovering a suspicious item
- Do not attempt to move or touch the item. The action of moving or disturbing the item may be enough to start off a reaction leading to an explosion or fire.
- Remain calm and composed. Try not to cause panic by shouting an alarm or running from the item. People and property can be injured through a disorderly or panicked evacuation.
- Report the matter to your supervisor or the police immediately. Check your establishment's procedures to find out whom you should inform.
- If possible, cordon off the area and move people away. It may be difficult to do this without causing people in the area to panic, but it is essential that no one attempts to move or touch the item, so you will need to warn people to keep clear.

● At some point it may be necessary to evacuate the building, or the part of the building nearest to the suspect package. This may be a decision taken by your supervisor, or the police if they are involved. If it is thought necessary to clear the area, follow your company procedures for the evacuation of the building.

Essential knowledge

● Suspicious items or packages must never be approached or tampered with in case they contain explosive materials which may be set off.
● Suspicious items or packages must always be reported immediately, to prevent serious accidents occurring involving bombs and explosives.

Reporting a suspicious item

If you are reporting a suspicious item make sure you are able to tell your contact:

1 what the suspicious package looks like:

2 the exact location of the suspect device:

3 the precautions you have taken so far:

4 the existence of any known hazards in the surrounding area, e.g. gas points:

5 the reason for your suspicion:

6 any witnesses to the placing of the package or item:

> **Do this** ✓
>
> 1 Carry out a survey of your work area to identify places where suspicious items or packages could be left.
> 2 Find out what procedures your establishment follows for dealing with suspect packages.
> 3 Carry out regular checks in your area.

DEALING WITH AN ACCIDENT

Within the normal course of your work, you may be required to deal with an accident or an emergency resulting in someone sustaining an injury. Often these injuries are not life-threatening, but occasionally they may be serious enough to warrant the person involved being taken to hospital, or being unable to carry on their work for that day.

Most organisations have several people trained in dealing with emergencies and administering first aid. These *first aiders* are often spread around the different departments to ensure that someone is available at all times. Organisations are legally required to have trained first aiders on the premises and to display a list detailing their place of work and contact telephone number on notice boards.

First aiders are usually the people who deal with an emergency before a doctor or an ambulance arrives (if necessary). They have a responsibility to respond to emergencies as they arise, and are trained to diagnose the course of action needed to deal with the injured person. You would immediately call a first aider when an accident occurs.

Recording an accident

All accidents need to be reported as soon after the event as practicable. Any accident is required by law to be reported and recorded in an *accident book* located on the premises. Any accident resulting in serious injury must be reported to the Health and Safety Executive within three working days. Your establishment should have procedures for dealing with this.

In the case of an accident to a member of staff, ideally the person who received the injury would complete the accident book. However, it may be necessary for an appointed person to report the accident on their behalf.

The following information is mandatory:
- the date and time of the accident
- the particulars of the person affected:
  - full name
  - occupation
  - nature of injury or condition
- where the accident happened
- a brief description of the circumstances.

If an accident happens to a customer or visitor, there will probably be different records available. Check the types of record kept by your own establishment.

Accident record-keeping is important, not only to comply with the legal requirements under Health and Safety legislation, but also to ensure details are available for possible insurance claims. Accident reporting can also be a great help when analysing trends and identifying where there may be a need for preventative training.

Complying with the regulations related to accidents

The current regulations governing the notification and recording of accidents are contained in the *Reporting of Injuries, Diseases and Dangerous Occurrences Regulations 1985* (RIDDOR). These regulations are about ensuring that a company has procedures in place to manage the reporting of accidents. There are five main areas:
- fatal or specified major accidents or conditions
- notifiable 'over three days' injuries
- reportable diseases
- dangerous occurrences (whether there is an injury or not)
- other accidents.

Each establishment is responsible for ensuring there are procedures in place which enable employees to comply with the regulations. Failure to follow the RIDDOR requirements can lead to prosecution under the Act.

Do this ✔

1 Establish where the Accident Recording Book is located in your establishment.
2 Find out whether there are different procedures and records for accidents involving customers and visitors to those involving staff for your establishment.
3 Find out the procedure for reporting accidents to the emergency services.

Who is a first aider?

The term *first aider* describes any person who has received a certificate from an authorised training body indicating that they are qualified to render First Aid.

The term was first used in 1894 by the voluntary First Aid organisations and certificates are now offered by St John Ambulance, St Andrew's Ambulance Association and the British Red Cross. The certificate is only valid for three years, to ensure that first aiders are highly trained, regularly examined and kept up to date in their knowledge and skills.

When a first aider is dealing with the casualty, his or her main aims are to:
- preserve life
- prevent the condition worsening
- promote recovery.

First aid organisations (left to right): St John Ambulance, St Andrew's Ambulance Association, British Red Cross

A first aider's responsibilities are to:
● assess the situation
● carry out diagnosis of the casualty
● give immediate, appropriate and adequate treatment
● arrange, without delay, for the casualty to be taken to a hospital or to see a doctor if appropriate.

Giving information to the first aider
Once the first aider arrives at the accident they will need certain information from you before they begin their treatment.

Be prepared to tell them as much as you know about:
● *the history of the accident*. How the accident happened, whether the person has been moved, what caused the injury
● *the symptoms*. Where the casualty is feeling pain, what other signs you have observed, whether the symptoms have changed
● *the treatment given*. What has already been done to the casualty and whether the casualty has any other illness or is receiving treatment or medication to the best of your knowledge.

Initial response to an accident

Whether you are a first aider or not, in the event of an accident it is the initial response to the situation and the way procedures are followed that can make the difference to the treatment received by the injured person.

You need to know what immediate response you should give if a person near you sustains an injury. Many of the points are common sense, and will depend upon the extent of the accident and the speed with which you can contact the relevant people.

When dealing with accidents the following points are important.
● *Remain calm when approaching the injured person*. The injured person will probably be frightened by the situation they are in, or may be in pain, and they will benefit from someone taking control of the situation. This may help reduce the feeling of panic, helplessness or embarrassment they may be experiencing.
● *Offer reassurance and comfort*. Keep the casualty (if conscious) informed of the actions you are taking by talking in a quiet, confident manner. Do not move the person but keep them warm, covering them with a blanket, or a coat if necessary. By keeping them warm, you are minimising the risk of shock which can often cause the condition of the injured person to deteriorate. By preventing them from moving, you are allowing time for them to recover and reducing the possibility of further injury.
● *Do not give them anything to drink*. If the casualty is given something to drink, he or she may not be able to have an anaesthetic if necessary. A drink may also make the casualty feel worse and may cause nausea.
● *Contact or instruct someone else to contact a first aider*.
● *Stay by the casualty* if you can, to reassure the casualty and ensure he or she does not cause further injury to themselves.

MEMORY JOGGER

What would you do if you were not a first aider and you were in the vicinity when someone had an accident?

Initial response to an accident

● *Minimise the risk of danger* to yourself, the injured person and any other people in the area.

In the case of:
● *gas or poisonous fumes*: if possible, cut off the source.
● *injury from electrocution*: switch off at the source – do not attempt to touch the injured person until he or she is clear of the current.
● *fire, or collapsing buildings:* move the casualty to a safe area after temporarily immobilising the injured part of the person.

Do this ✔

1 Find out the name and work location of your nearest first aider (a list should be displayed in your work area).
2 Find out how you can become a first aider.

Contacting the emergency services

If you or your supervisor decide that assistance is required from the emergency services, or you have been asked to call them by the first aider, you will need to pass on certain information:
● *your telephone number*, so that if for any reason you are cut off, the officer will then be able to contact you
● *the exact location of the incident*. This will help the ambulance or doctor to get to the scene of the accident more quickly
● *an indication of the type and seriousness of the accident*. This will allow the team to bring the most appropriate equipment and call for back-up if necessary
● *the number, sex and approximate age of the casualties involved*. If possible, you should also explain the nature of their injuries
● *any special help you feel is needed*. For example, in cases where you suspect a heart attack.

It might be a good idea to write down the information you need to pass on before calling the emergency services.

If you do call 999, you will be asked to state the service required: in the case of accidents you would normally state 'ambulance'. The officer responding to your call will be able to pass on messages to any other emergency services necessary, such as gas or fire.

Establishment procedures
Procedures vary from company to company as to who has authority to call the emergency services, so it is important that you find out how you are expected to deal with the situation in your own place of work.

CORRECT LIFTING TECHNIQUES

One of the most common sickness problems related to work is back injury. It affects not only those in manual jobs, but it can also affect sedentary workers. Under the Health and Safety Regulations, the *Manual Handling Operations Regulations* are intended to reduce the risk of injury and set out simple steps to take to reduce such injury. Back injury can put people out of work for a while as well as have a long-term debilitating effect on their health. Prevention of back injury is a must.

When lifting at work where there is a risk of injury, there are a number of questions to consider. For example, in the longer term:
● can the lifting operation be eliminated?
● is the lifting operation unnecessary?
● can the lifting operation be automated?
● could the lifting operation be mechanised?

As well as these longer term issues, it is also important that you think about how you are going to move an object – before you do it. You could:
● 'walk the route' to check how to lift and move the object without causing injury
● get someone else to help if the load is heavy
● get someone else to help if the load is bulky or an awkward shape
● use lifting techniques which do not put strain on the back (see the diagram below).

The correct way to lift a heavy object

If, as an employee, you are required to lift as part of your job, under Health and Safety legislation it is important you are trained in manual handling techniques. And, having been trained, it is then your responsibility to work to the correct procedures.

Case study

The area in which you are working is very busy and is used as an interim storage area for deliveries. You have often to step over boxes and crates as you work. Recently you have been asked, as part of your job, to help move the deliveries to their correct storage area. You are happy to help as it means you are learning a lot about storage of drink and receiving deliveries.

1 Before you get involved in this job, what are the main health and safety points to remember?

2 What should you find out from your supervisor?

3 What steps should you take to ensure you are complying with the HASAW Act?

DISCLOSABLE INFORMATION

During the time you are at work there may be people who ask you questions. These may be general questions about the operation of the bar, or may be specific about one aspect of the business. It is important that when this happens, you are discreet and careful about what you say. It may be that by answering such questions there could be a breach of security, or there may be a more indirect effect on the business (for example, an idea being used by a competitor).

If you are unsure what you can or cannot say to someone about the business or how it operates, it is best to say nothing and to check with your manager or supervisor.

It is also a good idea to mention to your manager or supervisor about the questions you have been asked. It may alert him or her and avoid a problem in the future.

REPORTING UNUSUAL/NON-ROUTINE INCIDENTS

Throughout the working day it is likely you and your colleagues have been busy. Much of the work we do does involve patterns of work and routines. If something disturbs that routine or seems out of the ordinary it is important these incidents are reported to the appropriate person (usually your manager or supervisor).

It may be that the incident does not need further action to be taken, but it also may result in a bigger problem being avoided. In cases where you see something which is a little bit out of the ordinary, it is important that it is reported.

FINDING OUT ABOUT AND COMPLYING WITH THE REGULATIONS

Health and safety is a responsibility of us all. Failure to comply with the requirements laid down may lead to an incident which could lead to prosecution. An injured person may be able to sue their employer, or a fellow employee for breach of their statutory duty. This could lead to damages being awarded through the civil courts, or being prosecuted in the criminal courts.

Information about the health and safety aspects of your work should be made available by your manager or supervisor. There may be a Health and Safety at Work handbook available when you join an establishment, which will detail your responsibilities and those of your colleagues. There will also be information available in the form of posters, statutory notices posted around the building and on staff notice boards.

During training sessions you will be given information about the regulations and how they affect your work. You should also be given guidance on working practices (such as lifting techniques) which will ensure you do not put yourself or others at risk from injury.

What have you learned

1 Why is it important that you are aware of your responsibilities under the Health and Safety at Work Act 1974?
2 What are the main responsibilities for employees under the HASAWA?
3 Why is it important to be involved and to carry out hazard spotting exercises?
4 Why is it important to report any suspicious packages or items you may spot?
5 What might make you become suspicious about a package or item?
6 Why must accidents be reported?
7 Where can you find the Accident Book in your establishment?
8 Why is it important to use correct lifting techniques?
9 Who can provide you with up-to-date information about Health and Safety matters?
10 List five potential Health and Safety hazards in your area of work.

ELEMENT 4: Maintain a secure environment for customers, staff and visitors

What you need to do

● Identify and report to the appropriate person potential security risks, in line with organisational procedures.
● Correctly secure customer and staff areas against unauthorised access.
● Secure all establishment storage and security facilities against unauthorised access.
● Report promptly, to the appropriate person and establishment, staff and customer lost property.
● Politely challenge, or report promptly to the appropriate person, any suspicious individuals.
● Work in an organised and efficient manner in line with appropriate organisational procedures and legal requirements.

What you need to know

● Which keys, property and areas should be secured from unauthorised access at all times.
● Why it is essential to be aware of potential security risks.
● Why procedures relating to lost property must be adhered to.
● Why it is important to comply with health and safety legislation.
● Where and from whom information on current health and safety legislation can be obtained.
● Why only disclosable information should be given to others.
● Why it is important to report all unusual/non-routine incidents to the appropriate person.

INTRODUCTION

Maintaining effective security should be the concern of everyone working within an establishment and is an essential part of good business practice. There may be staff within your own organisation employed as Security Officers whose role will include all aspects of protecting people on the premises, looking after the security of the building and the property contained within it.

Effective security practices can help protect the profit of the business by reducing the likelihood of losses through, for example:

- *theft*, whether through break-ins causing damage to the building or through walk-outs where customers leave without paying for their service
- *fraud*, by customers or staff
- *missing stock*.

Profitability can be affected both by the immediate loss of property or damage to the building and by bad publicity, which can damage the business through loss of custom.

Your role

Whether or not there are security staff employed within your organisation, you will find there are many situations within your working day where you need to be security conscious. It is easy to become complacent or lazy in your working habits, which can lead to an opportunity being seen and seized by a thief. A common example of this is a member of staff leaving a cash drawer open after transactions for speed or ease of use, allowing a customer to remove cash from the till when the cashier turns away.

Daily work patterns may also present an opportunity to be exploited by a thief. When we work in an area we become familiar with our surroundings, used to seeing things in a certain place and following procedures in a certain way. It is often these patterns that are observed by potential thieves and which can lead to break-ins or thefts.

Being aware of potential breaches of security and knowing how to report them or the action to take is an essential starting point. Think about the way you work and how security conscious you are. Make sure that you always follow the basic security practices listed below.

- Handle all cash transactions away from the customer and preferably out of their sight.
- To avoid disputes or potential for fraud ensure money tendered is confirmed with the customer before registering and giving change.
- Keep display materials beyond the reach of any customers and as far away from main entrances as possible, making it difficult for people to remove the items without being spotted.
- Keep security issues and procedures confidential: you can never be sure who might overhear you discussing a sensitive issue.
- Keep your own belongings, such as handbags or wallets, secure and out of sight in a locked compartment or drawer.
- Keep alert to anyone or anything which looks suspicious, for example: an occupied car parked outside the building for a long period of time, boxes or ladders placed near to windows, fire exits left open.
- Keep keys, especially master keys, under close supervision. You will probably find that your establishment has a log book for recording the issue of keys.

It is important for you to follow any particular security procedures that are in place in your establishment. These procedures are often there both for your benefit and to minimise any loss to the business.

MEMORY JOGGER

What are the guidelines to follow to help ensure there are no breaches of security in your working area?

Do this

1 Think about your working day. List the things you do where attention to security is essential.
2 Now write down your ideas for improving security within your job. Discuss your ideas with your supervisor.
3 Find out what security procedures you are required to follow within your work area.

DEALING WITH LOST OR MISSING PROPERTY

From time to time company, customer or staff property may go missing. This can be due to a variety of reasons, such as:

- customer property may have been left behind
- company property may have been moved without people knowing and may, in fact, be misplaced rather than lost
- a member of staff may have been careless about returning property, such as dirty linen to the linen room, or crockery to the crockery store
- items may have been stolen from the premises. You may hear this type of loss called *shrinkage* or *pilfering*, especially when referring to food or liquor missing from refrigerators or cellars.

In most establishments there will be procedures for dealing with any missing property. If you discover that property has gone missing, it is important you follow the correct procedure. The type of information you should report will probably include:

- a description of the missing item/s
- the date and time you discovered the item/s were missing
- the location where item/s are normally stored
- details of any searches or actions taken to locate the item/s.

In some cases your organisation may decide to report the loss to the police. This is common where the item missing is of value or where a substantial amount of goods has gone missing. In some organisations all losses are reported to the police whether theft is thought probable or not. If the police are involved, you may be required to give them information, so it is essential for you to be clear on the circumstances of the losses.

Essential knowledge	Keys, property and areas should be secured from unauthorised access at all times in order to:
	● prevent theft
	● prevent damage to property
	● prevent damage to the business from loss of customer confidence.

Recording lost property

In most establishments there are procedures for recording lost property. This usually covers personal property lost by customers, visitors or staff rather than property which may have been deliberately removed from the premises.

If someone reports they have lost an item, it is usual for this to be recorded in a Lost Property Book. An example page from a book is shown opposite.

- The information required should be recorded clearly and accurately. This information can then be used as a reference point for any property found on the premises.
- When recording lost property, it is particularly important to take an address or telephone number so that the person can be contacted should the item/s be found.
- If you find property, it is your responsibility to report the find so that it can be returned to the appropriate person.
- In some organisations, found property is retained for a period of, for example, three months and then either returned to the person who reported it or sent to a charity shop.

LOST PROPERTY RECORD					
Date/time loss reported	Description of item lost	Where item lost	Lost by (name, address, tel. no.)	Item found (where, when, by whom)	Action taken

A page from a Lost Property Book

Case study

A customer has reported to you that she thinks someone has stolen her handbag from the table at which she has been sitting all night.

1 What would you do if faced with this situation?

2 How would you record the incident?

3 What would you report to your manager?

SECURING STORAGE AREAS

Throughout the building there will be areas designated as storage, whether for customers or staff. These areas can often be used by a variety of people in the course of a day, so security of the area and the contents is essential.

Storage areas, particularly those allocated for use by customers such as coat racks or cloakrooms, are especially sensitive and can lead to a great deal of damage to the business if items from such areas are lost or go missing. Store rooms, refrigerators, freezers and cellars often contain a great deal of stock which constitutes some of the assets of the business and must be protected from potential loss.

Some items can be easily removed from the premises and are therefore of particular concern.

- *Small items* such as glasses, ashtrays, cutlery, etc. can be easily concealed in a carrier bag or suitcase and removed without too much difficulty.
- *Larger items* such as bar fixtures, bottles, table lamps, and if the bar has bedrooms, televisions, irons, hairdryers, etc. can also be removed, but will generally need more thought and planning beforehand.
- *Valuables* such as money and credit cards can be easily removed from coat pockets if left unattended in a cloakroom, or at a table when a customer goes to the bar for more drinks.

It is sometimes extremely difficult to make an area completely secure, especially as the premises are often host to a large variety of people. It is therefore important to minimise the risk as much as possible by following some fundamental guidelines.

Before we explore those guidelines, complete the exercise below. This will help you to identify areas which are not as secure as they could be. This may be due to a lost key, poor working practice or laziness on the part of the staff concerned.

Do this

1 Draw up a list of all of the designated storage areas within your department and indicate whether they are secured storage areas (i.e. lockable) or unsecured storage areas. Make sure you include every area in your list, including those made available for customers, staff and the storage of company property.
2 Once you have drawn up the list, tick those areas which are kept secure at all times. Identify the gaps, then discuss with your colleagues ways of improving the security of these areas.

Securing access

MEMORY JOGGER

How could you ensure you secure the areas within your establishment where access is restricted?

By carrying out regular checks like those given in the example above, you could highlight the need for improvement and increase the security of your area.

The following points show how you might prevent unauthorised access to certain areas.

- Where access to storage areas is restricted to certain people, ensure you comply with the rules. If you see anyone you think could be unauthorised, report it to your supervisor, or ask the person to leave the area.
- Limit the number of duplicate and master keys and keep a record of all key holders. Limiting access to keys makes it easier to control the movement of items around the building.
- Never leave keys lying around or in locks: this is an open invitation to an opportunist thief.
- Never lend keys to other staff, contractors or visitors; especially master keys. If you have been issued with a master key, you have responsibility for the access to that particular storage area.
- Follow any organisational procedures regarding the reporting of lost keys. It may be necessary to trace the lost key or have a new lock fitted to ensure the security of the area.
- If you have been issued with a duplicate or master key, keep it safe at all times. Ensure you follow any recording procedures there might be when you take and return the key.
- If you are working in a secure area, e.g. a liquor store room, always lock the room when you are leaving, even if only for a few moments.
- When closing the bar, check all windows, shutters and doors are secure and the area including toilets has been cleared of customers.

These guidelines are by no means exhaustive, but should help you maintain security within your area of work and raise your awareness about the potential risks.

Do this ✔

1 Add your own ideas to the guidelines listed above, taking into account the list of storage areas you drew up earlier.
2 Keep the list in a prominent position, such as your notice board or locker to remind you about the do's and don'ts of effective security practice.

DEALING WITH SUSPICIOUS INDIVIDUALS

Since you are working in the business of hospitality, there will inevitably and frequently be strangers within the building.

As part of your job, you should keep yourself alert to the presence of strangers in areas reserved for staff, i.e. in staff areas, offices and corridors. Non-staff may have a legitimate reason for being there: they may be visiting or delivering some material. On the other hand, they may have found their way in and be looking for opportunities to steal.

An individual may seem suspicious to you for a number of reasons. The following list will give you some pointers to potential problems, but remember that behaviour and situations may or may not indicate that an offence is taking place. An individual fitting any of these descriptions might be said to be acting suspiciously:

- someone wearing an incorrect uniform, or a uniform that is ill-fitting or worn incorrectly
- someone asking for directions to certain areas where you would not expect them to work
- someone carrying company property in an area not open to them
- someone who appears lost or disorientated (remember however that the person *may* be an innocent new employee)
- someone who just *looks* suspicious: perhaps they are wearing heavy clothing in summer, or carrying a large bag into the bar. Large bags or coats can be used to remove items from your premises
- someone who seems nervous, startled or worried, or is perspiring heavily
- someone booking into accommodation without luggage
- a customer asking for details of someone else using the establishment. (In this case, it is better to pass on the enquiry rather than give out information to a stranger.)

Responding to a suspicious individual

If you see someone on the premises you do not recognise, or who looks out of place it is important that you:
- challenge them politely: ask if you can help them, or direct them to the way out
- report the presence of a stranger to your supervisor immediately.

Procedures for dealing with strangers will vary depending upon the establishment in which you work.

In all cases, *do not put yourself at risk*. Do not approach the person if you feel uncomfortable or potentially threatened by them. Merely reporting any suspicions you have, whether about customers, staff or visitors, can often be of great help to the security and long-term health of the business.

MEMORY JOGGER

What would you need to do if you noticed someone acting suspiciously?

Do this ✔

1 Find out what procedures are laid down by your organisation for dealing with people acting in a suspicious manner.
2 Discuss with your supervisor how you think you might challenge someone should you need to.

What have you learned

1 Why is it essential to maintain secure storage areas within your establishment?
2 List any potential security risks within your own area.
3 Why is it important that you are aware of these risks?
4 Which keys, property and areas should be secured from unauthorised access at all times?
5 What should you ensure you do when leaving a secure area?
6 What should you do if you see someone acting in a suspicious manner?
7 How can you reduce the risk of items being taken from your own work area?
8 Why is it important you only give disclosable information to others?
9 Why is it important to report all unusual/non-routine incidents to the appropriate person?

Get ahead

1 Find out about the *recovery position* in first aid. When would you need to use this? Why is it effective?
2 Find out what immediate response you could give in the case of burns and scalds, fainting, strokes and heart attacks.
3 Talk to your security officers. Find out what kinds of event they commonly deal with in your establishment.
4 Invite a fire prevention officer to your establishment to talk about fire prevention and fire fighting in more detail.

UNIT NG2

Maintain and deal with payments

This unit covers:
ELEMENT 1:   **Maintain the payment point**
ELEMENT 2:   **Deal with payments**

INTRODUCTION

In many bars you will take money from customers for the service of drinks, either at the time of service, over the counter, or at a later stage in the service, perhaps when drinks are served at a table. In some bars, such as those in hotels, where the customers are also residents of the hotel no money may change hands – the bill is signed by the customer for later posting to the main bill. For more information about this method of payment see Unit 2NA5.

Cash handling is an important part of a bar person's job. It is also one of the most vulnerable areas and one that is open to fraudulent behaviour. For these reasons security is of vital importance when handling cash – security not only of the cash, but also of customer accounts and the back-up paperwork. Anyone who handles large amounts of cash is a target for thieves and conmen. The cash handling procedures within your establishment will have been designed to reduce the risk of theft and fraud, and your own vulnerability.

> ### MEMORY JOGGER
>
> Whom do company procedures protect?

Non-cash payments are not as vulnerable to simple theft as cash payments. However, they are more vulnerable to fraud. Another potential problem is that the credit card company or bank may refuse to honour a payment. It has the right to do this if the credit payment is not accepted correctly. You must never lose sight of the fact that any form of payment is always potentially fraudulent, as are any refund claims. You must, therefore, familiarise yourself thoroughly with the correct acceptance procedures and follow them carefully. If you do not understand why something is done in a specific way, ask your supervisor, but never deviate from the procedure without authorisation, because the system has been designed specifically to protect you and other members of staff as well as the bar.

ELEMENT 1:   Maintain the payment point

What you need to do

- Follow your establishment's procedures with regard to the handling of cash, and all other accepted methods of payment.
- Work efficiently and calmly under pressure and within the required time.
- Follow your establishment's proce-

dures regarding the security requirements and guarantees for all methods of payment.
- Replenish audit rolls, receipt rolls and customer bills as appropriate.
- Complete opening, closing and hand-over procedures correctly.
- Ensure sufficient change is always

available for use.
- Be aware of all the security aspects involved in the handling of cash.
- Produce all the accompanying documentation efficiently, accurately and neatly.
- Store the payment and accompanying documentation securely.
- Give receipts and vouchers where appropriate.

- Ensure that the payment point is secured from unauthorised access.
- Report or deal with any unusual or unexplained behaviour or situations in accordance with laid down procedures.
- Deal with customers in a polite and helpful manner at all times.
- Comply with all health and safety regulations at all times.

What you need to know

- Why you must be correctly prepared at the beginning of your shift with all the opening and hand-over procedures completed, and why you must complete all hand-over or closing down procedures at the end of the shift.
- Why you must follow company procedures at all times, especially when actually handling cash, handing over change or handing over cash to authorised persons.
- Why you should never hand over cash to unauthorised persons, and always maintain customer bills accurately and securely.
- Why you should always have a sufficient amount of change, and how to anticipate and deal with any shortages of change before they arise.

- What the bar's procedures are for processing non-cash payments.
- How to authenticate all forms of non-cash payment.
- How to prepare the appropriate documentation to accompany non-cash payments.
- How to deal with any problems or discrepancies that occur.
- Why security both of the payment point and access to the payment point are so important.
- How to deal with vouchers and tokens.
- How to deal with customers in a polite and helpful manner at all times, and work swiftly and efficiently.

OPENING, CLOSING AND HAND-OVER PROCEDURES AT A PAYMENT POINT

In bars customers are able to pay a bill at any time during opening hours. In residential catering establishments, such as hotels and hostels, the facility to pay bills may be available to customers 24 hours a day, seven days a week. However, there are always fairly regular high and low activity periods in establishments, although the actual routine varies from one establishment to another. For instance, in a bar, even if it is open from 11.00 a.m. until 11.00 p.m., the peak periods will be lunch time and evening. Thus, there are fairly standard shifts for most bar staff. Examples are as follows.
- An early shift will start sometime between 10.00 a.m. and 11.00 a.m. and go on until mid-afternoon, around 3.00 p.m. A late shift will start around 3.00 p.m. and continue until around 11.00 p.m.
- Some bars are open until the early hours of the morning. These are hotel bars where residents of the hotel are able to buy drinks at any time of the day. Bars in private clubs may also be open very late. In this case, they are often closed during the afternoon. If not, the change over between the early and late shift usually takes place between 5.00 and 6.00 p.m.
- Sometimes a bar may be required for a private function, in which case the opening times will be dependent upon the function requirements.

This means that the payment point is open for all of the time that the bar is open, and bar staff who handle cash upon starting or finishing a shift will have to go through various different procedures depending upon what time of day or night they are starting or finishing.

In most establishments the bar staff are responsible for handling their own bills, and operate their own payment points. They therefore open, close and hand over payment points as a regular part of their duties. The normal procedures which you, as a member of the bar staff, will have to follow in operating a payment point are described below. However you should always check to make sure that you are following your establishment's procedures.

Opening a payment point

When a start is made early in the morning, or as an establishment opens, you would be considered to be *opening a shift*. You would perform the following tasks.

- You will have to fetch, or receive the float and any other monies from where they had been stored overnight. This would normally be some sort of safe and would be authorised by the duty manager.
- When you have received the float you should count it, in the presence of the manager who is giving it to you. Both of you then agree on the amount that has been handed over. In most establishments there will be a book which you will sign to this effect.
- You will also have to set up the payment point and make it ready for your shift.
- Next ensure that the till or other billing machine is ready for use, and put the float securely in the cash drawer. How you ensure that the till or other billing machine is ready for use will vary from establishment to establishment. In essence, it means that you will ensure that the till rolls are in and working. In some bars you will also have to ensure that the paperwork necessary to create bills is available.
- You should then check to see if any transactions took place after the payment point had closed down at the end of the previous shift. This will mean that you will have to check with any staff who were on the previous shift to see what transactions, if any, took place and make sure that they are recorded correctly. In an hotel, this might entail making sure that late bar charges have been transferred to the reception payment point to be entered onto the customers' bills.
- You should also check to see if there are any special charges, discounts or promotions applicable during that shift.
- There may well be a hand-over book in which any such details have been noted which you should consult.

Date	Time	Amount	Till number/ Department	Issued by/ Handed over by	Received by

Example of a hand-over book

The exact procedure depends upon the policy of each establishment, which you will have to learn. Always follow your establishment's procedures, and if in doubt ask your supervisor.

Handing over a payment point

In a bar which is open for more than eight hours, it is normal for there to be a hand over (change over) of the bar staff. Normally this takes place during the afternoon, because it is usually the quietest time of the day. The hand over takes place when the late shift takes over from the early shift. The following points and tasks should be noted, but the exact order in which they are carried out depends upon the individual establishment.

Bar staff counting the float

- The payment point does not close during this procedure, which is why it is referred to as a *hand-over period*.
- During this time, the till rolls will be read, or some other computerised reading will be taken to show how much business has been done to this point. The cash, and other forms of payment, will be totalled up against the readings, and the float removed. The float should be the same amount as it was when the payment point was opened initially, and the cash, or other forms of payment should total the reading from the cash machines.
- The float will be formally handed over, and recorded as it was when the bar opened, and the till roll and takings removed by an authorised person to a secure place for banking.
- It is important to discuss any relevant points which have arisen during the shift. For example, perhaps one group of customers are paying in large denomination notes which means that the float is running short of change and action should be taken now.

Closing a payment point

At the end of the working day, the payment point will be closed down. The payment point closure procedures are along the lines listed below.
- A reading of all the business done to date will be taken, and the till roll removed.
- The takings will be counted against the cash point reading, and the float will be counted out again, but this time it will be handed back to management for safe storage overnight.

- All the customers' bills will need to be completely up-to-date, and, if applicable, made available to the authorised night staff.
- The hand-over/shift comment book will also need to be completed.

Exactly how these activities are completed varies from one establishment to another and is based upon its size and the number of payment points that it has. Remember that you must *never* deviate from your establishment's procedure because it is designed to safeguard you as much as anyone else.

Remember the following points

- If you do not open, close and hand over at a payment point correctly, the cash takings for the bar may be recorded incorrectly and mistakes will be very hard to trace.
- In some establishments, bar staff are required to make up any cash discrepancies at the end of their shift from their own pocket.
- If you do not open, close and hand over at a payment point *correctly*, all mistakes may be attributed to your shift and you may have to make up any cash discrepancies, whether or not the error occurred during your shift.
- Even when you are very rushed, never accept or hand over cash unless it has been signed for, or authorised in some way.

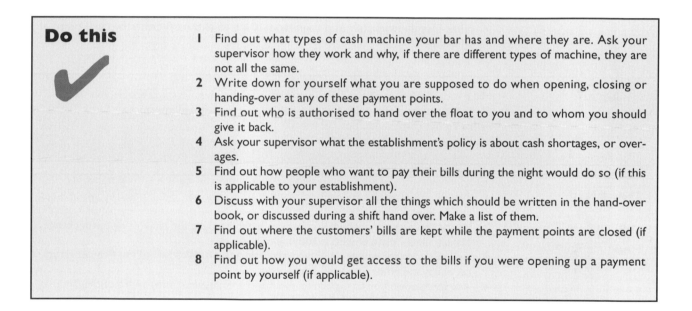

Do this

1 Find out what types of cash machine your bar has and where they are. Ask your supervisor how they work and why, if there are different types of machine, they are not all the same.
2 Write down for yourself what you are supposed to do when opening, closing or handing-over at any of these payment points.
3 Find out who is authorised to hand over the float to you and to whom you should give it back.
4 Ask your supervisor what the establishment's policy is about cash shortages, or overages.
5 Find out how people who want to pay their bills during the night would do so (if this is applicable to your establishment).
6 Discuss with your supervisor all the things which should be written in the hand-over book, or discussed during a shift hand over. Make a list of them.
7 Find out where the customers' bills are kept while the payment points are closed (if applicable).
8 Find out how you would get access to the bills if you were opening up a payment point by yourself (if applicable).

How to manage a float

The float which you receive at the beginning of your shift is to enable you to give change to your customers. It is not possible for you, or the management, to know exactly how all of the customers will pay – whether they will use cash, vouchers or some form of credit, or whether, if they give you cash, they will give you the exact amount or require change. This means that from time to time the change in your cash drawer could run out. *You should never let this happen.* If a customer is in a hurry to pay and does not want to wait while you try to find change, he or she will simply become annoyed at your inefficiency. To prevent this happening, you should always follow the procedure described below.

Procedure

1 When the change starts to run low, notify an authorised person about the situation. They will probably ask you what kind of change you are running low on

and how much more you think you need. This is something that you will learn to judge accurately as you become more experienced.

2   The change will then be brought to you by an authorised person, and they will usually ask you to give them the same amount of money back in large denomination notes. You may or may not be asked to sign for this transaction; it will depend upon company procedure. The total amount of money in your till should not be affected by this activity.

3   In some establishments when you receive the float, the exact breakdown of the float will be recorded, in others just the total amount.

4   Periodically during the day, authorised persons will remove the cash from all of the cash drawers. This is to prevent the build-up of cash, which would make the payment points a tempting target for thieves. When this happens, and when you are extracting the float from the takings at the end of the day, you should try to make sure that the money remaining in the cash drawer, or making up the float, is in small change so that change is always available for the customers' benefit.

5   On some shifts, everyone may pay by non-cash methods, so that you never run out of change. On other days, everyone may pay by large denomination notes and you run low frequently. This is a fact of business life, and you should not worry if you have to request more change frequently. You will not be able to provide an efficient service to the customers if you do not have the right equipment – in this case, enough change.

6   *Never* allow yourself to run out of change, so that in a panic you take change from other members of staff and then have to try to extract it from the cash point at a later date.

Essential knowledge	Make sure you have sufficient change available at all times. This will enable you to: ● give customers the correct change in the appropriate denominations ● carry out cash transactions efficiently ● keep the customer satisfied.

Do this ✔	1 Find out the float size for each payment point in your bar and, if possible, why it is set at that level. 2 Write down the procedure within your establishment for requesting extra change. Make a special note of who is authorised to do this. 3 Find out whether or not you have to list the exact breakdown of the float when you receive it and when you hand it back. 4 Ask your supervisor to explain to you how he or she becomes aware of the fact that they are running short of change. 5 Ask your supervisor if, because of the types of customer who use your bar, you require more change at certain times than others.

DEALING WITH AUDIT ROLLS, RECEIPT ROLLS AND CUSTOMER BILLS

Whenever you handle cash, tokens or vouchers there should be some paperwork to back up your action. This is for your own protection as well as to enable the establishment to judge how efficiently its business is running. It also enables any queries in the future to be traced back to the source and understood. For example, perhaps a customer may have paid too much for a round of drinks when the second identical round comes to a different total. The bar will want to confirm that this is what happened before they give a refund, and also why it happened so that they can prevent such an error occurring again.

There are two main ways of compiling and recording this information, and complying with legal requirements, either by using a conventional electronic till or via a computerised payment point.

At an electronic till

On a conventional electronic till there will be two rolls of paper. One is a till roll, or receipt roll, and one is the audit roll. When a payment takes place, the details of the payment will automatically be printed on both rolls. The receipt roll will be pushed out of the machine so that it can be given to the customer as proof of purchase, and the audit roll will remain within the machine, and have printed on it an exact copy of the information on the receipt roll.

A conventional till with receipt roll and audit roll

At the end of the day, when the payment point is closed down, and perhaps during the day, during hand-over periods, an authorised person will cause a total of the business to date to be recorded on the audit roll (and it may also appear automatically upon the receipt roll as well). They will then take away the relevant part of the audit roll and compare it with the actual takings to date, to make sure that there are no discrepancies.

You, the billing machine operator, will not be able to access the audit roll, but will be able to see it. You will have access to the receipt roll. At the beginning of each shift, you should check to ensure that there is enough of each roll to last throughout the shift. If customers are kept waiting while the till rolls are being replenished, it will make them impatient, and make the bar look inefficient.

At a computerised payment point

In a computerised payment point it is more likely that there will not be an audit roll. Instead there will be a program to which only authorised persons have access, and this program will automatically record each use of the payment point.

In both types of machine the receipt roll may be replaced by the customer's bill. This would be quite legal as long as the items on the bill are printed out by the machine and not recorded by hand. The customer's bill then acts as a receipt. However, it is customary in bars, other than those in hotels or restaurants, for the customer to pay for drinks as they are purchased. Thus the receipt roll is the usual type of customer bill in a bar.

If you work in an establishment where drinks are not paid for in cash when ordered, you must make sure that there is a plentiful supply of bills available for use during the shift, whether they be individual bills or an automatic feed supply to the payment point.

The exact procedure varies from establishment to establishment, and from one machine type to another.

Do this

1 Find out what kinds of audit roll, receipt roll and customer bill are used in your bar. Are they the same for each payment point?
2 Find out where the replacements are kept and if access to them is restricted.
3 Make a list of who is authorised to read the audit rolls or programs. Make a note of their job titles as well.
4 During a quiet period, ask your supervisor to show you how to change the receipt roll of any machine that you are likely to have to use.
5 If all the customer bills are numbered, ask your supervisor what to do if you have made a mess of a bill and it cannot be used. (Do not worry if you damage one or two bills at the beginning, your bar will have a procedure for dealing with this.)

Security of the payment point

Given that cash is such a temptation for thieves, it is obvious that all bar staff have to be very careful about security. You also have a duty to ensure that the customer is only asked to pay for those beverages, and perhaps meals, which they have consumed, and that they are charged for every item of food and drink consumed.

Remember the following points
● Any amount of cash is always a temptation to a thief.
● Members of staff are just as likely to steal from an establishment as a stranger.
● It is almost impossible to prove who is the real owner of a specific piece of currency. If £50 goes missing from the cash drawer and some people in the vicinity of the till have over £50 in their pockets, how do you prove who is the thief, or that none of them are?
● While you are the operator of a payment point, you are responsible for all the cash moving through that area. You are therefore responsible for any discrepancies between what should be there and what actually is there.
● If unauthorised persons gain access to the payment point, they may alter the billing machine entries for their own illegal reasons, with serious consequences for the business.

If you are the bar person authorised to deal with payments during a shift, then you are responsible for the security and safety of all the money in your cash drawer and for the safety and confidentiality of the customers' bills.

There are several golden rules which you should observe at all times:
● Never leave an unsecured cash point unattended for any period of time.
● Whenever you have to leave a payment point unattended, for example when clearing dirty glasses from a table, make sure that the payment point is securely locked.
● Never hand over cash, tokens or vouchers to, or receive cash from, anyone (even an authorised person) without the correct explanatory paperwork.
● Never allow anyone except the customer, or a properly authorised person, to look at a customer's bill.
● Never allow anyone without proper authorisation into the area of the payment point.
● If you have to make an adjustment to a customer's bill, get the proper authorisation and signature before you do so.

MEMORY JOGGER

What materials should you always have available in order to operate a payment point efficiently?

● Whenever you have the smallest doubt about the honesty of anyone's actions, contact your supervisor immediately.

In addition, each establishment will have a security procedure which has been set up to deal with each payment point's security needs. You must always follow this procedure.

In most bars, the payment point is incorporated within the bar counter itself

---

Essential knowledge

It is essential that payment points are secured from unauthorised access:
● to prevent strangers or members of staff stealing from the payment point
● to make sure unauthorised persons do not see customers' accounts
● to prevent anyone tampering with the payment point, for example by making false charges or adjustments to a customer's account
● to prevent damage to the payment points.

Do this

1 From time to time when you are in charge of a payment point you may need to leave it, for example, to go to the toilet. Find out what the procedure is within your establishment if this type of situation should arise.
2 Make a list of all those people who are authorised to have access to the customers' bills, and why they have that authorisation.
3 Discuss with your supervisor when you should hand over monies, to whom, why, and what is the required authorisation. Make notes of your discussion.
4 Do the same activity, but with monies received.

DEALING WITH CUSTOMERS AND UNEXPECTED SITUATIONS

MEMORY JOGGER

Why must customers always be dealt with in a calm and polite way?

The society in which we live teaches us to have certain expectations of various situations. When people do not act as we expect in a particular situation, they tend to stick out or cause problems for other people. For example, customers drinking in a bar expect to be asked to pay for the drinks as they are received, as required by law. Under normal circumstances this should be the case. Sometimes, however, it may not be, for example if there is a problem with the till. Another potential problem might occur if a customer says that he gave you a £20 note and you only gave change for a £10 note. If you are unable to deal with a customer immediately, or the situation is beyond the scope of your authority, remember to remain polite and calm, and contact someone who can help you deal with the situation.

Anticipating customer needs enables you to prevent most problems. If the busy period is between 12 noon and 2 p.m., make sure that you have plenty of spare bills, till rolls and a good cash float at 11.30 a.m. This is an example of being aware of a potential problem and defusing it before it occurs. The ability to do this comes through observation and experience.

However, you cannot anticipate all potential problems. If, on a summer's day, a customer walks towards a payment point with a heavy coat on, it may be that he has a gun or other weapon under the coat, as he intends to try to rob the establishment. But it may also be that the customer has just come to this country from a much hotter one, and is finding the English summer a little cold. If someone comes into the bar and has a glass of mineral water which he or she drinks very, very slowly and watches what is going on, it may appear that the person has dishonest intentions. But it may also be that he or she is early for an appointment or waiting to meet friends, and is merely killing time.

When you are responsible for a vulnerable area, like a payment point, you must learn to become aware of all unexpected behaviour, because of the potential trouble it could indicate. However, you must not overreact, and possibly embarrass a genuine customer who happens to be behaving in an unusual way.

Bearing in mind that you must never leave an open payment point unattended, the following points are useful guidelines as to what you can do and what you should not do.

● If you have any reason to believe that there is something unusual going on, you must do something immediately, such as contacting your supervisor, and not let it pass hoping that nothing will happen.
● You should always follow the establishment's policy in dealing with the situation. This would normally be to contact your supervisor, or the security department if your establishment has one, and report your suspicions.
● Approaching a potentially suspect person by yourself may not be a wise thing to do, nor possible if you are alone at the payment point. It could also be dangerous.
● Being aware of suspect behaviour also means keeping an eye out for packages left lying unattended. These may have simply been forgotten, or they may be much more dangerous.

Do this

1 Find out what your establishment's policy is for reporting unusual or suspicious behaviour.
2 Ask your supervisor, and other members of staff, about problems which frequently arise. Find out how they deal with them.
3 Make a note of when you have a problem at a payment point. After a week or so look at your notes and see if some problems are occurring regularly. If they are, discuss with your supervisor how you could anticipate them, and so prevent them from happening.

Case study

There was an accident on the way to work which blocked the traffic, and so you were late arriving for your shift. You had a very busy session and now you are cashing up at the end of your shift. The payments in your till do not match with the till readings.

1   How do you know that there is a discrepancy?
2   What action must you take?
3   What action can you take in the future to prevent this from happening again?

What have you learned

1   Why must you follow your establishment's procedures strictly with regard to the operating of a payment point?
2   What problems may you cause yourself if you do not open, close and hand over a payment point correctly?
3   What is a float?
4   Why should you always have a sufficient amount of change available in the cash drawer?
5   What is the difference between an audit roll and a receipt roll?
6   Why shouldn't the cash handler on duty have access to the audit roll or program?
7   Why must the customer have a receipt of some description?
8   Why must it be printed out by the cash machine?
9   What should you do if an unauthorised person wants access to a payment point?
10 Why should you never hand over any monies without the proper authorisation documents?
11 What should you do if you think that someone is behaving in an unusual fashion?
12 Why shouldn't you approach them directly?

ELEMENT 2:   Deal with payments

What you need to do

- Follow your establishment's procedures for handling and recording payments.
- Register or record correct price or code and inform customer of the amount due.
- Create a customer's bill.
- Receive cash, token and voucher payments, and give change when required.
- Issue receipts.
- Store payments securely, and in the required manner.
- Work swiftly and efficiently within the required time.
- Remain calm under pressure and deal with customers politely and helpfully at all times.
- Ensure that the payment point is secured from unauthorised access.
- Be aware of, and deal with, any unusual behaviour or situation.

What you need to know

- What all the prices in the bar are, and the codes for them on the cashiering machines, if applicable.
- How to issue a bill, calculate change, issue change (if applicable) and how to issue a receipt.
- How to store all forms of payment securely.
- How to work swiftly and efficiently, so that all work is done correctly by the required time.
- Why payment points must be secured from unauthorised access.
- How to deal with unexpected situations.
- How to deal with customers in a polite and helpful manner at all times.
- What the procedures of your establishment are for dealing with cash, token and voucher payments.

COMPILING A CUSTOMER'S BILL

In places like supermarkets, the customer's bill is often created by swiping the bar code on an item over a computer reader. This reader then tells the cash register how much to charge for the item, and then when all the items have been 'read', it totals up the amount automatically. The cashier does not need to know the price of any item individually, and so has quite an easy task when compiling a bill. This procedure cannot easily be followed in the service industries – you cannot put a bar code on a gin and tonic, for instance, or on a glass of wine. It would be especially difficult in bars which make mixed drinks and cocktails to order.

In some bars, the billing machine may be pre-programmed with the prices of standard drinks, such as an orange juice. However, even in these bars you will still need to know the correct code or symbol for each drink in order to press the correct key/s.

This means that you must be very skilful and accurate when compiling a bill, and know exactly what price to charge for each item of drink or food that the customer has purchased. Obviously you will not be able to remember the prices of everything which the customer can buy, especially in a very busy bar, or if there is a very long cocktail or wine list. Therefore the bar will have a set of procedures for keeping you up-to-date.

MEMORY JOGGER

When can you only accept cash payments?

The usual components of a bill in a bar are various drinks. There may also be snack items, such as crisps, or sometimes light meals. In England and Wales, it is illegal to give credit for alcoholic beverages. This means that, unless a customer is either staying in the establishment, where the bar is part of an hotel, or eating in it, where the bar is part of a restaurant, the customer must pay for drinks as and when they are ordered. Therefore compiling the bill is easy: it is for those drinks that you are serving to the customer at that time, with any food or snacks added on as necessary. However your bar may run promotions from time to time, such as a 'happy hour' where drinks are served for a reduced price within certain hours. Therefore you will need a list of any special promotions or discounts before you begin the service.

The basic principles of compiling a bill do not vary however, whatever items are on the bill. They are as follows.
- You must know what types of charge should be on the bill – if a customer had food as well as drinks, etc.
- If one type of charge appears to be missing, you should check. This can be done by contacting the appropriate department, i.e. if you are providing a table service and there appear to be no drinks charges while there is a food charge. You would then contact the dispense bar and ask if the customer had anything to drink with their meal. They may have only had tap water so no beverage charge would occur, but this is very unusual.
- Once you are sure that you have collected all the charges, you must ensure that you enter the correct figure on the bill. If the customer is a single person, he or she must be charged for only one portion of everything, ensuring that all discounts, etc. are taken into account, and so on.
- When all the charges are entered onto the appropriate cash register, they can be totalled, ready for presentation to the customer. If the customer is eating and you feel that they are likely to require some other services, for example they may decide to have coffee after their meal, then you might decide to delay the presentation of the bill. Common sense should tell you what is the most suitable action to take.

When compiling a bill, the most difficult part may be ensuring that the customer is charged the correct amount for any drink or food which they have consumed. This can be a problem, because you are not expected to remember all the possible prices within the bar, *and* because the bar may offer special discounts or promotions to certain people at certain times, so that the normal prices do not apply any way.

To prevent this problem occurring, there should be appropriate price lists at the pay-

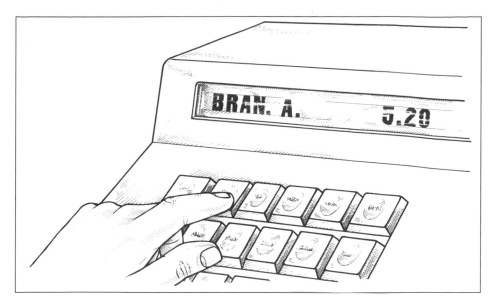

An electronic billing machine

ment point and, if any customers are receiving special rates, you should be given details of this before the customer arrives at the bar.

In some establishments which are highly computerised, it may not be part of the duties of the person operating the payment point to compile the bill because the charges are entered at source. In this case you may merely be required to total and print bills as and when required.

For instance, the bar person may take a food order on a computerised hand-held pad. This will automatically inform the kitchen of the dish ordered, and at the same time inform the payment point to start compiling this new bill.

Whatever system is used in any part of your establishment, there will be a set of guidelines for you to follow so that you will know, once you have collected all the necessary charges, how to record them and create a bill. Whatever system is used, you must take great care to make sure that the correct figure or code is entered accurately onto the right bill and that it is ready for presentation at the appropriate time.

Untidy, disorganised payment points will alienate customers

For certain bills it may be possible to anticipate when the customer is most likely to call for their bill. In these cases you can have the bill prepared in advance, to prevent possible delays if many bills are likely to be required at once. Likely busy periods, where bills can be prepared in advance, are immediately after lunch and dinner, if there is a popular food service as well. Otherwise most bills will have to be created at the time of service, even at peak periods.

Remember the following points
- It is illegal to charge a price other than the one advertised for any food or beverage.
- All basic prices must be displayed for the customer to see easily, whether for food, drink, accommodation or other services.
- It is very bad for the reputation of any establishment to accidentally over- or under-charge a customer.
- A messy bill, with lots of corrections, would indicate that the establishment, and its staff, are very inefficient.

Do this

1 Find out whether your bar uses a manual, computerised or semi-computerised system for compiling bills.
2 Practise compiling bills according to your establishment's procedures for any payment point which you are likely to have to work in.
3 Make a list of those bills which are compiled for immediate presentation and those for which you will receive payment at a later date.
4 If your bar uses codes to compile bills, make a list of all the standard codes and the charges they represent.
5 Make a list of all the different price lists within your establishment. Check to see that they are available at the appropriate payment point.

PRESENTING AND ACKNOWLEDGING CUSTOMER BILLS

There is always an *appropriate* time to present a bill to a customer – normally in a bar it is as the drinks are served. The bill may be presented either by the person working at the payment point, if the customer collects their drink themselves, or by a member of staff who takes the bill to the customer. This depends upon the type of bar it is (pub, hotel or restaurant), within which department the bill is required, and upon establishment procedure. If the customer is collecting the order themselves, it is usual for the bar staff just to tell the customer the amount owing and then, after payment has been received, a till receipt can be given with the change.

If payment is not taken immediately, for example if the customer is staying in an hotel and having a drink at the bar, when they do ask for their bill it should be presented in a written format. Normally it is printed by a cashiering machine, but in some establishments it is hand-written. In this case, great care should be taken to ensure that the writing is clear and legible. The customer should be given the bill in a written format so that they can see what charges are on the bill and therefore how the total amount was arrived at. The customer should be allowed time to study the bill, if they choose to do so, before the actual payment is collected.

When the bill is presented it should be done so discreetly. That is to say so that only the customer receiving the bill can see what charges are on it. There are several reasons for this.
- The customer may be entertaining someone else, perhaps for business or as a treat, and they would prefer the other person not to know how much was spent.
- The customer may simply not want the rest of the world to know how much they did or did not spend, or what discounts they received, etc.

Bills should be presented discreetly

When creating or totalling a bill, it is essential that the correct prices or codes are used, otherwise the bill will not be correct and unnecessary delays and embarrassment will be caused while the errors are corrected. It is also essential to use the correct price and code when accepting payment in any form. The correct price must be entered so that:

● you can give the correct change, if applicable
● the reading on the receipt roll and audit roll match that of the amount of payment received
● you charge the customer the correct amount of money.

By law, there must be a price list displayed near the point of service, which is large enough for both you and the customer to read.

On a computerised till, most prices will be indicated on the keyboard by a code. The correct code (or ledger information – if a bill is not being paid immediately, it may be sent to a company for payment, then it is called a ledger payment) must be entered when receiving payment so that the accounts department will know how much money to expect in cash and how much in other forms of payment. Again this information will either be indicated on the keys of the billing machine, whether

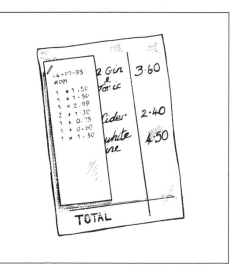

A bill with a receipt attached

computerised or not, or there will be a list of codes available at the payment point. You must make yourself familiar with the bar's procedure and codes.

Once payment has been made, even if it is for a non-cash payment, the customer must receive a machine-printed receipt showing the amount that they have paid. If the bill was created by machine rather than by hand, then it can be used for this purpose. However, if the bill was hand-written, the customer must be given a receipt from the billing machine's receipt roll as proof of the transaction.

The exact procedure will vary from establishment to establishment and from one machine to another.

Do this

✔

1 Find out whether your bar creates its customers' bills manually or by machine. If more than one system is used, find out why.
2 Learn how to compile the bills according to your establishment's procedures for any payment point which you are likely to have to operate. For example, you may have to work in two different bar areas at some time during your training.
3 Find out how your establishment presents bills to different types of customer, and in different departments, if applicable.
4 Make a list of all the codes which are used when operating a payment point within your bar, and what they mean.
5 Find out what types of receipt are issued at each payment point that you are likely to work at, and learn to create them yourself.
6 Ask your supervisor whether there are specific times of the day when certain customer bills are most likely to be required. If there are, ask why these busy times occur and what action you can take to anticipate them so that you will be able to react swiftly and efficiently to them (what work should you have done in advance, what should you have checked?).
7 Ask your supervisor what you should do if someone other than the customer, another guest perhaps, says that they have come to collect the bill on the customer's behalf.

ACCEPTANCE OF CASH PAYMENTS, RECEIPTS AND CHANGE

You may not always be able to give change to a customer, it depends upon the method they choose to pay by, but by law you must always give a printed receipt for each transaction which takes place.

In this section payment by cash, token or voucher is considered. Other methods of payment, such as credit cards, are discussed later in this Unit on page 55.

Cash payment means payment using the coinage and/or printed money of the country that you are in. If a customer pays by this method they are entitled to the appropriate amount of change, again in the coinage or printed money of that country.

When voucher or token payments are made no cash changes hands. This is a method of payment where the actual exchange of cash took place before the customer visited your establishment. For instance, a company may buy Luncheon Vouchers for its employees and include them as part of their pay package. Each voucher represents a certain cash value, which is written on it, and it can be exchanged for food and drinks in establishments which accept this type of voucher or token. When the customer has consumed their meal, they will pay for it using these vouchers instead of money. If the bill comes to £5.60 and the customer gives £6.00 worth of vouchers or tokens, they would not normally be entitled to any change.

SUB TOTAL	54	50
LESS PROMOTION	5	50
TOTAL	49	00

A bill showing an allowance against a person for a meal

Sometimes bars may have gaming machines which pay out the winnings in tokens which are redeemable in purchases from the bar. The tokens have no monetary value outside the bar. In this case, the same procedure as for accepting vouchers would be followed. Drinks to the face value of the tokens would be supplied, and any extra charge would be paid in cash. If the value of the tokens came to more than that of the drinks, change would not normally be given.

Some tokens or vouchers may be a form of part-payment. Sometimes organisations promote themselves by having special offers. They may say, for instance, that upon presentation of the voucher the customer can have a pint of beer at a reduced price. When this type of token or voucher is presented at the payment point, a certain portion of the bill is not charged to the customer, i.e. the reduced price pint, but the rest is, i.e. the other beverage and food charges.

Although a customer is not entitled to change when using a voucher, if for instance they did not have their free drink because they were taking antibiotics at the time, the management might allow them to use the unused facilities on their voucher at another time. However, this would be a decision which the manager would make and not you.

Whatever method of token or voucher payment is used, you must make sure that it is one which is accepted by your bar. There should be a list of those which are acceptable at the payment point. Normally, if a customer is going to settle their account using a voucher or token they will tell you when they arrive, or check in advance, perhaps by telephone. However there may be customers who present the voucher when they pay for their drinks. If the voucher or token is one which is

A promotional voucher from a brewery offering a pint of a new beer at a reduced price

accepted by the bar, it would simply be accepted and the appropriate information recorded on the bill. If, however, it is not a token or voucher which is acceptable to your bar, then you would have to say that you cannot accept it and ask for some other form of payment. If there are any problems here, perhaps if the customer insists that the voucher should be accepted, then you should be courteous and polite, explaining that you are not able to help them, and ask your supervisor to deal with the problem. Problems often arise if people do not read the expiry dates, or exact terms on special offers.

When a voucher or token is accepted in place of a cash payment, it must be cancelled immediately so that it cannot be used again. There are various methods for doing this. There may be a section on the token or voucher which should be filled in by you, it may be company policy to write 'cancelled' across the voucher or token, or the bar may have special date stamps which can be used to show when the voucher was accepted and by what department.

A cancelled voucher

Assuming that everything is fine, the payment in cash, token or voucher form should be accepted, cancelled where appropriate, and stored in the correct compartment of the cash drawer.

In some bars, it is establishment policy that payments by large denomination notes are not placed in the till until after change has been given. This is in case a dispute should arise as to the value of the note. You must follow your establishment's procedure in this area, as always.

As soon as the payment has been placed in the cash drawer it must be closed, for security reasons, to make it less vulnerable to theft, etc. (See Essential knowledge, page 66.) On some machines it is not possible to start a second transaction unless the cash drawer has been fully closed from the first one.

If cash, tokens or vouchers are not placed neatly in the cash drawer then it will be much harder, and much slower, finding change when it is necessary, and if the notes are muddled up into different denominations it is quite easy to give out the wrong change.

Once payment in any form has been accepted, the customer is entitled to a printed receipt. The receipt does not necessarily have to show the exact breakdown of the bill, but should show where and when the transaction took place, how much it was for and what type of service it covered, i.e. drink, food, snacks, etc. If the customer's bill was printed by the billing machine, this can act as the customer's receipt. This saves the customer having an extra piece of paper to carry around, and saves you time having to produce the receipt, and is the normal practice in bars. If the customer's bill is also their receipt, it is customary for the bill/receipt to be duplicated on the audit roll so that the establishment retains a copy of it.

A well-organised till drawer   *A disorganised till drawer*

If the customer's bill was hand-written, it would often be in duplicate, and they would have to be given a printed receipt from the till roll. The bottom copy would be kept by the bar and used by the accounts department to make sure that all trans-actions have been correctly charged for, and all monies taken correctly recorded.

Exactly what you will have to do depends upon the type of billing machines which your establishment uses, the vouchers and tokens they accept and the establishment's procedures for accepting payment. You must find out all this information as quickly as possible.

Do this ✔

1 Make a list of all of the vouchers and tokens which your bar accepts.
2 Make a list of how to cancel them once they have been accepted.
3 Find out what the bar's policy is if a customer wants to pay with a voucher or token which the establishment does not normally accept.
4 Find out whether the billing machines tell you how much change you should give a customer when they pay by cash, or if you have to work it out.
5 Find out what type of receipts your establishment issues. Are they the same for all payment points?

ACCEPTANCE AND VALIDATION OF NON-CASH PAYMENTS

There are various types of non-cash payment. Each must be treated slightly differ-ently, but no matter what establishment you work in the basic acceptance and vali-dation procedures for each type of payment remain the same. The main types of payment are:
- cheques, for example bank, giro or building society cheques, sterling travellers' cheques, Eurocheques
- credit cards, for example Access/Mastercard, Visa/Barclaycard
- charge cards, for example American Express, Diners Club
- direct debit cards, for example Switch, Visa.

Cheques

People tend to carry cheques with them rather than cash if they are not sure how much their bill will come to and because it is a more secure form of payment than cash. If cheques are stolen, the customer can report this to the issuing company which can cancel them, and no money is lost. This is not possible with cash. This does mean, however, that when accepting a cheque payment you must always consult the establishment's cancelled/invalid lists. These lists will also record the number of any bank cards which are no longer valid and which should also not be accepted in payment.

ACCESS INVALID CREDIT CARD LIST 25.2.96

Card Number	Expiry Date
5534 9948 7535 9630	10/96
7984 5555 2341 9804	9/96

A cancelled/invalid cheques and credit cards list

Bank cheques

Cheques are issued by banks, the post office (giro cheques) and building societies. If you are presented with a cheque, then it means that the customer has an account with the issuing establishment into which they pay money with which their cheques will be paid. A cheque can only be used in the country and currency in which it was issued. This means that a cheque from a Barclays Bank, for example, anywhere in the UK can be accepted anywhere within the UK and the amount written on it will be in pounds sterling.

A cheque that has been filled in

Eurocheques

A Eurocheque is similar to a normal cheque but it can be accepted anywhere within the European Union and written in any currency. This means that a customer from France can bring a Eurocheque, issued by a bank in France, to the UK and pay for goods and services in sterling.

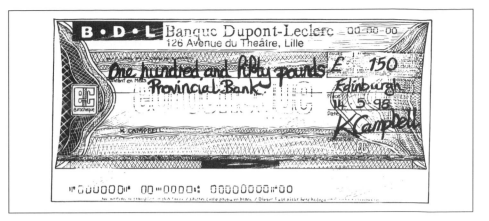

A Eurocheque that has been filled in

Travellers' cheques

A sterling travellers' cheque is slightly different. In this case the customer will usually have bought, and paid cash for, the travellers' cheques from a financial institution, for instance Thomas Cook or American Express, because carrying cheques is safer than carrying large amounts of cash around. When your establishment accepts the travellers' cheque, it will eventually get its money from the issuing company, which already has the customer's money.

A travellers' cheque that has not yet been counter-signed

Bank cards

A bank card is a small plastic card issued by a bank, post office or building society which contains information to enable an establishment to verify the ownership of a cheque.

Bank, giro, building society and Eurocheques should all be supported by the relevant bank card. The bank card has a cash figure on it, usually a multiple of £50, and the signature of the customer. This is to enable you to check that the bill total is not for more than the issuing establishment will accept (the cash amount on the bank card). By checking the signature on the card against the signature on the cheque you can make sure that the cheque has been written by the correct person. Travellers' cheques are usually supported by a passport or official ID card. Here you will be able to look at the photograph and signature and establish the identity of the customer. If there is no supporting card or passport you should not accept the cheque.

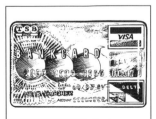

A bank guarantee card

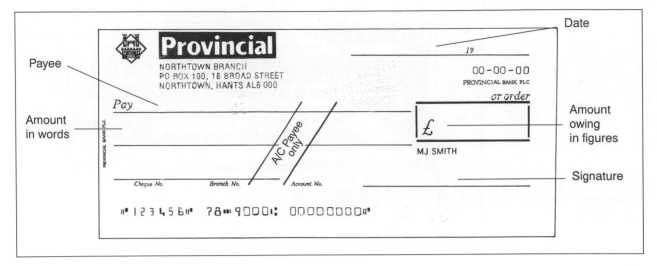

A blank cheque

Basic procedure for accepting bank, giro, building society and Eurocheques

1 Show the customer the bill, so that they can write out the amount owing on the cheque.
2 Take the completed cheque from the customer and check the following points:
   - the date is written in correctly
   - the amount, both in writing and figures, is written correctly
   - the signature on the cheque is the same as that on the bank card
   - that the signature on the bank card is written on the original paper strip (if a new strip has been pasted to the bank card, when you run your thumb over the back of the card it would catch on the different surface)
   - if your establishment has a validation machine, hold the card under the ultra violet light to check that the hologram is a true one and not a two-dimensional fraud
   - the bank card is valid, not out of date, etc.
   - it is the correct bank card; you can check this by making sure that the sort code on the cheque is the same as the sort code on the bank card (except with a Barclays Bank bank card because the bank card is also able to be used as a credit card under certain circumstances)
   - the total of the bill does not exceed the guarantee figure on the bank card (if it does you must follow your establishment's procedure for dealing with the cheque)
3 Compare the bank card and cheque with the cancelled/invalid list; make sure that it does not appear on it.
4 Write the card number on the back of the cheque. (You may also be asked to write down other information but that will depend upon your establishment's procedures.)
5 Place the cheque in the cash drawer.
6 Give the customer back their bank card, plus a copy of the bill, and a printed receipt if applicable.

If the bill total is for more than the amount guaranteed on the bank card your establishment will have a set of procedures for you to follow. This usually means that other information is entered on the back of the cheque, so that if the cheque is not honoured (paid) by the issuing company, the customer can be traced and asked to pay by another method.

Your establishment will also have a procedure to follow if the cheque or bank card number show up on the cancelled/invalid list. Make sure that you are familiar with the procedure and follow it, always remembering to be as discreet and tactful as possible. If you accept payment from a cheque or bank card which has been withdrawn, the issuing company will not honour the cheque and your establishment, and perhaps you, will lose money. If, on the other hand, you retain an invalid card correctly you may be financially rewarded.

In some bars cheques are not hand-written, they are printed out by the billing machine. In this case the above procedures remain the same except for point (1). The procedure would then be:

1   Show the customer the totalled bill, and take a cheque from them. Print the cheque on the billing machine and return it to the customer for checking and signature.

Then continue as before.

Basic procedure for accepting sterling travellers' cheques

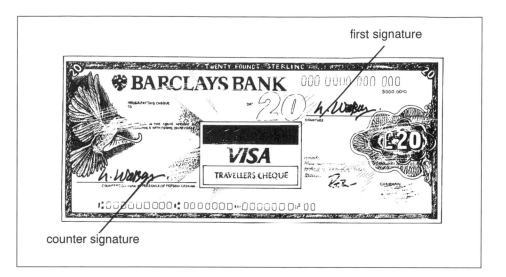

A sterling travellers' cheque, complete with counter signature

Before accepting a sterling travellers' cheque, you should note the following.
●   An unauthorised travellers' cheque is one on which the second signature is not yet filled in. The first one was filled in when the customer bought the travellers' cheques.
●   Travellers' cheques are issued for standard amounts – £5, £20, £50, etc. This means that when a customer uses this method to pay, the amount on the travellers' cheque is unlikely to be the same as the amount on the bill.
●   If the value of the travellers' cheque is greater than the value of the bill, you should give the customer change for the difference. For example, if the bill is for £19.50 and the customer gives travellers' cheques worth £20, they would be entitled to £0.50 change. If on the other hand, a customer's bill came to £25 and they gave the bar staff £20 in travellers' cheques, the difference would have to be made up, usually by the customer paying £5 in cash.
●   Often a customer may use more than one travellers' cheque to pay for one bill. For example, they may use two £50 cheques to pay for a £100 bill. This is an acceptable, standard practice.
●   Customers who are entitled to change may only be given change in sterling. Only banks and suitably licensed premises are legally allowed to issue foreign cash.
1   Show the customer the totalled bill.
2   Accept from the customer unauthorised travellers' cheque(s), usually for more than the total of the bill.

3 Accept from the customer an authorised form of identification, usually a passport or an official ID card.

4 Ask the customer to date the travellers' cheque, and countersign it (that is, to enter the second signature). This second signature should only be entered in front of the person receiving the payment so that they can authenticate the signature.

5 Check the signature and the photograph in the passport or on the ID card against the signature and person in front of you.

6 If it is your establishment's procedure, write down the passport or ID card number on the back of the travellers' cheque.

7 Receive the difference between the total of the travellers' cheques being offered and the total of the bill, if applicable.

8 Give the correct change, the identification documents and a printed receipt to the customer.

9 Place the travellers' cheque(s) safely and correctly in the cash drawer.

Credit cards and charge cards

Some cards are issued by banks, such as Barclays, and others are issued by large financial institutions, such as American Express. Some are only acceptable within the UK and some are acceptable internationally. Not all bars accept all credit and charge cards. This is because they have to pay commission to the issuing company. Your bar will have a list of those charge and credit cards which it accepts, and you should familiarise yourself with it so that you only accept the listed cards.

Credit cards

As far as accepting payment by credit or charge card is concerned, you will follow the same basic procedures. This is because the main difference in the type of card is how the establishment receives its final cash payment from the issuing company. Another difference which you will notice is that the internationally accepted cards, which tend to be charge cards, normally have a higher guarantee limit, and the restaurant will have a higher floor limit (see below) for this type of card.

A cheque is guaranteed by a bank card, and checking against the cancelled/invalid list. A charge card or credit card payment is guaranteed by the card's printed limit, by the floor limit of the establishment, by an authorisation code and by checking the cancelled/invalid list.

Floor limits
The floor limit is the bar's credit limit – the maximum amount that can be accepted without authorisation for a credit or charge card payment. Its purpose is to try to reduce the potential for fraud. Normally there is a different floor limit for each type

of card which the establishment accepts. If the total of a bill exceeds the floor limit, an authorisation code must be obtained from the issuing company otherwise they may not honour the payment.

Authorisation codes

An authorisation code is needed whenever the bill total is for more than either the card's stated limit, the bar's floor limit, or both. In this case, you must contact the issuing company by following the bar's procedure. This will normally be to telephone a special number. You will give the issuing company the following information:

- the name of the bar
- the reference number of the bar
- the name, number and expiry date on the card
- the total of the bill.

If everything is in order, the issuing company will give you a number. This is the authorisation code. It guarantees that the issuing company will reimburse the bar for the total of that bill even if the customer should run out of money. Once an authorisation code has been obtained, no adjustments may be made to the customer's bill. If an adjustment has to be made, a new authorisation code for the new amount must be sought.

If there is a problem, you will be asked to retain the card and inform the customer why you are doing so. If this happens, your bar will have a standard procedure to follow to help you do this. It will probably recommend that you contact your supervisor.

Always remember that when a card is cancelled, while it may be that the customer is trying to defraud your restaurant, it could also be that they are a genuine customer whose last payment was simply held up by something like a postal strike. If they are a genuine customer, they will be deeply embarrassed, and would not want anyone else to know what has happened. Therefore you must be discreet. In all circumstances you must follow your bar's procedures, as well as asking for another form of payment.

Basic procedure for accepting credit and charge cards

In some bars, the method of accepting credit and charge cards is manual, and in others it is incorporated into a computerised system. The procedures vary slightly so both are described below. It may also be useful for your future career to learn both systems.

Procedure for a manual acceptance system

1 Give the customer the totalled bill.
2 Accept from the customer the credit or charge card.
3 Check that this is a card which is accepted by your bar, and the floor limits for this type of card.
4 Check the following details on the card:
   - that it is still valid, i.e. the expiry date has not yet been reached
   - the cash guarantee limit of the card
   - check that the signature is the original one by running your thumb over it (if a new paper strip has been added with a new signature written on it, your thumb will catch on the edge of the new strip)
   - if your bar has a validation machine, place the credit or debit card under the ultra violet light to check that the hologram is real, and not a two-dimensional fraud.
5 Take a blank voucher and the credit card, and run them through the imprinting machine.
6 Write the following information on the voucher:
   - date
   - department, if applicable

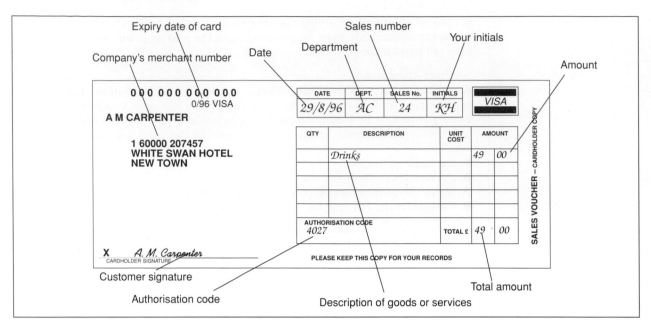

A credit card voucher

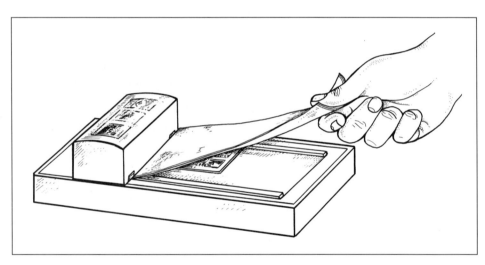

*A credit card and voucher
in an imprinter*

- sales number, if applicable
- your initials
- a brief description of what is being paid for, such as 'drinks'
- the amount of the bill in the amount section and the total section
- the authorisation code, if applicable.

7 Give the voucher back to the customer to sign.

8 Check the customer's signature on the voucher against the signature on the card. (The card may be valid, but it may not be the owner of the card who has presented it to you.)

9 Give the customer the customer's copy of the voucher, their card and a printed receipt.

10 Place the bar's copies of the vouchers in the correct place in the cash drawer.

Procedure for a mechanised acceptance system

1 Give the customer the totalled bill.

2 Accept from the customer a charge or credit card.

3 Check that it is a card which is accepted by the bar.

4 Swipe the card through the appropriate machine. (There will either be a separate machine through which to swipe the card, or it may be incorporated as part of the billing machine.) The machine will automatically check the card and provide an authorisation number. When the checks have been successfully completed the machine will print out a duplicate voucher.
5 Ask the customer to sign the voucher.
6 Check the signature on the voucher against that on the card. (The card may be valid, but it may not be the owner of the card who has presented it to you.)
7 Give the customer the customer's copy of the voucher, their card and their copy of the bill.
8 Place the bar's copies of the voucher in the correct place within the cash drawer.

In some bars, there may be a combined manual and mechanised system. Here the normal procedure would be for you to validate the card by swiping it through an authorising machine and entering the total of the bill. The machine would automatically show the authorisation code on a digital display, and you would complete processing the card via the manual system. This system is more popular now than an entirely manual system, because it saves time and all cards can be validated quickly and efficiently at any time of day or night.

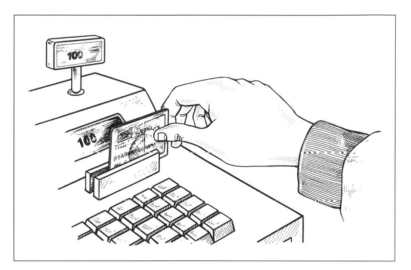

An authorisation machine

If at any stage you are not happy with the transaction, you cannot get an authorisation code or the signatures do not look the same (even after you have asked the customer to sign for the second time on the back), etc., you should not accept the payment, but follow the bar's procedures and get assistance from another member of staff.

This is especially necessary if the payment point is very busy. If you take a long time to deal with one customer, others will start to ask where their bills are and become frustrated. It is also very difficult to be discreet when there is a problem with lots of other people around, like customers and bar attendants, all trying to collect or pay bills, and therefore able to overhear any conversation which might be going on.

Direct debit cards

These are cards which directly debit the customer's bank account with the total of the bill, and place that amount into the bar's bank account. It is therefore similar to accepting cash, in that there is no waiting period for the payment. However the procedure for accepting payment by this method is very similar to the mechanised credit or charge card system. The most common card of this type is a Switch card.

Many people choose to carry them in preference to cash, as a security measure. Bars are happy to accept them because, as long as they are correctly accepted, the bar is guaranteed its money straightaway.

Basic procedure for accepting a direct debit card

1 Give the customer the totalled bill.
2 Accept from the customer the direct debit card.
3 Check that it is a card which is accepted by the bar.
4 Swipe the card through the appropriate machine. (There will either be a separate machine through which to swipe the card, or it may be incorporated as part of the billing machine.) The machine will automatically check the card. When the checks have been successfully completed, the machine will print out a duplicate voucher.
5 Ask the customer to sign the voucher.
6 Check the signature on the voucher against that on the card. (The card may be valid, but it may not be the owner of the card who has presented it to you.)
7 Give the customer the customer's copy of the voucher, their card and their copy of the bill.

As with any other form of non-cash payment, if you are not happy with any part of the acceptance or validation procedure, you should follow your bar's procedure for dealing with problems in a non-cash payment situation. This will normally involve explaining the problem to a more senior member of staff, in the first instance.

Dealing with errors or spoilt cheques or vouchers

From time to time, especially when you first start training, you will make errors. Your supervisors will expect a few problems to occur, and there will be an establishment policy for dealing with them. However, when a cheque or voucher is spoilt or written incorrectly there are several basic steps to follow which will be part of your establishment procedure.

Cheques

If any part of the cheque is written out incorrectly (most often the date), the customer can cross the error through, write down the correct information and initial the error. As long as the cheque is still clearly legible, it will not matter if there is more than one correction on it, but all the corrections *must* be initialled by the customer.

If there are a lot of corrections it is better to cancel the cheque by tearing it up in front of the customer so that they can see you doing it, and giving them the torn cheque if they require it. A new cheque can then be written.

Credit or charge cards

Manual system

If there are any errors the voucher must be voided. The voucher should be torn up, in front of or by the customer, and they should be given the torn voucher if they require it. A new voucher should be written out.

Mechanised system

If you are using a mechanised method of accepting credit or charge cards and an error is made in the creation of the bill before it has been signed, there will be a method of cancelling the voucher immediately. Your establishment will have a procedure for this. There is probably a void key on the machine which will cancel the transaction. However you must always follow your establishment's procedure, keeping all paperwork that is generated by the error, i.e. the incorrect voucher and the cancellation slip. These should be placed in your cash drawer and handed over with the rest of the money at the end of your shift.

Do this

1 Write down the procedure for accepting a cheque if it is for more than the guaranteed cash limit on the card.
2 Make a list of forms of ID, other than a passport, acceptable to your establishment when accepting sterling travellers' cheques.
3 Make a list of all the credit cards and charge cards which your bar accepts.
4 Make a list of your establishment's floor limits for each card which is accepted.
5 Find out where the cancelled/invalid lists are kept. Make sure that there is one beside the cash point.
6 Write down exactly what you should do if you are at all worried about accepting a non-cash payment.
7 Find out whether your bar uses a manual or mechanised credit and charge card authorisation system, and learn how to use it.
8 Write down the procedure which your bar uses to cancel unusable cheques and vouchers.

SECURITY OF THE PAYMENT POINT

The bar is generally one of the most secure areas, by nature of its trading practice. However, any form of payment is a temptation to dishonest people, so it is obvious that security of the payment point is very important. If unauthorised persons gain access to a payment point they will be able to gain access to the customers' bills, as well as cash and other forms of payment.

Unauthorised people may also behave in other dishonest ways, for example they may alter the totals of the customer's bills, i.e. lower their own. They may also simply steal, i.e. remove cash and other valuable items.

For these reasons payment points must be kept secure, and are sometimes physically separate from the other parts of the bar, and may even be within a secure cubicle. In other establishments the payment point may be incorporated within the main bar counter.

If you are the person authorised to deal with payments during a shift, you are responsible for the security and safety of the contents of your cash drawer and for the safety and confidentiality of the customers' bills.

There are some golden rules which you should observe at all times.
● Never leave the open payment point unattended for any period of time.
● Never allow anyone except the customer, or a properly authorised person, to look at the customers' bills.
● Never allow anyone without proper authorisation into the area of the payment point.
● If you have to make an adjustment to a customer's bill, get the proper authorisation and signature before you do so.
● If you have to void a voucher or cheque, actually tear it up in front of the customer so that they can be certain that it has been destroyed.
● Whenever you have the smallest doubt about the honesty of anyone's actions, contact your supervisor immediately.

In addition, each establishment will have a security procedure which has been set up to deal with each payment point's security needs. You must always follow this procedure.

MEMORY JOGGER

Why must you never leave the payment point unattended?

A bar counter with a closed off end/area, such as is often found in cocktail bars or where the payment point services both the restaurant and the bar

Essential knowledge	It is essential that payment points are secured from unauthorised access:

Essential knowledge

It is essential that payment points are secured from unauthorised access:
- to prevent members of the public or members of staff stealing from the payment point
- to make sure unauthorised persons do not see customers' accounts
- to prevent anyone tampering with the payment point, for example by making false charges or adjustments to customers' accounts
- to prevent damage to the payment points.

Do this ✔

1 From time to time when you are in charge of a payment point you may need to leave it, you may need to go to the toilet for instance. Find out what the procedure is within your bar if this type of situation should arise.
2 Make a list of all those people who are authorised to have access to the customers' bills, and why they have that authorisation.
3 Discuss with your supervisor when you should hand over any form of payment, to whom, why, and what is the required authorisation. Make notes of your discussion.

DEALING WITH REFUNDS

You may be the first person to hear about a problem for which a customer feels that they are entitled to a refund. This is because the payment point is where they settle their account. When dealing with such customers you should remember the following points.

- From time to time refunds either in cash or credit will need to be made by all establishments.
- Not all refunds are the results of errors, or bad service, etc. However, most are.
- A customer requiring a refund will usually be unhappy about something and therefore will require especially sympathetic handling.
- Applications for refunds are as open to abuse, such as fraud, as payments are.
- Because all applications for refunds are potentially fraudulent, all refunds must be appropriately authorised.
- The issuing of a refund must be authorised and recorded. If cash is handed over without being recorded, the person who handed it over is open to accusations of cash discrepancies, i.e. theft.
- All applications for refunds must be recorded so that management can take action to prevent the problem reoccurring

There are three basic reasons why a customer may ask for a refund, but in each case they may be, or appear to be, very angry and so need to be treated very politely and diplomatically. The reasons are as follows.

- If something has gone wrong. For example if the customer asked for slimline tonic in their gin and tonic and were served ordinary tonic, then they are entitled to be angry. If they requested an extra napkin, and it did not arrive before the end of their meal, they are caused great inconvenience. This means that when you are dealing with them you will have to be especially tactful.
- A customer may be 'trying it on'. That is to say, seeing if they can get a price reduction even if they are not really entitled to it. After investigating the incident, a senior member of staff will have to give authorisation, once they are satisfied that the incident has occurred. The customer usually appears very angry in order to intimidate the establishment's staff. This is why a senior member of staff should investigate it and deal with the problem.
- A customer may have a problem, but they may have caused it themselves. For example when they ordered their cocktail, they did not mention that they were taking antibiotics, and so should not drink alcohol; alcohol was used in the preparation of the cocktail, and so they became ill. Again a senior member of staff will have to investigate the incident, and make a decision about whether or not the guest is entitled to some form of compensation.

In all these cases, it is you who often gets the first blast of anger. Your bar will have a procedure to deal with this. If you follow it and remain calm, the incident can be defused and remedies offered. But if you take the customer's anger personally and become angry in return, the problem will get worse. For more information about how to deal with customer complaints see Unit 2NG3.

Validating and issuing a refund

Your bar will have a procedure for validating and issuing refunds. You must never deviate from this procedure because it is designed to protect staff as well as the bar.

Issuing a refund means giving money away from the business. It can only be done if a senior member of staff has authorised it. Giving money away means that the money in your cash drawer will be short. You must have documentation to justify the shortage. As a refund claim is as potentially open to fraud as any other payment transaction, the claim must be validated before the refund is issued.

Most establishments will follow the same basic rules and only the fine detail will vary from one establishment to another. The basic procedure is:

1 The bar becomes aware of a problem. This may happen in two ways:
- In the first incident the bar's staff become aware of the problem, and alert the appropriate senior member of staff. For instance, a customer who has arranged a surprise party at the bar asked for a special keg beer to be available, and paid a deposit in advance for it as it was an unusual request. The

wrong type of beer has arrived, and the brewer has closed for the day. Here the management know that there is a genuine problem before the customer is aware of it and complains. They can work out the remedial action to take, i.e. arrange for the similar beer to be available for the party's arrival, but charge a reduced amount for it.

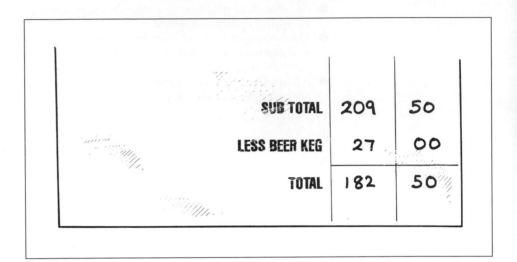

SUB TOTAL	209	50
LESS BEER KEG	27	00
TOTAL	182	50

A customer's bar bill with a reduction against the price of the beer

- In the second type of incident the customer becomes aware of the problem first. For instance, they may have ordered one dessert after their meal but the cost for two has been put on their bill. Your first action, after apologising, would be to contact the appropriate senior member of staff. The senior member of staff will quickly investigate the incident.

2 Once the senior member of staff is sure that the incident happened, they will authorise you to make a refund. They will do this by writing up the incident in a Refund Book, which will be similar to the example given below:

Date	Details	Cash Refund	Credit Refund	Authorised By	Cashier

A page from an example Refund Book

Where there is a very simple manual or semi-mechanised payment system in operation, a cash refund may be authorised without the above paperwork, but simply by an authorised person initialling on the till/audit roll.

3 If the refund is a cash refund then cash is removed from the cash drawer and given to the customer. There will normally be a duplicate book for the customer to sign saying that they have received the cash, with the bottom copy going into the cash drawer to justify the reduction in cash. If the refund is a credit refund

(that is to say that there is an adjustment made on the customer's bill), then no cash changes hands, but when the customer comes to pay their bill there will be a reduction on it for the agreed amount.

4   If the refund is a credit or charge card refund, you will have to fill in a voucher which is very similar to a credit or charge card voucher, but it will say refund. You will take an imprint of the customer's card, or run it through an authorisation machine, according to your establishment's procedures. The customer will sign the voucher and retain their copy. However when the customer eventually receives their statement from their credit or charge card company they will find that the refund amount has been deducted from their statement, not added on to it.

As previously mentioned, if your establishment has a mechanised method of accepting credit and charge card payments, and you make an error which you notice before the voucher is signed, there will be a method of voiding the voucher which you have just created. Always follow your establishment's procedure for doing this.

5   If the senior member of staff is not satisfied that the refund is justified, they will not authorise it and will deal with the customer in private, away from the public work areas. If there is no authorisation, you must never give out a refund, even if it is only for a tiny sum like £0.50, because you may not know the whole story.

In all bars, the basic procedures will be as described above. However there will be variations in the documentation to be completed and in the members of staff who are authorised to issue refunds. You must learn the procedure for your bar.

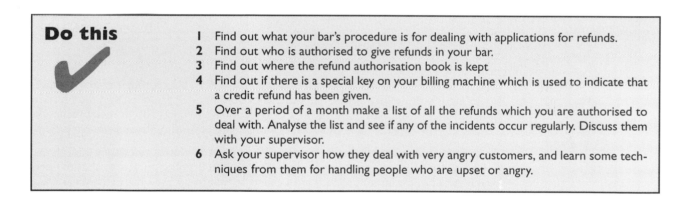

Do this

1   Find out what your bar's procedure is for dealing with applications for refunds.
2   Find out who is authorised to give refunds in your bar.
3   Find out where the refund authorisation book is kept
4   Find out if there is a special key on your billing machine which is used to indicate that a credit refund has been given.
5   Over a period of a month make a list of all the refunds which you are authorised to deal with. Analyse the list and see if any of the incidents occur regularly. Discuss them with your supervisor.
6   Ask your supervisor how they deal with very angry customers, and learn some techniques from them for handling people who are upset or angry.

DEALING WITH CUSTOMERS AND UNEXPECTED SITUATIONS

Customers expect an efficient service at all times. This should always be provided, but sometimes it may not be. If you are unable to assist a customer straightaway, remember to remain polite and calm at all times, and if you are unable to deal with the customer at all, contact someone who can.

Anticipating customer needs will enable you to prevent most problems. If most people use your establishment between 6 p.m. and 11 p.m. make sure that all the documentation for creating bills is ready by 5.30 p.m. This is an example of being aware of a potential problem and defusing it before it occurs. The ability to do this comes through observation and experience.

A customer who may have criminal intentions

You cannot, however, anticipate all potential problems. If a customer walks towards a payment point with a folded paper held in both hands, it may be that they have a gun or other weapon under the paper, as they intend to try to rob the establishment. It may also be that the customer has a strange way of holding their newspaper.

If someone comes into the bar and just orders a mineral water which they take a very long time to drink, while sitting and watching what is going on, it may that the person has dishonest intentions. But it may also be that the person has arrived early for a meeting with a friend and is merely killing time.

The ability to deal well with unexpected situations comes mainly through personal experience, and observing how others deal successfully with incidents. The bar's procedure for dealing with unexpected incidents has been set up to provide a set of guidelines to work within, but common sense is also required.

When you are responsible for a vulnerable area, like a payment point, you must learn to become aware of all unexpected behaviour, because of the potential trouble it could indicate. However you must not overreact, and possibly embarrass a genuine customer who happens to be behaving oddly.

Bearing in mind that you must *never* leave an open payment point unattended, reread page 46 to remind yourself of the action you should take.

Do this

1 Find out what your bar's policy is for reporting unusual or suspicious behaviour.
2 Consciously try to become aware of anyone who is behaving in an unusual fashion when they enter a vulnerable area, like a payment point.
3 Ask your supervisor, and other members of staff about problem areas which frequently arise. Find out how they deal with them.
4 Make a note of when you have a problem at a payment point. After a week or so look at your notes and see if some problems are occurring regularly. If they are, discuss with your supervisor how you could anticipate them, and so prevent them from happening.

Case study

You are working in a bar in Cardiff, and one group of customers have got a bit merry and decide to try to confuse you. They offer you payment in Irish pounds or Scottish pounds, saying that they have no British currency on them.

1 What should you do?
2 What must you not do?
3 Is there any action which you can take to prevent an incident like this happening again?

Read Unit 2NG3, Element 2 if necessary.

What have you learned

1 If a customer gives you a form of payment which is more than the total of the bill, under what circumstances should you not give them change?
2 Why must vouchers and tokens be cancelled immediately?
3 Why must cash drawers be kept closed when not in actual use?
4 Why must the customer be charged the correct price for food and beverages?
5 Why should the customer be able to look at the bill before they pay it?
6 Why must price lists be displayed?
7 Why must printed receipts be given?
8 What do you need to guarantee a bank, giro or Eurocheque?
9 What do you need to guarantee a sterling travellers' cheque?
10 Which type of cheque can you give change for? In what currency?
11 If an error is made on a credit or charge card voucher, what is the most secure way of voiding it?
12 Which credit cards and charge cards are accepted by your bar?
13 How should all cheques and vouchers be held securely at a payment point?
14 Who should cheques and vouchers be given to and why?
15 Why shouldn't unauthorised people have access to a payment point?
16 Why must all refunds be authorised?
17 Who is able to authorise refunds?
18 What should you do if a refund is not authorised?
19 Where should a refund be recorded if it is:
    (a) a cash refund?
    (b) a credit refund?
20 Why must you remain calm and helpful all the time?
21 What should you do if you see an unusual occurrence within the bar?
22 Why must you never leave a payment point unattended?
23 Why must you report all unusual situations?
24 Why must you follow company procedure at all times?

Get ahead

1 Find out what fidelity bonding means.
2 Learn how all the payment points in your establishment work, not just the ones in your area.
3 Find out how all the charges on a customer's bill are arrived at, and how they get to the various payment points in the establishment.
4 Find out what a ledger payment is, and how the account is settled with your establishment.
5 Find out why your establishment only accepts certain vouchers and tokens.
6 Find out why some vouchers and tokens can only be used at certain times.
7 The government says that customers must have a printed receipt for each transaction; it will protect them. From whom will it protect them and how?
8 Your establishment should have a list of procedures which you must follow when operating a payment point. Some of those procedures are to protect the establishment, some are to protect the cash handlers, some cover both areas. Identify which procedures protect the establishment, which the cash handlers, which both. How do they do this?
9 Find out why it is useful for management to have the details of all refunds recorded. What use do they make of this information?
10 Find out the most common reasons for your senior staff to refuse to give a refund. What do they do when this type of situation occurs?
11 Find out how much commission your bar pays for each type of credit or charge card it accepts.
12 Find out why your bar accepts the cards it does.
13 Find out how long it takes for the bar to actually receive the money in the bank if it accepts payment by any non-cash method.
14 Make a list of the most common ways that conmen are able to defraud bars using non-cash payment methods.
15 Find out the legal position if very confidential information about customers is given out to unauthorised persons by your bar.

Develop and maintain positive working relationships with customers

This unit covers:
ELEMENT 1: **Present positive personal image to customer**
ELEMENT 2: **Balance needs of customer and organisation**
ELEMENT 3: **Respond to feelings expressed by the customer**
ELEMENT 4: **Adapt methods of communication to the customer**

INTRODUCTION

When serving food and drink in the bar one of the most important tasks is dealing with customers. For some customers you will be the first and last person they deal with, and for a few the only one. This means that how you behave is crucial to how the customer perceives the rest of the establishment, and whether or not they use it or any of its facilities again. You will have to develop great skills of tact and diplomacy in order to cope with all the situations which will arise, and learn to remain calm under all circumstances. Without customers you will have no work.

All customers are individuals and need to be treated as such. Most of the work involved in dealing with customers will be routine, and you will easily be able to help them if you have a good enough knowledge of the food and drink you are serving, how your establishment works and the facilities available within the local environment.

However you must also remember that you have obligations, or limitations upon your behaviour, with regard to the establishment that you work for. Some of these are legal requirements, and so you must try to achieve a balance between the needs of the customer and the limitations of the establishment.

ELEMENT 1: **Present positive personal image to customer**

What you need to do

- Deal with all customers in a polite and professional manner at all times.
- Work efficiently under stress.
- Identify all individual customer needs accurately and anticipate them, where possible.
- Help customers without being pushy or rude.
- Identify how your establishment requires you to present yourself.
- Maintain the required standards of behaviour and personal presentation at all times.
- Identify the equipment and supplies which you will need to work efficiently.
- Make sure the equipment is available, up-to-date and in good working order.
- Work within current health and safety, and all other relevant, legislation.

What you need to know

- What standards of behaviour and personal appearance your establishment expects you to maintain.
- Why you must always be polite and courteous to customers.
- What equipment you will need for each job that you may be asked to do.
- How to maintain and replenish that equipment.
- How to constantly seek to improve your relationships with your customers, within the professional limits of your establishment.

> ### MEMORY JOGGER
>
> Why must you always be polite to customers, even when you are very busy?

When you are at work, especially in a bar area you are acting as the public representative of your establishment, and how you behave will affect what the customers think about your establishment. Sometimes, when you are very busy, you may feel very pressured, for example if your customers can't make up their minds what to order and there are several customers to serve. If you snap at the customer, perhaps ask them to hurry up, they will become offended and very difficult. Remember that your customers have come out to enjoy themselves, do a business deal, or drown their sorrows, not to deal with your problems.

You must learn to deal efficiently with these pressures in a way that pleases the customer and enables you to use your time most effectively. For instance, if the customer can't decide which beer or cocktail to have, you can recommend one or two, which will both speed up their decision-making, and make them feel that you have contributed positively to their enjoyment. You could also suggest coming back to take their order later, if they are enjoying their discussion about what to have. Then you can serve someone else who knows what they want, but neither group of customers will feel neglected, and the first group will feel that you understood just what they wanted, thinking time. However, you must not forget your first group of customers, if they have chosen to think awhile, otherwise you risk losing the positive images which they have about the establishment.

If the customers require assistance which you are unable to give, perhaps about the different types of malt whisky served, ask your supervisor or another member of staff for assistance. However, you should never be unable to serve a customer because you have forgotten to prepare some equipment correctly for your shift.

> ### MEMORY JOGGER
>
> What problems can occur if you have not made sure that all the equipment and supplies you need for your shift are ready before you start?

When you first start work you will not know about every product which the establishment sells, nor how to present them, but you must make it a priority to find out as soon as you can, so that you are able to:
- answer customer enquiries correctly, and make positive recommendations when required
- ensure that all the equipment which you need to serve your customers is available, such as glasses, order pads
- work as efficiently as possible, because you know what you are serving and how it should be served
- give your customers the best, most efficient service possible
- reduce pressure on yourself at busy times, so that you can react more positively to your customers' requirements.

Your establishment will set certain standards of behaviour and personal appearance for all staff. For instance, you may be required to wear a uniform. This is partly to help to create the correct establishment image, but also for hygiene and safety reasons. For more information on health and safety at work see Unit NG1.

However your behaviour, as much as your appearance, will affect how the customer perceives you, and the establishment will have standards of behaviour which they will expect you to maintain. For instance, in all establishments you will be required to present a cheerful face to all of your customers, no matter how much your feet hurt, etc., but in some establishments you will need to go out into the room and take customers' orders, in others you will be required to wait behind the bar for the customer to come to you.

From time to time you may notice that a customer needs something, and be able to offer it to them before they request it, for instance a clean ashtray, or more peanuts. When this happens, the customer will feel that they have been well looked after, and so will feel more positive about your establishment. They may even stay longer and place another order!

Essential knowledge	A customer will always respond positively to a positive member of staff and negatively to a negative one.
	● Organisational standards are designed to enable you to provide the customer with the level of service which they expect.
	● If you do not prepare your equipment and supplies correctly at the start of your shift, you will not be able to work efficiently.

Do this

1 Make a list of all the equipment and supplies you need to have ready at the start of each shift in order to do your job efficiently.
2 Find out how to order new supplies when that is necessary.
3 Find out how to have equipment repaired if it should become faulty.
4 Ask your supervisor what standard of dress and behaviour is expected of you, and always stick to it.
5 Ask your supervisor about legislation relating to safe working practices.
6 Practise smiling even when you are under pressure.

Case study

A new member of staff has just been employed. They do not like the uniform shirts you all have to wear. Neither do you. They suggest, as only you two will be on the bar for the next shift, that you wear your own shirts.
1 What would you like to do?
2 What are you going to do?
3 Why?
If necessary read the relevant section in Unit NG1.

What have you learned

1 Why must you always be courteous, even when you are very busy?
2 Why must you always maintain the standard of behaviour required by your establishment?
3 How can you find out what these standards are?
4 How can you build a positive working relationship with your customers? Why should you do so?
5 Why must you always be properly prepared at the start of your shift?
6 Where do you get more equipment and supplies from, when you need them?
7 Why must you maintain health and safety regulations?

ELEMENT 2: Balance needs of customer and organisation

What you need to do

● Help the customer whenever you are able to do so.
● Identify all company procedures for dealing with customer needs.
● Only give that information to customers which is within your authority.

● Identify what senior management are available and at what times, should any difficulties arise outside your ability to act.

What you need to know

- Why you must always try to assist your customers.
- Why you should not give assistance to a customer which is beyond your authority.
- What assistance you are unable to give.
- Why you are unable to give that assistance.
- When to get assistance from your supervisor.
- How to record any incidents.

INTRODUCTION

To be able to meet the needs of your customers and balance those needs with the abilities of your establishment, you must have a detailed knowledge of your establishment's facilities. You must also be aware of the type of information that is confidential, and the legal requirements in force. This will enable you to deal with most of the situations you are likely to find yourself in. Typical situations are described below.

DEALING WITH CUSTOMER ENQUIRIES

Enquiries fall into two categories, those that require confidential information, which you may not answer, and those which require non-confidential information, which you may answer.

Non-confidential enquiries

Many customers have a belief that every member of staff will be able to answer any query that is put to them, and nine times out of ten you should be able to do so. This is because although you will be asked many questions most of them will be about the same subjects. As long as you know about these areas you will be able to help. Most questions fall into five categories.

- **Questions about the establishment and its facilities.** In this situation you may be asked if you can make up a special drink, about the opening times of the restaurant or about the type of food it serves. You must therefore make sure that you know what facilities your establishment has, when customers can use them, and if there are any supplementary charges, perhaps for specialised food or drink and its service. You must also be able to direct the customers accurately to any part of the establishment that they wish to get to.
- **Local facilities**, for example, how to get to the local station, what time main-line trains run, telephone numbers of local taxi companies, and so on. If you have a good working knowledge of the facilities or have easy access to guides and other sources of information, you will be able to help. If your establishment is an hotel, it will have a reception desk or it may have a concierge's or porter's desk. It may be company policy that they deal with certain enquiries and bookings. In this case, you should explain to the customer and direct them to the correct place.
- **Enquiries that need to be referred to another member of staff.** Sometimes the customer may need to speak to another member of staff, perhaps if they have special dietary needs, they want to book a special party, or want to know if they can bring a baby into the bar, for example. In this case you should locate the required member of staff and enable the customer and staff member to talk to each other. To deal with this type of enquiry you will have to know the names and responsibilities of all the supervisory staff in the establishment and how to contact them.
- **Product enquiries.** Sometimes customers may ask about a product that you sell. For instance, when ordering a customer may ask 'Can I have a Perrier water please?' If you serve them another type of mineral water, you will not have provided them with what they asked for, and in fact, will have broken the Trades Description Act. You must always be accurate. You could have said, 'I'm sorry

we don't have Perrier water, but we do have (whatever type of mineral water your establishment serves).' The customer then knows what type of drink they are getting and you remain within the law.

● **Questions you are unable to answer.** Sometimes customers may ask you questions to which you don't know the answer. In this case you should tell them that you don't know, but that you will find out or pass them on to someone who can help them. If you give out the wrong information, because you think that it may be right, you may actually cause the customer a lot of inconvenience and embarrassment. For instance, if you say that the establishment does have a Children's Certificate within the bar area and the customer arrives with his family to find out that they do not, the customer will feel angry and foolish, the children will be irritable and the staff greatly inconvenienced. An even worse incident would occur if you were to say that the establishment has easy access for wheelchair users, but when the customer arrives they find out that it has not and they are unable to enter the establishment without help.

It is not possible to be able to anticipate every single thing that a customer could ask you, but if you say that you do not know when you do not, it will give you a breathing space to find out the answer or to find out whom to pass the enquiry onto. When customers ask very unusual questions they do not normally expect you to be able to answer them immediately, but they do expect that the answer they get will be accurate.

Don't give misleading information to customers

Confidential enquiries

From time to time you may be asked for information which it would be indiscreet for you to give out, or for confirmation of details that you are not authorised to give. In this situation you must exercise great tact and diplomacy. For instance if someone came to you and asked for the name of another customer, you have no way of knowing whether or not the customer wants to be identified to the person who asked their name. Someone might also ask you who supplies certain products to your bar, and you have no way of knowing why they want that information, or

MEMORY JOGGER

What should you do if one customer asks about another one?

MEMORY JOGGER

Why should you continuously try to help the customers?

what use they will put it to. Your establishment will have a code of practice for this type of situation. You must learn what it is and not deviate from it.

This does not mean that you should be unhelpful however. You can always say that you will take and pass on a message. Remember that if you do take a message, you must see that it reaches its destination, whether it be for a customer or a member of staff. The message may be very important, or trivial, but you don't know which. To pass on information accurately you should always write it down at the time that you take it.

If it is a formal message, such as a complaint, there will be an establishment procedure to follow, and forms to fill in. For more details see page 81 on customer complaints. If it is an informal message, for example Bill Jones can't wait any longer for Charles Smith and has gone back to work, a note on a memo pad will be sufficient, as long as the message is passed to Charles Smith as soon as he arrives.

You should remain calm, professional and discreet in these circumstances as it is nothing to do with you why one person may or may not want to talk to another, nor why one person might enquire after something or someone else. However, if you give out information which you do not have the authority to give out, you may inadvertently break the law, and/or cause your company great embarrassment.

DEALING WITH CUSTOMER COMMENTS

It is always important to treat all comments seriously. If a customer has been sufficiently motivated to bring some point to the notice of a member of staff, then you should have the courtesy to listen politely, so that the customer feels that they are being taken seriously, and are important.

Customer comments differ from customer enquiries in that they are not asking you something, they are telling you something. This may be good or bad, and may or may not require you to take some form of action.

A comment might range from someone saying that they like the floral arrangement on the bar counter, to someone saying that the draught beer tastes different from the one they had yesterday. In the first case, no action other than an acknowledgement of the guest's comment is required. In the second case, a message should be passed on to the bar supervisor or the cellar man, according to establishment policy.

From the establishment's point of view, dealing with a comment quickly and efficiently may prevent a major problem occurring. If a guest says that their beer tastes different, there may be a problem in the pipes that needs correcting as soon as possible so that other customers do not have the same bad experience. If the comment is favourable, for instance the customer said that the service in the bar had been extremely good, this should also be passed on as it encourages the staff concerned to keep up their standards of service.

PROMOTING THE ESTABLISHMENT'S FACILITIES CORRECTLY

You will often be asked questions about the establishment. To be efficient and professional, as we have established, you will need to know about all of the facilities of your establishment. Having this knowledge means that there may be times when you can encourage a customer to use more of your establishment's facilities or services than they had originally intended.

Most of the services and facilities of any bar are promoted in tariffs, menus and beverage lists. These are usually given to the customer upon request, or are displayed in the bar area. In an hotel they would be included as part of the guest packages in the bedrooms. However, simply because something is left on a table or given to a customer does not mean that it will be read fully. This is especially true if the guests are unable to read English, or if the customer has poor eyesight.

Your customers may not use your facilities either because they do not even know that they exist or because they are not aware that they can cater for their needs. For example, when a customer asks what there is to do in the evening in the vicinity of your establishment, besides telling them about activities locally, if your establishment has a suitable facility, an excellent restaurant, a cabaret night, its own leisure facilities, etc., then you can take this opportunity to draw their attention to them.

Not all of the establishment's services remain the same all of the time. It may be company policy to offer special packages or promotions at certain times of the year, such as at Christmas. You need to become aware of these activities so that you can promote them to your customers.

The more that the facilities of your establishment are used, the more likely it is that it will remain in business.

Essential knowledge

A comprehensive, accurate knowledge of the beverages which you serve, menu and dish composition, if available, as well as information about the local area will enable you to answer 90 per cent of enquiries.

- Inaccurate information will result in angry and embarrassed customers.
- Inaccurate information can result in you breaking the Trades Description Act and so the law.
- When you are unable to deal with an enquiry, someone else will be able to, and the enquiry must be passed to them as soon as possible so that the customer's needs can be attended to swiftly.
- Some information is confidential, it must never be given out. To do so may break the law and/or cause the customers (or staff) great embarrassment.
- Not all comments require action, but all should be acknowledged so that the customer does not feel ignored.
- Comments which need action, good or bad, should be passed to the appropriate person for action as soon as possible.
- You can have a direct bearing upon the success of the business if you encourage the customers to use facilities which they might not otherwise have done.
- If you over-promote ('hard sell'), you will may put the customers off, and prevent them from using one of the establishment's facilities.

Do this

1 Make a list of all the special features of your bar list and menu which your customers may like, and when they are available, if applicable.
2 Make a list of all the reference books that it would be useful to have available in the bar. If they are not available, ask your supervisor why.
3 If your establishment has a concierge's or porter's desk, find out what types of enquiries they deal with.
4 Make a list of all the supervisors in your establishment, what they are responsible for and how you would contact them, i.e. via a paging system, a telephone extension, or some other method.
5 Write down your establishment's policy on the handling of written messages, if there is no one available to deal with a specialist enquiry immediately.
6 Ask your supervisor what your company's policy is about giving out any type of information about the guests in your establishment.
7 Write down what you should do when someone asks you for information which it would be indiscreet and against company policy to give out.
8 Write down how you feel when you are praised for doing something well.
9 Discuss with your supervisor the types of comments which should be passed on and those which should just be acknowledged. Make a list.

10 Find out what your establishment's method of passing on comments is and make yourself familiar with it.

11 From your tariff, menu or beverages lists highlight those special features that could be offered as an alternative when a customer asks about a local facility. For example, if a foreign visitor asked about a traditional pub, is your establishment's bar a suitable alternative?

12 Make a list of all the special activities coming up in your establishment so that you can recommend them at the appropriate time.

Case study

A customer who is very drunk comes into your bar and asks for a double Bacardi and coke.

1   What are you not allowed to do by law?

2   Give two suggestions as to what you can do.

If necessary read the relevant sections in Unit 2NC8.

What have you learned?

1 What knowledge should you seek in order to be able to answer 90 per cent of the questions you will be asked?

2 Which is the most unprofessional:
   (a) to be unable to answer a query immediately?
   (b) to give inaccurate information?

3 Why is some information confidential?

4 What should you do if you are unable to answer a question?

5 What is the difference between a comment and an enquiry?

6 Why should good as well as bad comments be passed on?

7 In what ways can you directly influence the success of the establishment?

8 Even when promotional material is available, why should you draw customers' attention to the special facilities of the menu or beverages list?

9 Why are you a sales person as well as a provider of food and drink?

10 What is a code of conduct?

11 What problems can result if you say that your establishment has facilities or serves products which it does not?

ELEMENT 3:   Respond to feelings expressed by the customer

What you need to do

● Observe whenever a customer is feeling very strongly about something.

● Identify an incident from a complaint and assess its seriousness.

● Prioritise your response to the event.

● Identify quickly any incident or complaint you are unable you deal with and refer it to the appropriate person as soon as possible.

● Be familiar with your establishment's procedure for dealing with those events which have aroused strong feelings in your customers.

● Reassure a customer that they are being taken seriously.

What you need to know

● Why an angry or upset customer must be dealt with straightaway.

● Why tact and diplomacy are very important.

● Why any complaint or incident must be accurately identified and its seriousness assessed.

● Why the situation should be resolved as soon as possible, either by you or the appropriate person.

● Why it is important to deal with all incidents quickly and seriously.

● When an incident is beyond your ability to respond to it, how and to whom to refer it.

● Why you must follow the company procedure when dealing with and recording complaints or incidents.

Whenever strong feelings are roused in a customer, it is important that you find out why. The customer may be very happy with the service which they have received, but often these feelings are raised because they are not. Customers may also become very upset by something over which the establishment has no control, but which they must deal with as it has affected a customer, such as a customer having their pocket picked before they enter your establishment, and thus no money to pay for what they have just ordered. As mentioned earlier, when customers are very happy, they usually just pass comment, so when they start to express a strong feeling about something it is serious and you must listen. These feelings will usually be expressed either as complaints or incidents.

Essential knowledge

- A person who is angry or upset does not always act in a rational fashion.
- A customer who is angry or upset will be very impatient.
- If you do not start to deal with a customer who is upset immediately, they will simply become more angry and more irrational.
- As a representative of the establishment you are responsible for any problems which your customers come across.
- All complaints or incidents are serious, because they have caused upset to your customers who are no longer satisfied with your establishment.
- When some incidents occur, as in the case of lost property or an accident to a customer, the establishment may have a legal responsibility.
- You must never admit responsibility for an incident, because you may have committed the establishment to some legal liabilities in the future.

DEALING WITH CUSTOMER COMPLAINTS

MEMORY JOGGER

Why must you respond fast and accurately to customers feelings?

When dealing with a customer who has a complaint, you must always remember that they will be angry. Perhaps not angry enough yet to shout and threaten, but certainly unhappy enough to be extremely short with you if you do not act in a very efficient and diplomatic way. This would be true even when you, personally, are not responsible for the problem, because you as a representative of the establishment bear a collective responsibility for everything that happens within it. You must remember, therefore, to remain calm and polite no matter how upset the customer may get with you. Do not take the anger personally.

To defuse the situation as swiftly as possible you should follow the course of action recommended below, always remembering to act within your establishment's policy:
- The first thing to do is to acknowledge the guest immediately and apologise to them. If they are not attended to swiftly, all it will do is make them more angry.
- Listen very carefully, without comment, unless the customer asks you to say something. Remember that when someone is angry they often tell you about lots of minor things before they get to what is really wrong. If you jump in too soon, you may prevent the customer from explaining the real reason for their annoyance. Sometimes just by describing what has made them so angry will enable the customer to become more rational and calm.
- Start to deal with the complaint immediately, with the customer able to see that you are taking them seriously and actually doing something. Tell the customer what action you are taking.

The situation and the customer should now become calmer.

When listening to the customer's complaint you should have a calm, but interested expression on your face. This is one time when a smile could be taken as a sign of a lack of interest or seriousness, and could make the situation worse.

Some complaints are very easy to deal with. Examples include:
- if the taxi a customer has ordered has not arrived, you can phone up and find out why there is a delay

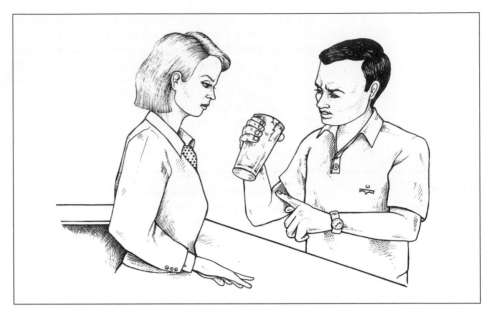

When listening to a customer's complaint, have a calm but interested expression on your face

MEMORY JOGGER

What should you do if a customer decides to lodge a complaint?

● if the customer wanted to order food at the food bar and the attendant has gone missing, you can take the order and pass it directly on to the kitchen.

However there are other complaints which you cannot do anything about at the time. Examples include:
● a customer may say when leaving that they ordered a low calorie tonic with their gin, but an ordinary one was served
● a customer says, as they are leaving, that there were no pickles on their ploughman's lunch.

In this type of case you should write down all the details of the incident, the date, the name of the customer and what the problem is, and then you should pass on this information to your supervisor, or other appropriate person as soon as possible (according to your establishment's code of practice), and tell the customer that this is what you are going to do. If it is appropriate you may thank the customer for drawing your (the establishment's) attention to the problem, for example if a group of customers are getting a bit drunk and rowdy.

If you are unsure about what to do or if the customer is being very difficult to deal with, rather than allow the situation to deteriorate, you should ask your supervisor to deal with them. If you allow the customer to get angry with you, then this will be another thing for them to complain about.

If the customer is allowed to leave the bar still feeling that their problem has not been dealt with then that dissatisfaction is what they will remember about your establishment and is what they will describe to their friends as typical of it. This will seriously damage the reputation of the establishment

DEALING WITH CUSTOMER INCIDENTS

There are many things which can happen to customers while they are in your establishment. In most cases, no matter what the incident is, they will report it to you. This is especially true if the customers are strangers to the area or from overseas, and so unfamiliar with the locality or the regulations of the country. As a consequence, unlike when dealing with enquiries, you will often not be able to help immediately, and will have to report the incident or redirect the customer.

A customer who has been involved in some incident, such as losing their wallet or being mugged, may appear agitated, or feel frightened and vulnerable. They will need to be reassured in a very tactful manner that they are being taken seriously.

The first thing to do is to listen, very carefully, to what the customer says has happened. Then you will be able to decide what action to take. It may be helpful to jot down some notes.

When property is found in an establishment, it should be recorded in a lost property book, and stored for safekeeping (see Unit NG1). If the customer remembered paying for something in the gift shop, and is now unable to find their wallet, you could check with the gift shop and with the lost property book to see if it can be located in either place. If that is not successful you would have to record and report the incident according to your establishment's code of practice.

However some incidents may be much more serious, for instance if the customer has been mugged or a child is lost outside the establishment. In this type of incident where outside bodies such as the police have to be involved, senior management may also be involved and you must become familiar with company procedures for reporting such incidents to the appropriate person as soon as possible.

No matter how serious the incident is, or how agitated the customer is, you must remain calm. If you do not then you will not be able to find out what has happened and take the appropriate action.

Do this

1 Find out what your establishment's policy is about how to deal with a complaint or incident.
2 Find out if your establishment has a book in which complaints or other incidents are recorded, and if it has, how to fill it in.
3 Find out where the lost property book is kept.
4 Find out who has the authority to deal with very serious complaints.
5 With a friend, role-play a situation in which one of you is a bar person and one of you is a customer with a complaint. See if the bar person can deal with the incident to the customer's satisfaction.
6 Make a list of the things that make you angry at work, and another list of how you think that these problems could be sorted out. Discuss this with your supervisor.
7 Ask your supervisor about the most serious incident that they were involved in and how they dealt with it.

Case study

A customer orders one gin and tonic, one vodka and tonic, one gin and bitter lemon and one pint of lager. By accident you serve two gin and tonics. The customers start to drink them and then you realise what you have done.
1   What action should you take?
2   What laws have you broken?
3   How are the customers likely to react?
If necessary re-read the relevant section Element 2 of this Unit.

What have you learned

1 In what sort of mood will a customer with strong feelings be?
2 Where can incidents involving your customers take place?
3 Why should all incidents be treated seriously, no matter how trivial?
4 What might be the consequences of an unnecessary delay in dealing with an incident?
5 What will be the consequences of dealing with an incident swiftly and efficiently?
6 Why must the problem be solved before the customer leaves the establishment?
7 Why might you find yourself doing things which are not strictly speaking within your job description?
8 Will your management always be unhappy to receive complaints?
9 What is the procedure for dealing with complaints that you cannot solve immediately, within your establishment?

ELEMENT 4:   Adapt methods of communication to the customer

What you need to do

- Communicate with people from different cultures, of different ages, and with differing needs.
- Ascertain whether the communications have been understood correctly by both parties.
- Identify other personnel within the establishment who are able to communicate by different methods, i.e. using a foreign language or sign language.
- Respond to people with different needs.

What you need to know

- The importance of communicating accurately with your customers.
- Why it is particularly important to establish a good rapport with customers from the moment they enter your establishment.
- What facilities there are within your establishment for people with special needs.
- All of the facilities which your establishment is able to offer to its customers.
- When and how to seek assistance when there is a problem in communicating with a customer.

Accurate communication with your customers is essential if you are to be able to provide them with whatever service they require. Not all communication is verbal – body language (non-verbal communication) is also important, as can be supplementary methods of conveying information to people with special needs, for example people with impaired hearing.

Essential knowledge

- You will probably be the first representative of the establishment that the customer meets. You may also be the only and last person as well, and so the impression which you make on them will colour their views about the rest of the establishment and what they tell their friends or colleagues.
- If you do not understand a customer, you will not be able to help them satisfactorily.
- If you smile, most people will smile back and feel relaxed.
- Non-verbal communication is as important as verbal communication.
- A person with individual, specific needs wants useful, accurate information, not embarrassed sympathy.

VERBAL AND NON-VERBAL COMMUNICATION

Verbal communication is using speech. Non-verbal communication is the information which you convey by your body language. For instance, if a customer comes up to you and you continue with what you are doing, without acknowledging them in any way, they will feel ignored and angry. You may be busy, perhaps making up a drink. However, you can still smile at the new customer at the bar, so they will then know that you have seen them, and will be with them as soon as you can. They will feel noticed and welcome.

Make customers feel welcome

Verbal communication is an important skill for you to develop, and you should try to become aware of the following points.

● Customers must be able to understand what is being said to them.
● You should, therefore, be very careful about the words you use and their pronunciation.
● If you use slang words, the customer may never have heard of that word, or never have heard it used in that context, and so not understand you.
● If you do not enunciate your words clearly, if you slur them or mumble, even the most intelligent and patient customer will not be able to understand you and will become dissatisfied.
● Just because a customer does not respond to you immediately, it does not mean that they are either rude or stupid. It may mean that they have impaired hearing, or that they are having difficulties trying to reply in a language which is not their own.

Welcoming and addressing customers

Everyone likes to be made to feel welcome when they arrive somewhere, especially if they may have had a long and difficult journey. Saying 'Good morning' or 'Good afternoon' with a smile on your face as soon as the customer appears is a very good start. If you know the customer, they may be a regular visitor or have been staying for a while, use their name to personalise the conversation, for example 'Good afternoon Mr Johnson. It's nice to see you again' or 'Good morning Mrs Smith. How can I help you?'

Useful pointers
It is useful to learn the following points so that you become more skilled in talking to customers.
● If you do not know the name of the customer, you should use the more impersonal forms, such as 'Good afternoon sir/madam. How can I help you?'
● When you do find out the customer's surname, you can start to use it, but you should never use their first name, as this would be considered to be overfamiliar.

MEMORY JOGGER

When a child asks you for a coke, how should you respond?

- If the customer is a small child, you should use their first name. This is because most children would be very puzzled to be addressed by their surname and to do so would not put them at their ease.
- Note that children are not allowed into all bar areas (check the licence for your establishment).
- It requires great tact and experience to know when a child is old enough to be addressed as an adult. Addressing a young person as a child when they consider that they are an adult may be seen by them as patronising and insulting.
- If the customer you are talking to has impaired hearing or does not speak English well, speak slowly and clearly while looking directly at them.
- Check to see if any other member of staff speaks the appropriate language.
- If a customer does not understand what you say, repeat yourself using other words and appropriate gestures. For instance, if the customer does not understand when you ask them what they would like to order, show them the order pad or beverages list, if available. You could also show a customer where the toilet is if they are unable to follow your directions.
- Listen very carefully when the customer says something to you, and don't be afraid to ask them to repeat themselves if you did not understand the first time. Accuracy in helping people is more important than short conversations. This is especially true with telephone conversations where you are unable to see the person, and so confirm that accurate communication has taken place, for example by seeing a nod of agreement.

If a second customer should require your attention while you are still dealing with the first, you should greet the second customer immediately and explain that you will attend to them as soon as you have finished with the first one. As long as the second customer knows that they have been seen, most people are happy to wait a few minutes. They will not be if you ignore them.

Bidding the customers farewell is as important as greeting them correctly, because this is often the last impression of the establishment which they will take away with them. It is also a good opportunity to try to encourage the customer to return in the future. It does not mean that you should ignore the customer for the rest of the time that they are in your establishment. However, most customers do understand that you are busy, and will not expect individual attention throughout their visit, especially if the communications at the start were well done, efficient and accurate, and the service they required was provided.

Be helpful and attentive to customers

A simple farewell, such as 'Goodbye Mr Johnson. I hope you enjoyed your evening with us and that we will see you again in the future', or to a regular guest 'Goodbye Miss Easton. It was nice to see you again and I look forward to seeing you again soon', is sufficient. (Notice the use of the customer's name to make them feel like an individual not just part of the daily business.) This may encourage the guests to pass any comments that they might have been wondering whether or not to make and, if applicable, it may also stimulate the customer to make their next booking there and then if they already know the date.

Specific individual needs

All the time that you are communicating with a customer you will need to consider them as a unique individual with their own special requirements. This is especially true if your customer has any impairments or disabilities. As mentioned previously if the customer is hard of hearing or does not speak English well, you will need to be very precise and clear in what you say. You might also use other methods to communicate. For instance you could show a customer who was deaf where the restaurant was within the establishment from a plan in the brochure, or direct them to signs. You could do the same with a customer who spoke little English, or find another member of staff who spoke the language. You may also find that there can be difficulties understanding very broad dialects. For instance a person from Newcastle on holiday in Cornwall may have a very broad accent, and the same care will need to be taken in communicating with them as with someone who is not British.

If your customer had a speech impediment, perhaps a slight stammer, you must listen carefully to their request, and repeat it back to them to be sure that you have understood what they wanted. If they are unable to speak you can ask them to write down their requirements.

Those with physical disabilities will also need special attention. As already noted people in wheelchairs will need to know about access, lifts and toilet facilities. But even people less disabled, such as a person who has a broken leg and is on crutches, will need extra information, again often relating to access, where the lifts are, the shortest way to walk from one point to another, how to avoid stairs, etc.

People with learning difficulties, that is to say those who have great trouble in absorbing and retaining information, or have a very short attention span, can present other problems. If a customer who has learning difficulties approaches you to ask the way somewhere perhaps, it may be more sensible to take them there especially if the route is quite complicated. If they ask you to explain an item on the menu you must be careful not to appear patronising, but choose the simplest words that you can think of to explain, and speak slowly and clearly.

MEMORY JOGGER

What information would a customer in a wheelchair need to have about your establishment?

Do this

✔

1 Try to put yourself in the position of a customer. Next time you are in a shop, observe and remember how quickly they served you and whether you felt happy with the service or not.
2 Find out whether your establishment has a particular way in which they would like you to address the customers.
3 Practise becoming aware of people entering the bar, and smiling a greeting to them as soon as they appear.
4 Get a friend to put on a pair of ear muffs and try to explain something to them.
5 Make a list of all the people who work in your area who speak a foreign language and list the languages they speak.
6 Find out what phrase your establishment feels is suitable for bidding a customer farewell.
7 If applicable, make a list of the names of all the people who have reservations for tomorrow, then upon arrival and departure you will be suitably prepared to say goodbye to them all.

Case study

Your beer supplier phones up when your supervisor is not immediately available. They need to change the day of the next delivery of beer to your establishment.

1   What should you not do?
2   What information should you ask for?
3   What should you do with this information?
If necessary re-read the relevant section in Element 2 of this Unit.

What have you learned

1   How will your customers feel if you ignore them?
2   Why do your customers like to be remembered and recognised?
3   Why should you address children by their first names?
4   Why must you find out exactly what the customers want?
5   What should you do if you are unable to communicate accurately with one of your customers?
6   What alternative methods could you use to communicate with people who have difficulty in understanding you?
7   Why is bidding farewell to a customer so important?

Get ahead

1   Find out what legislation, other than health and safety, affects the way that you are able to work.
2   Find out how to check that large pieces of equipment, like tills, are working properly.
3   Find out which supplies take more than a day to arrive.
4   Make a point of actively asking each customer how they have enjoyed their visit, and make a note of their comments. You may want to discuss these with your supervisor later.
5   Find out what the difference is between orange juice and fresh orange juice under the Trades Description Act.
6   Find out how many codes of practice your establishment has and how they relate to you and your job.
7   Write down all the formal communication routes within your establishment.
8   Find out what the Children's Certificate is and what other licencing laws relate to your place of work.
9   Find out what the most common complaints are which occur within your establishment, and why they occur.
10   List the nationality and complaint of your customers over a period of time. Is there a correlation between the things people complain about and the culture they come from?
11   Make a list of all the types of incident which occur which require you to contact people outside your establishment, such as the police. List those people that you would contact for each type of incident, and why.
12   When there is a serious problem, which you have to pass on to your supervisor, find out how your supervisor dealt with it, and why.
13   Find out what the most common legal problems are, which occur if you do not handle an incident correctly.
14   Find out whether it would be possible for you to learn another language, so that you could communicate with more people.
15   Some people have titles, like doctors and religious people. Find out how people with titles should be addressed.
16   Find out what the most common mobility disabilities are and what special facilities each type of disability needs to have provided.

UNIT 2NG4

Create and maintain effective working relationships

This unit covers:

ELEMENT 1: Establish and maintain working relationships with other members of staff

ELEMENT 2: Receive and assist visitors

ELEMENT 1: Establish and maintain working relationships with other members of staff

What you need to do

- Identify your responsibilities as an employee, in respect of health, safety, equal opportunities and confidentiality.
- Identify the working structures of your organisation so that you can seek and obtain advice and support in difficult or serious situations.
- Be familiar with the correct proce-

dures and communication channels should an incident, breach of security or difficult situation occur with customers.

- Recognise the importance of passing important information on promptly and accurately within acceptable time scales to establish and maintain constructive working relationships.

What you need to know

- What your own job responsibilities are.
- How to adapt methods of communication to suit the person you are dealing with.
- Why you should comply with equal opportunities policies and legislation.
- Where, when and from whom you

should seek information.

- What the most appropriate methods of communication are when proposing change.
- Why it is important to ensure, when using any form of communication, that the information is complete and accurate.

INTRODUCTION

In a service industry one of the most important parts of your job will be dealing with people. You may work within the same organisation with these people or they may be external, for example customers, suppliers' delivery people, maintenance personnel. The way that you deal with them will not only affect your relationship with them, but will also help them to form an impression of your company. Good 'people skills' are not just about relationships, they are good for businesses too.

Dealing with people is a difficult skill because people are all individual. You will need to develop many skills to deal with people. These skills relate to communication, team work and attitude, as well as developing your knowledge about procedures, policies, legal requirements, structures, systems, products, services, and the facilities of your organisation.

To maintain relationships you need to pay constant attention to behaviour. This is often easier with external customers, because you are aware that the relationship you have with them is service- or product-related. However, we seldom consider what our colleagues or managers needs are. They are your customers too – they also need a product or a service from you as a team member. Teamwork is vital to the quality of the service and product being delivered by your organisation. Everyone has a role to play.

WORKING WITHIN THE COMPANY STRUCTURE

It is important to understand your own job role, and in a well-structured company a written job description is usually available. This normally contains the key tasks and duties that you should perform, along with details of your responsibilities to your immediate supervisor and colleagues. In certain situations the details may not be written down. If that is the case, it is important that you discuss and clarify your job role with your immediate supervisor and develop an agreed written job description.

Do this ✔

1 Obtain an organisational chart for your establishment/department and identify your own job role within the establishment/department.
2 Obtain a copy of your job description.
3 Using the chart obtained in 1 above, draw lines showing links that you have within your department.
4 List the people that you have to deal with.
5 Place all of the above in your portfolio of evidence.

Teamwork

What do you need from others to provide a service? What do others need from you to provide a product or a service? These questions are vitally important – as important as the relationships with external customers. To provide a quality product or service, you need the help of your colleagues. You must take the time to understand the pressures, priorities and schedules of other members of the staff.

For example, a waiter and a chef are reliant upon each other to deliver the service to the customer. The waiter must ensure that the tables are laid out well with clean cutlery, the menu is explained and the order taken efficiently. The chef is then responsible for producing a meal to the desired quality and quantity within an acceptable time .

Other relationships within organisations are less apparent, such as the relationship between reception and the bar. However links do exist. Every job role within any organisation is interdependent on other departments. This relationship is based upon communication, which is the life blood of every organisation. The channels of communication will vary from one organisation to another. They fall into two basic types:

- **formal communication**, which takes the form of standard operating procedures, organisational policy, procedures, legislative information, team briefings, memos, appraisal discussions, training sessions, coaching, telephone calls and letters
- **informal communication**, which usually occurs as one-to-one conversations, face-to-face or in a brief telephone conversation.

Whether communication is informal or formal, the importance of a constructive exchange cannot be over emphasised. Some of the benefits that flow from effective communication are that it:

MEMORY JOGGER

What are the two channels of communication?

- helps you to improve the service
- strengthens the team effort
- informs both internal and external customers of the latest situations.

Good communication is the key to successful businesses. Everyone needs to be kept informed. Well-informed people know what to expect and what is expected from them, and understand what they can contribute to situations. Wherever you work, good communication skills are necessary to achieve results. You need to know about appropriate communication channels, company structures, your role and the different situations that require contact with your line manager.

COMPANY STRUCTURES

Your own role and the role of others is formalised in the company structure. All companies, large and small, have some form of *hierarchical structure*. Within all organisations there are levels which relate to job responsibilities and indicate a line of command. For example, as a waiter your immediate line manager would be the restaurant supervisor. But in the absence of the restaurant supervisor, you would report to the next level of line manager, the Food and Beverage Manager. The line of command is important to you because it indicates who you should contact if you find yourself in a situation that you cannot resolve.

A simple example of a hierarchical structure for a department might look like the example below:

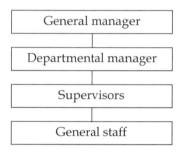

You can then add all other departments and the illustration might then look like this:

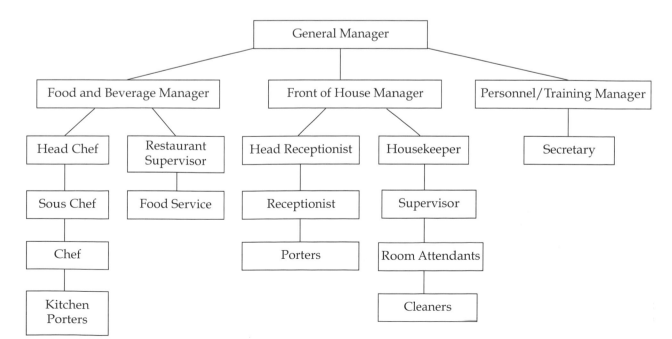

MEMORY JOGGER

All companies have hierarchical structures. What is the name of the most common form of this structure?

This structure, when completed with all departments and names, forms a pyramid shape and is known as a *pyramid structure*. However, more companies today are taking away the levels of management to produce a flatter structure, where the responsibilities are shared. In this type of organisation the communication channels are also likely to be easier because there are less levels involved. These companies may also rely more on informal communication rather than more formal memos and meetings.

Do this

Using your establishment's organisational chart indicate:
(a) who you report to
(b) who requires a service from you and your deparment and who you require a service from.
State whether communication is formal or informal in each case.
Keep this information in your portfolio of evidence.

YOUR OWN ROLE WITHIN THE ORGANISATION

You will have certain responsibilities wherever you work. Some of these you will be aware of, while others will affect you without you realising that they exist. The latter are laid down in legislation (laws). The information below on legislation which affects you at work is not exhaustive, and additional information will be found in other units.

Common law rights and obligations

MEMORY JOGGER

You are affected by rights and obligations under common law. What are the three most significant?

These rights and obligations affect both you and your employer. For the purpose of this unit, a number that affect you have been identified. They are:
● **a duty to serve** – in simple terms this requires you to be ready and willing to work to your contract
● **a duty of competence** to carry out your job to a level expected within the organisation
● **a duty of good faith** – the most important part of this relates to confidentiality. You must ensure that nothing is done to damage your employer's business. Information relating to the company's profits or to customers must not be divulged.

Essential knowledge

It is important that you know:
● what your role is within your organisation, where you fit in, what you should do, and the legislation affecting you
● who your line managers are and how to contact them
● in what circumstances you should refer problems to line managers
● the most appropriate methods of communication in different situations.

Equal opportunities policies

You need to be aware of your responsibilities under equal opportunities legislation. All companies should operate an equal opportunities policy. This relates to the equal opportunity of every employee regardless of colour, gender, age, race, nationality, ethnic or national origin.

However, it is less well-known that it is illegal for hotels and similar establishments to discriminate against *anyone* with whom they do business. You will obviously be affected by this law and must serve people in these categories unless there are other reasons, for example if they are drunk or pose a threat to others.

Other legislation

You will also be affected by other legislation, which is covered in more detail in other units and relates to:
● health and safety – in general terms, the Health and Safety at Work Act (HASAWA) states that you must take reasonable care of yourself and others, and that you must cooperate with your employer, so far as it is necessary, to enable them to comply with any duty or requirements of the Act or associated acts
● hygiene regulations – these relate to personal hygiene, the wearing of appropriate clothing and to your working environment
● COSHH, which relates to the safe use and storage of hazardous materials
● fire regulations
● reporting of accidents
● licensing laws.

In summary, therefore, you need to be aware that your employer not only has a responsibility to you, but that you also have responsibilities to your employer, to internal and external customers.

Do this

Collect examples of the statutory laws affecting you. Retain a copy of these documents in your portfolio.

COMMUNICATION SKILLS

People are the most important part of any business, whether they are internal colleagues, managers, external suppliers, visitors or customers. The way in which you communicate with them will make a difference to you, to them and to the business. It is important that, when you communicate with others, you establish and build up a rapport.

The type of communication you use will depend upon:
● who you are communicating with
● what you need to communicate
● why you need to communicate
● the speed with which you need to communicate – is it urgent or can it wait?

There are three general types of communication:
● **verbal** – face-to-face, one-to-one, within a group, over the telephone
● **non-verbal** – face-to-face or within a group
● **written** – letters, notes, memos, faxes, computer generated.

Face-to-face communication (verbal and non-verbal)

If communication is face-to-face, both verbal and non-verbal communication will play a part. First impressions are formed in the first few minutes of contact and are based largely upon non-verbal communication although stereotyping and prejudices will also play their part.

Non-verbal communication

This is also known as *body language*. It is more likely to convey attitudes rather than verbal communication, which conveys information.

Body language accounts for nearly 55 per cent of communication with people, so it is easy to see why it is so important to understand body language, and also why some people prefer face-to-face contact, rather than communication via the telephone, computer or fax machine.

Body language can convey lots of messages. Without realising it, we all send out these messages. They are likely to be based upon:

- whether we like or think we might like the person we are dealing with
- how the person is reacting towards you
- the situation in which the meeting takes place
- other situations which may have conditioned you.

The whole of the body is used when using non-verbal communication, hence the use of the term body language. However, the most expressive part of the body is the face, which can convey many different emotions and feelings. Facial expression can include the use of the eyes and mouth, although the head is used as well when nodding to replace the spoken 'yes' or shaking for 'no'. The facial expressions used will be linked to other body movements and gestures which will also need to be read.

When you start to read body signals, you must look at all of them to decide what they mean. Taking any one in isolation can be misleading.

> **MEMORY JOGGER**
>
> Body language conveys lots of messages. The way that we act towards others is likely to be affected by four reasons. What are they?

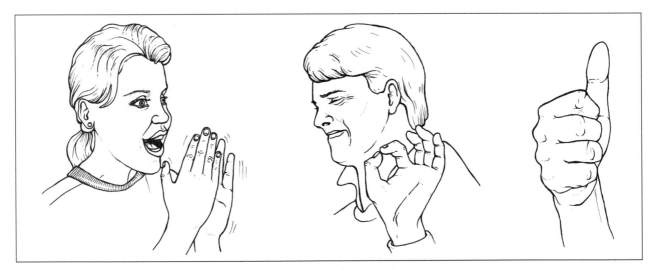

Face-to-face communication: 'Isn't it exciting!', 'Everything's OK!', 'No worries!'

Do this ✔

Identify and list your own prejudices which may affect your body language and communication skills. (Recognising them will help you to avoid using them.)

Verbal communication: using the telephone

The use of the telephone as a means of communication is very common. It is immediate and enables you to talk with someone straightaway because you know where to contact them. However, care needs to be taken when using the telephone because calls can often be overheard by others. So if the information is confidential, the telephone may not be the best method of communication.

When you use the telephone as part of your job you need to make sure that you:
● speak clearly
● establish who you are, who the other person is and what the call is about
● give clear information, taking notes if necessary
● action any points that you may have agreed during the conversation.

The organisation that you work for may also have a procedure to follow when using the telephone, for example, how you should answer the telephone, how many rings the telephone makes before being answered, what you should say, how you should record the messages, when you should pass a call on, and how to pass the call on.

Do this

Find out whether your organisation has any laid down procedures for using the telephone. If it does, obtain a copy for your portfolio of evidence. If not, write down what procedures you use and include examples of messages as well as a summary of how, when and why this method of communication was chosen.

Difficulties with verbal communication

When communicating with people there may be barriers, the most common being language. Dialects, jargon and accents can cause difficulties. If you have to deal with people with language difficulties you will need to check that they have understood you and that you have understood them. This is achieved by using questions or gestures to confirm the level of understanding.

Emotions are conveyed in language by pitch, tone and volume. You will use a variety of skills to interpret and react to the person that you are dealing with. For example, if you encounter someone who is annoyed or aggressive they will often speak with a raised voice. You should avoid shouting too, otherwise the situation is unlikely to calm down. You will also need to control your body language so that you do not appear to pose a threat or appear aggressive in return.

Written communication

Written communication has many forms: letters, memos, notes, computer-generated information, facsimile messages and so on. When using writing as a method of communication you must ensure that:
● the style is appropriate to the audience
● it is clear who it is from, and what it is about
● it is well-worded, with accurate spelling, grammar and facts.

It is also vital that all written communication is circulated only to the intended audience. It is therefore important to establish whether it is the most suitable method of communication in a given situation and ensure that anyone who needs to see it does so.

Confidential information needs to be handled discreetly and may require a combination of communication methods to ensure confidentiality is maintained.

Do this

✔

Obtain some examples of written communication to a variety of people within your organisation. Keep copies for your portfolio.

EFFECTIVE WORKING RELATIONSHIPS

Communication is a tool used to establish and maintain relationships with internal and external customers in an organisation. It is important to keep other people around you informed about what is going on, what you need to deliver the product or service, and any problems you have encountered. By using communication effectively the quality of the product and/or service of your organisation can be maintained and improved.

Different organisations will use different methods of communication to achieve results. You need to demonstrate that you have taken appropriate opportunities to discuss work-related matters using the correct communication channels.

Here are some simple rules that you need to follow to maintain effective working relationships.

- Always keep other people informed of the situation.
- Take care in selecting the method of communication, consider what you want to say, the best method of communicating it and how you phrase the communication.
- Always use the correct communication channels, based upon your organisation's structure.
- Always deliver promptly whatever you have promised to others.

MEMORY JOGGER

What action should be taken to ensure effective working relationships?

Case study

You have recently joined the staff of a large bar in a hotel. It is company policy that members of staff should not be served in the bar area. However, during the night shift one member of the bar staff serves other members of staff. You become afraid that you will be placed in a difficult situation of either serving the staff and breaking the rule or keeping to the rule and alienating the other members of staff.

1 How do you think you would feel?
2 How should you react?
3 Why do you think hotel and other establishments make these sort of rules?
4 What should you do?
5 Why do you think this is the best course of action?
6 What method of communication should you use and why?

COMMITTING TO RESULTS

The success of any organisation is reliant upon gaining the commitment of the people who work within it. It is vital to establish the role that each person has within the organisation and to appreciate how everyone fits together to form a team. As part of a team, your individual contribution to the organisation, other team members and external customers is all of fundamental importance to achieving results.

As well as knowing your own job role, the role of others and the channels of communication, you will also need to know about the products, services, standards for service and organisational policies. To achieve this unit, you need to ensure that you obtain as much information as you can about the organisation where you work.

ELEMENT 2: Receive and assist visitors

What you need to do

- Identify the working structures of your organisation so that you can seek and obtain advice and support in difficult or serious situations.
- Become familiar with the correct procedures and communication channels should an incident, breach of security or difficult situation occur with customers.
- Identify why it is important to receive customers in a polite and professional manner.
- Identify why it is important to promote the products and services available within your organisation.

What you need to know

- What the company procedures are for dealing with awkward or aggressive customers.
- How to adapt methods of communication to suit the person you are dealing with.
- What the products and services of your organisation are.
- Why it is essential to be discreet when handling confidential information.
- What systems are in place for dealing with emergencies, incidents and breaches of security.
- Why it is important to operate paging systems effectively.
- Why you should receive guests in a polite and professional manner.
- Why it is important to ensure, when using any form of communication, that the information is complete and accurate.

DEALING WITH VISITORS

MEMORY JOGGER

Why is it important to create a good first impression when receiving and assisting visitors?

Receiving visitors is one of the most important duties that you will perform for your organisation. When you deal with visitors, whether they are internal, external, expected or unexpected, it is essential that you always maintain a degree of professionalism to maintain standards and ensure security.

The visitors' impression of an organisation is created by the people who work there just as much as by the environment. First impressions are considered to be the most important impressions that are left with us. Creating a good first impression is therefore vital. Many companies have recognised the importance of creating a good impression, and have developed detailed procedures for dealing with visitors.

> **Do this**
>
> ✔
>
> Find out what procedures your organisation has in place for:
> (a) dealing with visitors
> (b) routing visitors to other departments
> (c) dealing with emergencies, including aggressive customers.

Wherever you fit within the organisation, if a visitor arrives you should be able and willing to deal with them. Working behind the bar puts you into contact with many different sorts of people. Disney recognised this when they created their theme parks. They found that the most likely people to be asked directions were the staff keeping the parks tidy. So these staff were given the same amount of knowledge about the parks as the information staff. Other companies too have recognised the importance of 'people skills'. Working behind the bar you are likely to be asked about almost anything. Your level of knowledge about the hotel or organisation needs to be as good as that of the receptionist.

Most of the time the service we give and receive is adequate. If the service falls below expected norms a complaint may be made. It is possible to learn a lot from a complaint and so improve the level of service. Compliments come from service that exceeds expectations, and must therefore be exceptional. Hence the fact that we are much more likely to receive letters of complaint than we are complimentary letters.

Here are some simple rules that you should always follow to ensure that the service given to visitors fulfils both their needs and the needs of the organisation.
- Greet visitors promptly – a smile helps to break the ice.
- Establish the nature of their business or their needs efficiently.
- Give prompt and helpful assistance or guidance, directing visitors to the appropriate people, products or services within the organisation.
- Acknowledge any difficulties and seek assistance from the most appropriate person.

There are different procedures for dealing with visitors which detail how you should greet customers and deal with them, depending upon where you work in an organisation, for example whether, rather than simply giving directions to a customer, you should accompany them to their destination. This will help to maintain health, safety, security and confidentiality.

PROMOTING BUSINESS

It is important that you know about the products that your organisation offers. You should be aware of the products of each department, not just of your own. This offers you the opportunity to sell the products, services and facilities of your organisation, not just of your own department. For example, the receptionist usually provides basic information about the facility and offers the customer the opportunity to book a wake-up call, breakfast, papers and a meal in the restaurant. But in the bar area you too should be aware of such facilities that the hotel or organisation offers, particularly the restaurant. You should be able to advise customers of what is on the menu and what special meals may be available, for example.

The opportunity exists for all staff to be able to promote the organisation's products and services. To do this you need to be able to describe what these products and services are. Equally important, you need to be able to direct visitors or customers to the correct facility or person.

Essential knowledge	● You need to be familiar with your organisation's procedures. ● You should be able to promote the facilities of the hotel or organisation by being familiar with what your organisation has to offer. ● You need to have a knowledge of the local area, local tourist attractions and transportation facilities.

Do this ✔

Describe or obtain copies of the procedures your organisation has in place for:
(a) dealing with visitors
(b) routing to other departments
(c) dealing with emergencies, including aggressive visitors
(d) promoting the facilities of the organisation.

Promoting the services and products is good for business. You should always recognise this when dealing with both internal and external customers, because it is that business that keeps everyone in employment at all levels within the organisation. Knowing about the place where you work is good for business, but it also has many benefits for you, the organisation and the customer:

● for you:
  – it makes you feel part of the organisation that you work in
  – it allows you to act professionally
  – it creates good team spirit.
● for your organisation:
  – it creates a good impression to customers
  – it maintains security
  – it is cost effective
  – it promotes sales.
● for the customer:
  – it creates a good first impression
  – the external customer is likely to return, the internal customer is likely to be more helpful towards you when you need some help, information or a product
  – they are likely to return or contact you again.

Do this ✔

1 Write a description of the organisation's products and services. Include all departments.
2 Find out what the procedure is for evacuation of external customers if there is a fire where you work.

COMMUNICATION

Choosing the most appropriate method of communication is very important when dealing with any person that you come into contact with. You need to choose the right method of communication, suited to the needs of that person. You will need to take in to account:
● who they are
● what they want
● whether they have any special needs, for example if they don't speak English, if they have impaired hearing, or, if they use a wheelchair, where access could be a problem.

Routine enquiries

Most of the time the enquiries that you will be dealing with will be routine, for example directing people to other parts of the organisation. For this you will clearly need to know the layout of your place of work, and the best way to reach different areas. You must also be aware of any routing policies that your organisation may have. If someone asked if Mr Smith was in room 36, what should you do? Your answer to this particular example would be affected by the need to protect confidential information and there is usually a company policy covering this. Confidentiality is very important, and you must be careful not to divulge information. If in doubt, you should always check.

Complex enquiries

You are likely to have to deal with people in many complex situations – people who are angry, upset, aggressive, drunken or perhaps distressed as the result of an emergency. There may be procedures for dealing with problem situations, for example aggressive customers or emergency situations. You need to check whether there are such procedures in place and what the procedure states you should do. Where a procedure does not exist, the following tips should provide some guidance.

- Always try to stay calm.
- Try to move the angry customer away to a quiet area.
- If a customer is very angry, let them have their say. This time will allow you to think.
- Try to identify what their needs are.
- Don't argue. In fact, try to speak softly as this will have several effects:
  - it is likely to calm them down
  - it is more difficult to argue with someone when they are speaking softly.
- Acknowledge your own difficulties as quickly as possible and seek help from the most appropriate person within the organisation.
- Try to move them away from other customers to minimise disruption.

Eventually the customer usually runs out of steam. It is important to establish as soon as possible whether you can deal with the customer or whether you require assistance, otherwise the customer will have to explain the situation all over again, which is likely to make them even more angry or distressed.

Most organisations have procedures and policies for dealing with emergencies. You will need at least a basic knowledge of these.

Do this ✔

Find out whether there are procedures in your establishment for the following:
(a) fire
(b) suspicious packages
(c) bomb alerts
(d) unknown visitors
(e) dealing with aggressive visitors
(f) dealing with drunken visitors.

Essential knowledge

You need to know what your own responsibilities are. For example:
- What do you do if you find a package?
- What must you do if there is a fire or a fire alarm sounds?
- Why you should challenge people that you might find wandering around your establishment? Who you should contact?
- When and how should you contact someone else in difficult situations?
- What are your organisation's products and services?

PAGING SYSTEMS

Paging systems are used in many large organisations where people have to be contacted in places where there is no telephone extension. There are two types of paging systems used:

- an electronic bleep that simply identifies that the person is required and should report back to a central point of contact, often Reception
- an audible message transmitted using strategically placed speakers, usually used in reception areas of public rooms.

HEALTH, SAFETY AND SECURITY

Security is becoming an increasing problem for organisations. With fewer people employed, large areas are left unattended. Wherever you work, because it is visited by numerous people, it is very difficult to control access. Many catering organisations, such as hotels, have a large number of exits, so security is of vital importance. It is therefore essential that any person entering your place of work is challenged about why they are there and what they want.

You should make sure that you are familiar with any procedures your organisation has, as you may need to react quickly, without stopping to think of a course of action. Most of the time in these situations you will refer the matter to the appropriate line manager. However, there may be occasions when that person is not available, in which case your knowledge of the company structure is vital, so that you can contact the next most appropriate person.

DEALING WITH EMERGENCIES

There are a few basic rules that you should try to follow in any emergency situation.

- Do not panic. Try to stay calm.
- Try to think about the situation. If you feel it is beyond your control, contact someone who can help quickly, before the situation gets out of hand.
- Always try to speak calmly to avoid panic in others.
- Try to use the procedures that your organisation has developed. They are there to help.

The best preparation is *knowledge*, so you need to make sure that you know your job well and that you understand your role and how that fits into your responsibilities and those of other people in the organisation.

Case study

You are working in a small hotel bar. You are called in early one day due to staff shortages to prepare the bar prior to service. A man arrives in overalls. He claims that he has come to check on the redecoration of the bar, cellar and store room area, and asks for access. He can see that you are busy and says that he is quite happy to be left alone to check the areas, and that your supervisor knows about it.

1 *What should you do?*
2 *Who might you contact to verify his story?*
3 *What might you be able to ask him for, to check his story?*

What have you learned?

1   What are the systems for security in place within your organisation?
2   What are the procedures for dealing with:
    (a) aggressive visitors?
    (b) emergencies?
3   What are paging systems and when might you use them?
4   Why is it important to allocate roles and responsibilities clearly via the organisational structure?
5   What products and services does your organisation have available?
6   What are your responsibilities for dealing with visitors?
7   What are your responsibilities in complying with equal opportunities in relation to visitors?
8   What are the systems in operation in your establishment to maintain security?

Get ahead

1   Find out if there are other legislative laws affecting your job role.
2   Find out what legal problems might occur if you did not handle an incident correctly.
3   Look at the other units and see what evidence or additional material they could provide for this unit.
4   Find out the names of all the companies that carry out work for your establishment and make a list including the name of the internal contact person.

UNIT 2NC6

Receive, store and return drinks

This unit covers:
ELEMENT 1:   **Receive drink deliveries**
ELEMENT 2:   **Store and issue drinks**
ELEMENT 3:   **Return unsaleable items and containers**

INTRODUCTION

Cellar management includes:
- having a clean, tidy, well-ordered cellar which provides the correct storage temperatures for stock
- controlling stock rotation and stock levels
- keeping accurate, up-to-date records when stock is delivered, issued to the bars and returned to the brewery
- preventing loss of stock through wastage, spillage or stealing.

ELEMENT 1:   Receive drink deliveries

What you need to do

- Prepare the areas where drink is received and stored before the delivery arrives.
- Check that the quantities of drinks delivered match up to the quantities listed on the order form and delivery note or invoice.
- Check that the goods delivered are undamaged, are of the right quality and can be sold before their 'sell-by' date.
- Sign for the goods delivered and retain a copy of the delivery note to give to your employer.
- Prevent any person who does not have your employer's permission from entering the area.
- Transfer the goods delivered to the appropriate storage area carefully and safely.
- Clean and tidy up the area to be ready for the next delivery.
- Deal effectively with any unexpected situations that might arise and report them to the appropriate person.
- Carry out your work in an organised and efficient manner taking account of priorities, organisational procedures and legal requirements.

What you need to know

- How to prepare the areas where drink is received and stored.
- Why you should check all deliveries to make sure that they match up to the order and delivery documentation.
- Why you should check the drinks delivered for damage, quality and 'sell-by' date.
- Why you should take care when transporting goods from the receiving area to the cellar and

storage areas.
- Why it is important that receiving areas should be left clean and tidy after a delivery.
- Why the area where drink is received should not be open to customers or other members of staff.
- How to deal effectively with unexpected situations.
- How to organise your time in order to complete the work safely, in line with current relevant legislation.

PREPARING THE DELIVERY AREA

The area into which deliveries are brought will vary from one establishment to another. Storage areas should be prepared prior to deliveries. Old stock is normally pulled forward to allow newly-delivered stock to be placed behind it. See Element 2 of this Unit.

Underground cellars

These cellars often have flaps which open outwards and upwards and ramps or slides, sometimes with steps.
- Make sure that, when the cellar flaps are open, the bolts holding them are in good condition and hold them securely.
- If the cellar flaps open onto a public area, make sure that chains, ropes or webbing are securely fixed around the opening to prevent accidents to people passing by. 'Trap Open' warning signs should also be placed around the opening.
- If dropping rings, posts or hoists are used, check that these are securely fixed and in good condition.

Delivery ramps and barrel slides can become slippery and dangerous in bad weather. They can also become dirty very quickly if the flaps are left open at delivery times. Make sure:
- that any steps and the ramp or slide are clean and clear of any obstacles
- that everyone stands clear of the ramp and that dump pads are correctly positioned
- that all lights are in working order
- that you report any defects in fastenings, equipment, ramps, stairs or lighting as soon as possible so that they may be repaired.

General rules
- The delivery area should be clean and tidy.
- All passageways should be clear and well-lit.
- All equipment used during deliveries should be checked regularly to ensure that it is operating properly.
- All structures such as ramps, slides and steps should be in good repair, clean and clear of any obstacles.

Security

The value of a delivery may amount to several thousand pounds. You should, therefore, be aware of the need to protect the stock against theft or damage.
- Whenever the delivery area is left open, you should not leave it.
- Whenever the delivery is finished, all the entrances should be securely locked.
- If possible, keep all newly-delivered stock completely separate from other cellar stock until an accurate count and check is made.
- Do not allow people making deliveries to distract you or to enter other areas of the premises where they are not authorised to go.

MEMORY JOGGER

What four actions can you take to maintain security in the cellar and storage areas?

Essential knowledge

The main reasons why you should not allow people to enter the receiving area without your employer's permission are:
● Goods may be stolen. Remember, many of the items delivered are of a high value and can be easily concealed under clothing.
● People standing around during a delivery may cause accidents if they get in the way of the delivery man and the stock might be damaged.
● The cellar can be a dangerous area for people who are not familiar with the hazards involved.
Ideally, access to the cellar and storage areas should be limited to one or two people and they should be kept locked when not in use.

Do this

1   Draw up a table, similar to the one below, giving details of the suppliers, type of goods, delivery day(s) and time, if possible, of all goods being supplied to your establishment in a typical week.

Name of Supplier	Goods Supplied	Delivery Day(s)	Time (approx.)
ABX Brewery	Bottled, draught, cider, spirits	Monday Friday	9.30 a.m. 11.00 a.m.
Hollytrell and Donane	Minerals, Coke, Fanta	Tuesday	3.00 p.m.

2   Draw a sketch of the cellar and indicate the area where goods are delivered. Write a description of the area indicating whether it is at ground floor or underground level, and how goods like casks, kegs and crates are brought in.

TAKING DELIVERY

Normally, bar or cellar staff would be supervised by a senior member of staff during a delivery. However, in the event of illness or other absences, you may be required to take delivery of goods. The procedure for taking a delivery is normally as set out below. However, you should always follow your organisation's procedures.

Procedure

1   Obtain a copy of the order form

There are several ways that bars order goods. These include:
● goods ordered by telephone
● verbal message to a trade representative. See the figure at the top of page 106. Note the various sections of the pre-printed form and the different sizes of bottle available for some brands
● written forms of order.

Typically, an order form contains a number of columns into which details of the order are written. See the figure at the bottom of page 106.

MEMORY JOGGER

What four details should you check when taking in a delivery?

| ACCOUNT No. | | | | | | ORDER No. | | | | | NAME/ADDRESS | | | | |

DATE   /   /

METHOD OF ORDER

SPECIAL DELIVERY INSTRUCTIONS

| CUST. | REP. | COLLECTED | | | AM/PM |

DESCRIPTION	Product No.	Cases	Sgle.	Prom. Code	DESCRIPTION	Product No.	Cases	Sgle.	Prom. Code	DESCRIPTION	Product No.	Cases	Sgle.	Prom. No.
										Benedictine Bt.	311012			
Walker Black 75 Cl.	151012				Hennessy 1.5 Lt.	210006				Campari 6 x 75 Cl.	367112			
Walker Red 1.5 Lt.	150006				70 Cl.	210112				Cointreau Bt.	313012			
75 Cl.	150212				½ Bt.	210024				Creme de Menthe 50 Cl.	330018			
					200 Ml.	210045				Drambuie 70 Cl.	303013			
Buchanan 75 Cl.	120012				71 Ml.	210128				Dubonnet 75 Cl.	365013			
White Horse 75 Cl.	156012				Remy Martin Bt.	213212				Galliano Bt.	308012			
37.5 Cl.	156024				Beauregard Bt.	216012				Grand Marnier Bt.	320012			
18.75 Cl.	156048				Bikini Rum Lt.	237009				Green Chartreuse	312012			
John Barr 1.13 Lt.	110008				Bt.	237012				Irish Mist 70 Cl.	302012			
75 Cl.	110012				McK Dem. 1.13 Lt.	250008				Malibu Bt.	318012			
35 Cl.	110124				70 Cl.	250112				Midori Bt.	324012			
200 Ml.	110045				37.5 Cl.	250024				Peachtree 70 Cl.	361012			
5 Cl.	110192				200 Ml.	250045				Pernod 70 Cl.	373012			
					Sailor Rum 70 Cl.	251012				50 Cl.	373118			

A pre-printed order (courtesy of Guinness (NI) Ltd)

ORDER

Order no. 0245

Name: _____

Address: _____

_____

_____

Product Code	Quantity	Description of Goods	Price per Unit	Total

An example of a written form of order

Whenever a delivery is due, you should obtain a copy of the order form for the goods from your employer or supervisor, if it is available.

2 Request the delivery note

Whenever goods are being delivered, you should ask for the delivery note before you accept the goods. See the figure below. Note the headings and the sections to be signed. Do not allow a delivery to begin until you have been given the delivery note or invoice

Order No: 533937 Delivery No: 464187 Date: 15/11/96

Account No: Rep: Your Ref: Page: Sale Type:

QUANTITY UNITS/ PART UNITS	DELIVERY UNIT	PRODUCT DESCRIPTION	PRODUCT CODE	RETURNS DESCRIPTION	DOZ	SGLE
8/000	DOZEN	COD GUINNESS 1/2 PTS	700104	LARGE PLASTIC CASE		
2/000	DOZEN	KALIBER HALF PINT	712201	SMALL PLASTIC CASE		
2/000	DOZEN	SATZENBRAU '1/2 PINT'	715101	LARGE BOTTLES		
10/000	DOZEN	HARP LAGER PINTS	710201	SMALL BOTTLES		
2/000	DOZEN	NEWCASTLE BROWN PINTS	751201	PALLETS		
2/000	DOZEN	7UP SPLIT	765201			
8/000	DOZEN	COCA COLA 7OZ	815201			

DELIVERY DATE

RECEIVED BY

DELIVERED BY

PALLETS DELIVERED   TOTAL

34/000

NOTES:

FOR TERMS AND CONDITIONS OF SALE SEE OVERLEAF

An example of a delivery note (courtesy of Guinness (NI) Ltd)

3 Compare the order form and delivery note

Check that the goods listed on the delivery note match up exactly with those on the order form.

● Do not accept delivery of any goods which are not listed on the order form.
● Mark any goods that have not been delivered on the order form and inform your supervisor or employer that the delivery was not complete.

4 Check the delivery

Before you sign the receipt, you should check the delivery against the delivery note or invoice.

- Stand where you can see all goods coming into the receiving area. Do not allow yourself to be distracted.
- It is very important that you check the quantities on the order form and the delivery note or invoice against the goods received.
- Do a check on the contents. If a case or cardboard carton should contain 12, 24 or 48 bottles, check that all cases are full. Note any breakages, missing labels or faulty closures like corks or bottle caps. Pay particular attention to crates at the bottom of stacks.
- For bottled and keg beers, you should check the 'sell-by' date to make sure there is sufficient time to sell the stock. This is normally punched onto the bottle label or fixed as a date label on kegs. Do not accept goods which are at or have passed their 'sell-by' date or do not allow sufficient time for sale.

Essential knowledge

When breakages are discovered during a delivery, you should draw them to the attention of the person making the delivery and:
- make a note of them on the delivery note or invoice
- report details of all breakages to your supervisor or employer when giving them the delivery documentation.

You should report all breakages because:
- the cost of breakages will be deducted from the cost of the goods delivered and your employer will not be charged for them
- it may be necessary to re-order or replace quickly the stock that was broken
- if breakages are not reported the cellar stock records will not be accurate and staff, including yourself, may be wrongly accused of theft.

---

5 Sign the receipt

If the goods delivered are of the correct quality and quantity and the order form and delivery note match up, sign the delivery person's copy of the delivery note.

- Do not accept alternative brands or types of stock without consulting your supervisor or employer. They may be inferior or more expensive.
- Note any breakages or shortages on the delivery note or invoice before you sign it.
- Never mix stock. It may only be possible to make spot checks during delivery. Newly delivered stock should never be mixed with stock already in the cellar until it has been completely checked.
- Never use 'unexamined'. Never accept goods without checking them or write 'unexamined' on the receipt. Don't be rushed. Delivery people may have to wait while you check the delivery, but this is often necessary.

6 Retain the delivery note and order form

The delivery note and order form should be attached together so that details can be entered into the cellar records and they can be given to your employer afterwards.

Essential knowledge

You should retain your copy of the purchase order/order form and the delivery note or invoice because:
- these are the only record of the delivery that has taken place.
- the delivery note may be used to enter details into the records of cellar stock.
- your employer will need details from the delivery note or invoice to pay his bills and for VAT purposes.

7 Carefully check the delivery

You should pay particular attention to partially filled or incorrectly sealed containers, breakages, shortages or substitutions of different brands. It may also be necessary to dip casks or weigh in kegs.

Notify your employer or supervisor about any differences or problems you find so that the supplier can be contacted as soon as possible after the delivery has been checked. Also make a note in your diary or tell your supervisor if you have noticed anything suspicious or unusual during the delivery.

As the cost of shortages and breakages can be claimed from the supplier, these items should be removed to the despatch area or disposed of safely and a written record kept.

8 Return the order form and delivery note to your employer

After completing the necessary checks and paperwork, you should return both documents to your employer or supervisor for filing or store them safely until they are needed.

Essential knowledge	It is important to check that the goods delivered match up with those on the order form because:
	● the sizes and quantities of the goods may not be the same
	● the supplier may have sent other goods of a lesser quality or higher price than those ordered.
	It is important to check the delivery note against the order form:
	● to make sure that you do not accept goods that have not been ordered
	● to identify goods which have been ordered, but not delivered which may mean you will run out of stock of a particular item.
	It is important to check the goods delivered against the delivery note to guard against:
	● goods being lost or stolen while being brought to your establishment
	● not receiving the right sizes or quantities of goods during the delivery
	● entering stock into the cellar record from the delivery note when you have not received the goods.

Do this

1 Find out what types of order form are used in your establishment. Ask your supervisor/employer if you can make copies of two orders that you have checked during deliveries.
2 Examine the delivery note from a brewery. Make a list of the headings.
   (a) Are they different from those on the order form? If so, how are they different?
   (b) Try to obtain photocopies, if possible, from your supervisor/employer of two delivery notes that you have checked and signed.
3 Find out what record is kept of shortages and breakages. Make a note in your diary or evidence record of the date, details of any breakages you have reported and who you reported them to.
4 What happens to the order form and delivery note after the new stock has been entered into the cellar records? Find out where they are stored or sent.

TRANSPORTING GOODS TO STORAGE AREAS

After the delivery has been thoroughly checked and the entrances to the delivery area have been locked, you should move the goods received to the appropriate storage areas as soon as possible. Care must be taken when moving goods to prevent damage to them and to yourself.

Handling hazards

- Always wear strong footwear, protective gloves and clothing when handling crates and metal containers such as kegs and gas cylinders. If equipment like trolleys or hydraulic hoists are available to move heavy loads, use them rather than your own strength.
- Be careful when carrying boxes or crates. Never carry so many boxes in front of you that you cannot see where you are going. Remember, cardboard boxes can become soggy if delivered on a wet day and goods can fall out. Shrink-wrapped goods can also be difficult to handle, especially on a wet day.
- Be careful when handling wooden boxes and crates. Edges may be split or splintered and nails or broken wires may be sticking out.

Lifting hazards

The drayman should have placed most of the heavy goods such as casks close to where they will be used. However, some lifting will be necessary. It is important that you lift goods properly. Learn the correct method for lifting heavy objects to prevent putting unnecessary strain on your back.

Remember that a drop of only a few inches is enough to damage wooden casks or break glass bottles.

Trips and falls

Falls are one of the commonest accidents in cellars and passageways. Although keeping the cellar areas tidy and well-organised will reduce the risks, you should always be careful.

- Make sure all stairs, floors and passageways are well-lit, dry and clear so that you can see any problem areas before you reach them.
- Report defects in steps and stairs, torn or raised carpet or linoleum or problems with equipment so that they can be repaired as soon as possible.

Essential knowledge	To obtain information about the relevant legislation relating to safe working practices when receiving and transporting goods, such as the Health and Safety at Work Act, Manual Handling Operations Regulations and the Personal Protective Equipment at Work Regulations, you should contact one of the following: ● your employer, or safety officer if you work in a large organisation ● the nearest office of the Health and Safety Executive (HSE) or the HSE Information Centre at Broad Lane, Sheffield S3 7HQ ● your local Environmental Health Department.

TIDYING UP AFTER A DELIVERY

After you have checked the delivery and moved the goods to the appropriate storage areas, tidy up and clean the delivery area.

- Brush up any loose material lying around the floor, steps and ramps.
- Broken bottles or glasses should be carefully wrapped and disposed of safely as soon as possible in a rigid bin outside the premises.
- If any spillages have occurred, you should wash down the delivery area with an appropriate detergent and mop it as dry as possible.

The area in which you receive deliveries should be included in the regular cleaning schedule operating in the cellar. See Unit 2NC7 for details.

MEMORY JOGGER

What actions can you take to ensure that goods are transported safely from receiving areas to storage areas?

Do this

1 Find out where goods are stored in your establishment. Either:
  (a) draw a diagram of the cellar showing the delivery area and stores and show the route you would take, or
  (b) describe the route you would take and note any steps, stairs or other obstacles on your route.
2 Find out how to lift goods properly. There are often wall charts or leaflets showing you how this should be done. Make a copy of the instructions.

Case study

At 3.00 p.m. a barman was called into the manager's office and asked to explain about a delivery he had signed for that morning. He explained that the assistant manager had gone to the bank with the previous day's takings when two delivery men arrived from the local brewery. He opened the cellar and allowed them to start the delivery. Some wines and spirits had been delivered just before the assistant manager left and he had not had time to store them.

The barman had asked for the delivery note, but the drayman had told him that it was in the lorry and he would get it for him later as he was in a rush. While the kegs were being delivered to the cold room, one of the draymen told him that he could hear gas escaping. The barman had spent a few minutes listening along the lines while the rest of the kegs and some crated drinks were being delivered, but could not find a leak. When the delivery was over, he wanted to check the goods, but the draymen became aggressive and said that they couldn't wait. The barman had signed the delivery note and written 'Unexamined' on it. He was called back to the bar before he could check the goods.

The manager showed him the delivery note. It was for a different pub several miles away. He also informed him that when the delivery was checked, it was three kegs and two crates of beer short and that six 1.5 litre bottles of whisky from the previous delivery had disappeared. The barman was then sacked on the spot.

1 *Identify three basic mistakes the barman made when receiving the delivery.*
2 *How should he have dealt with it?*

What have you learned

1 What should you do when you have opened the cellar flaps to receive a delivery?
2 State two reasons why you should not allow people into the delivery area without your employer's permission.
3 What are the three main methods of ordering goods for licensed premises?
4 Why is it important to check the 'best before' or 'sell-by' date on any draught or bottled products when they are delivered?
5 Why should you keep a record of any shortages or breakages in newly-delivered stock?
6 Give three reasons why you should check that deliveries match up with details on the order form and on the delivery note.

ELEMENT 2: Store and issue drinks

What you need to do

- Store drinks and gas cylinders correctly in the right conditions.
- Follow the correct procedure for storing and rotating stock.
- Keep accurate records of deliveries and of stock issued to other areas in the establishment.
- Follow the establishment's procedures when issuing stock from the cellar.

- Report to your employer when stock levels are low and new stock should be ordered.
- Keep all storage areas clean and tidy.
- Keep all storage areas secure to prevent theft from or damage to the stock.
- Deal effectively with any unexpected

situations that might arise or report them to the appropriate person.
- Carry out your work in an organised and efficient manner, taking account of the priorities, following organisational procedures and adopting safe and hygienic working practices.

What you need to know

- What the correct storage conditions are for drinks and gas cylinders.
- Why you should store your stock correctly and use the 'first in, first out' principle of stock rotation.
- Why you should keep accurate and up-to-date records of deliveries, the amount of goods in stock and any stock that leaves the cellar.
- Why you should keep the cellar stock at a constant level.

- Why storage areas should be kept clean, tidy and free from rubbish.
- Why you should not allow other people in the cellar without your supervisor's or employer's permission.
- How to deal effectively with unexpected situations.
- How to plan your work and carry it out in an organised and efficient manner.

STORAGE CONDITIONS

When drinks are brought into the cellar they must be stored in the correct position and at the appropriate temperature to keep them in the best condition possible.

Bottled drinks in crates

Drinks in bottles or cans are normally stored upright in their crates.
- Each brand should have its own stack. The crates should be stacked securely on top of each other so that stacks are firm, level and even. Normally, crates should not be stacked above shoulder height.
- Full crates should be stacked on the lower layers and any part-full crates placed at the top of stacks.
- All these drinks should be stored at the normal cellar temperature of between 12.5–14.5°C (54–58°F).
- Bottled beers should be stored in the dark away from direct sunlight or any heat sources, both of which can cause them to deteriorate quickly.

Bottled wines

Wine is a very delicate product and requires great care to be kept in good condition. Some red table wines and fortified wines such as vintage port contain a sediment and care must be taken to leave this undisturbed as far as possible.
- Wine should be stored on its side with the label upwards in racks or bins. Ideally, the angle of the bottle should be such that the wine is kept just in contact with the bottom of the cork to keep it moist.
- Large bottles of wine which are not sealed with cork but with a plastic or metal cap should be stored in an upright position.
- Wines should be kept at a constant temperature, ideally between 10–13°C (50–56°F). They should not be exposed to draughts or sudden temperature changes.
- Wines should be stored in darkness and not exposed to too much light.
- Wines should be stored away from walls and there should be no vibration from traffic or other sources.

<table>
<tr><td>
MEMORY JOGGER

In what position and under what conditions of temperature, lighting and ventilation should bottled wines be stored?
</td></tr>
</table>

Most fortified wines like sherry, madeira and non-vintage ports, along with aromatised wines like vermouths, can be stored upright at the normal cellar temperature.

Bottled spirits

- Spirits and liqueurs should be stored upright on shelves at the normal cellar temperature.
- Do not mix different brands of the same spirit together. Group each brand separately to make it easy to count the number of bottles of each particular brand that you have in stock.

Keg beers

Most keg beers and lagers have been filtered and pasteurised and require little attention. See Unit 2NC7 for details of the correct storage methods.

Gas cylinders

Gas cylinders can be stored in either an upright or horizontal position. It is important that they are safely secured and not stored close to any heat source. The ideal storage temperature is around 7°C (45°F). See Unit 2NC7 for further information.

Ventilation

The need to avoid draughts and sudden temperature changes has been mentioned already. At the same time, the air in the cellar must be changed regularly to keep it fresh and to prevent dampness.

(For a detailed description of cellar environmental conditions, see Unit 2NC7.)

Essential knowledge

It is essential that you use correct and safe lifting techniques when storing goods
- to reduce the risk of injury to yourself
- to prevent accidental damage to or breakages of stock.

If you have not received training in manual handling techniques, you should ask your supervisor or employer to provide you with the necessary training.

STORING AND ROTATING STOCK

An essential part of stock control is that old stock must be used before new stock. This process is known as *stock rotation*.

MEMORY JOGGER

How should you operate the FIFO principle in the storage and issue of bottled spirits, bottled wines and keg beers?

The 'first in, first out' principle (FIFO)

Beer and other beverages deteriorate, whether they are bottled or draught, so they must be used before their 'best before' or 'sell-by' date. It is very important, therefore, that old stock is issued before newly-delivered stock. The 'first in, first out' principle should be used for all stock with the exception of vintage wines.

The FIFO principle means that new stock is almost always stored *behind* old stock in stores and on shelves.

Stock rotation

- As stock is issued from the front of stacks, pull old stock forward before new stock is delivered or before the new stock is brought from the delivery area.
- Wine is normally stored ('binned') on racks which do not allow new stock to be placed behind old stock. Move the old stock to the left of each rack and fill in new stock from the right.
- Spirits, liqueurs, fortified wines and less expensive wines in large bottles should be pulled forward and new stock placed behind old stock.
- Newly-delivered kegs should be stored behind old stock.
- Gas cylinders should also be used following the FIFO principle. These cylinders have to be checked for safety every five years and empty cylinders should be regularly returned to the supplier.

Mixed deliveries

Don't assume that just because goods are delivered at the same time that all have the same 'sell-by' or 'best before' date. When you find a mixed delivery, store those goods with the earliest 'sell-by' or 'best before' dates in front of those with later dates.

Thefts

You should report to your employer if any of the following events occur.
- Goods present when you checked the stock on delivery are missing when you do a complete check later.
- Bottles are missing from crates in the lower levels of stacks which should be full.
- There are signs of tampering with the stock, such as broken seals on spirit bottles.
- Stock in the cellar does not match the amount recorded in the stock book or bin card.
- There are signs of tampering with the locks of doors leading to storage areas.
- Keys to storage areas have been lost or are missing.

Do this

1 Find the areas in the cellar where bottled drinks in crates are stored. Make a sketch of the area and indicate where crates are stacked. Put the brand name against each stack.
2 Obtain a copy of the brewery's order form. Are the crates stacked in the same order as they appear on the form or are the fastest moving stocks stored close to the doors of the storage areas?
3 Find out how and when stock is rotated in the cellar.
   (a) What stock is pulled forward?
   (b) When does this happen?
   (c) If stocks of wines are kept, how are they stored and rotated?

Essential knowledge

The main reasons you should store and rotate stock correctly are:
- to prevent damage to the stock or injury to staff if crates are unevenly or loosely stacked and either fall or are knocked over
- to allow cellar staff to move freely without damaging the stock or having an accident
- to make sure that all stock is stored in the way that will keep it in its best condition
- to make sure that old stock is used before new stock and that all stock is sold before its 'best before' or 'sell-by' date
- to make sure your customers get the product in the best condition possible and provide a high quality service to them.

KEEPING STOCK RECORDS

In order for a licensee to control his or her business, they must keep accurate, up-to-date records. A lot of money is tied up in the bar and cellar stock, and accurate records of these are needed.

At regular intervals, the licensee will call in a stock taker who will count the stock and help the licensee in preparing his accounts. The stock taker will require the cellar stock records in order to do this. The licensee may also want to do regular checks.

So that the licensee and stock taker can do their job, you may have to keep:
● a goods received book
● a cellar stock book/bin cards
● a cellar transfer book.

The amount and type of records you are required to keep will depend on the size of the establishment and the procedures operated in the establishment.

Goods received book

Although the delivery note can act as a record of goods entering the premises, some employers may wish you to maintain an accurate record/diary of all deliveries which are entered into the cellar stock.

An example of a page from a typical goods received book is shown below.

Date	Del. Note	Supplier	Quantity	Description of Goods	Unit Price	Total

Headings in a typical goods received book

● The information should be entered from the delivery note and price list.
● Quantities of bottled items or glasses were traditionally recorded as whole numbers representing 12 (one dozen) and fractions of a dozen. For example, 18 bottles of whiskey would be recorded as $1 \frac{6}{12}$. Computerised stocktaking, however, usually uses whole numbers like the 18 above.
● The unit price of the goods is the price of a single item without VAT being added.
● The total is the total cost of units of that item. For example, if a case of 12 bottles of wine is delivered at the unit price of £10 per bottle, the total is 12 x £10 or £120 before VAT is added.

Details should be entered into the goods received book as soon as possible after the goods have been delivered and completely checked. At the same time you can complete the next set of records you may be required to keep, the cellar stock book or bin cards.

Cellar stock book or bin cards

All licensees will keep records of the deliveries to the cellar stock, issues from that stock to the bars on the premises and the balance of stock in the cellar. The records should be kept for each item of goods in the cellar.

These records may be kept either on separate pages of a cellar stock book (one item per page) or by keeping a bin card for each item. The term 'bin' is the name given to the storage location of each item in the cellar.

A typical example of a bin card or page of a cellar stock book is shown below.

Guinness (bottled)						Bin 9					
		Issued						Issued			
Date	Received (dozen)	P	L	C	Balance (dozen)	Date	Received	P	L	C	Balance
09.11.97	20	–	–	–	20						
10.11.97	–	2	1	–	17						
12.11.97	–	3	2	1	11						
13.11.97	–	3	1	–	7						
14.11.97	–	2	–	–	5						
16.11.97	20	–	–	–	25						

A sample bin card

- The 'Issued' section of the bin card would list all those areas in the establishment that draw their stock from the cellar. The larger the number of sales outlets on the premises, the greater the number of 'Issued' columns.
- It may be necessary to record breakages of expensive items such as bottles of spirits on the bin cards (initialled by a supervisor) to keep an accurate stock balance.
- The 'Balance' column of the card records the amount of stock of a particular product left in the cellar after stock is issued.

The cellar stock book or bin cards should be completed after each delivery and after stock is issued each day.

Essential knowledge	If breakages occur during the storing and issuing of drinks, you should retain the broken bottles and inform your supervisor or employer: ● so that your supervisor can witness that the stock was really broken and not stolen ● because breakages may have to be noted in the records of cellar stock ● so that your employer can claim the cost against tax and VAT ● to prevent staff being wrongly accused of dishonesty.

Cellar transfer book

Whether a cellar transfer book is kept or not will depend on:
- the size of the establishment and the number of areas that stock is issued to
- the establishment's procedure for issuing stock.

Establishment procedure

Some licensees in small premises operate the Imprest System, where a constant stock level (a 'par' stock) is held in each service point. Full bottles are issued from the cellar stock to match the number of empty bottles returned from the bars, which reduces the need for written records of issues and transfers.

The cellar transfer book is used to record the issues from the cellar on a day-by-day basis. See below for an example of the information that is usually recorded.

Date	Requisition number	Details of goods (units, quantities, brands)	Unit price	Total	Bin card

Headings in a typical cellar transfer book

- When a requisition is made up for a service point and taken to the cellar, the cellar man should keep the top copy.
- Details from the requisition should be entered into the cellar transfer book and the bin card for each product changed to show the issue and balance.
- The bin card column in the cellar transfer book is marked when the information about the issue has been recorded on the bin card or in the cellar stock book.

Essential knowledge

It is important that the correct documentation is received before stock is issued:
- to ensure that stock is not taken without permission
- to enable accurate records of the cellar stock to be kept
- to prevent stocks of certain items running out if low levels are not reported
- to enable the employer to check the movement of stock and the level of sales in each area of the establishment.

Do this

1 Find out what records are kept in the cellar. Is there:
   (a) a goods received book?
   (b) a cellar stock book or bin card system?
   (c) a cellar transfer book?
   If these records are not kept, find out how the cellar stock is checked.
2 If written stock records are kept, make a note of the type of heading used in the records. List them from left to right as they appear on each record.
3 Find out how accidental breakages of cellar stock are recorded in the establishment. If a record is kept, copy down how you should write in an entry. Do you need to call another member of staff or manager to witness the breakage? If so, find out why this is necessary.

MAINTAINING STOCK LEVELS

Most licensed premises like to keep a minimum level of stock of all the products on sale. Often what decides the level will be:
- how often a supplier delivers goods, for example twice a week, weekly, and so on
- how long it takes a supplier to deliver after an order has been placed.

The lowest level of stock that is held for each product is sometimes called a 'buffer stock' and usually allows for problems that can occur like bad weather or strikes which can prevent delivery.

> ### Essential knowledge
>
> It is important that low levels of stock should be reported to prevent stock running out and customer satisfaction being affected.
> - Ideally, the minimum level of stock should be noted for each product in the cellar stock book or on the bin cards.
> - When the figure in the 'Balance' column is close to the figure for the minimum level of stock, draw your employer's attention to the bin cards so that he can order a new supply of the products.
>
> The main reasons why you should maintain a constant level of stock are:
> - to prevent loss of sales because you have run out of stock
> - to prevent unnecessary delays in providing drinks for your customers because you have run out of stock
> - to prevent wastage by keeping stock past its sell-by date
> - to avoid taking up too much cellar space with slow-selling products.

MAINTAINING THE STORAGE AREA

As beer and other beverages are classed as a food in the Food Safety and Food Hygiene Regulations, it is important that all storage areas should be kept clean, tidy and free from rubbish.

Cleaning the stock

- When stock is delivered and you are checking each crate and case, you should clean each bottle by wiping it with a damp cloth to remove superficial dirt.
- Where packs are sealed with plastic film, you should keep the film intact until the goods are to be used.

Keeping the cellar clean and tidy

- Spilled beer and other drinks should be mopped up immediately to prevent both accidents and the growth of moulds and bacteria.
- Do not leave crates, cases or cartons lying in passageways where their contents can be damaged or they can cause accidents. Remove them to the collection area as soon as possible.

Dispose of all rubbish safely

During the unpacking and storage of goods, there will be an accumulation of cardboard cartons, packing material and other items which should not be allowed to remain in the cellar where they could become fire or safety hazards. After storing the goods:
- wrap broken glass in thick paper and dispose of it safely in a metal or plastic bin with a tight-fitting lid
- fold and compress large cardboard cartons and boxes and store them in a dry area outside the cellar.

SECURITY IN THE CELLAR

An important part of stock control is to prevent theft from or damage to the stock in the cellar. See the section on maintaining security in the cellar in Unit 2NC7.

> **MEMORY JOGGER**
>
> What are the three main activities involved in maintaining the storage area and why should they be done?

Strangers in the cellar

If strangers claiming to be from gas or electricity companies wish to gain access to the cellar, you should:
● ask to see their identification – don't be rushed, check it carefully
● inform you employer that they are on the premises
● be present all the time that they are in the cellar to observe their movements.

If you find a customer in the cellar or in a storage area you should:
● politely ask them to leave straightaway
● escort them out of the area
● inform a senior member of staff or your employer as soon as possible.

It is important that you follow the establishment's procedures in these circumstances.

Essential knowledge

The main reasons that you should keep storage areas secure at all times are:
● to prevent stock being stolen or drunk by dishonest staff, tradesmen and customers
● to prevent stock being damaged by inexperienced or untrained staff mishandling it
● to prevent stock being removed without a requisition or other record being kept
● to make sure stock is used in the correct order.

Do this

1 Find out the minimum and maximum stock levels for the following items:
   (a) draught beers
   (b) bottled beers
   (c) wines
   (d) spirits
   (e) minerals
   (f) cigarettes (if sold).
2 List the methods of disposal you find for the following:
   (a) non-returnable glass bottles
   (b) plastic film and containers
   (c) metal cans
   (d) paper and cardboard.
3 Talk to your employer/supervisor and make a list of:
   (a) those people who have keys to the storage areas in the cellar
   (b) those people who have permission to enter the cellar area.

Case study

On the cellar man's day off, two members of staff were sent to obtain the drinks needed to restock the saloon bar. While fooling about in the spirit store, they knocked down and broke two 1.5 litre bottles of cognac brandy. As they were afraid of the consequences of telling the manager, they cleaned up the area and disposed of the broken glass, hoping that no one would notice. On the following Monday, they were called into the manager's office. He told them that there had recently been a spate of thefts from the cellar and that when he had performed a spot check on Sunday night he had found that two bottles of cognac, a bottle of whisky and a case of Budweiser were missing. As they were the only staff known to have been in the cellar, he suspected them.

When they tried to explain what had happened, they were asked to produce the evidence to support their story. They could not and were dismissed for suspected theft.

1 What is happening in this establishment?
2 How did the actions of the two members of staff result in them being suspected of theft?
3 How should they have dealt with the initial breakage?

What have you learned?

What have you learned?

1 How should you store crated drinks?
2 How should you store:
   (a) wine sealed with a cork?
   (b) wine sealed with a metal screw-cap?
3 What is the principle on which the storage of new stock is based?
4 Give an example of how stocks of wines can be stored to follow normal stock rotation procedures.
5 What should you do if you find several different 'sell-by' dates in a delivery of a particular brand of drink?
6 Give the main reasons why you should store and rotate stock correctly.
7 When should you enter details of deliveries in:
   (a) the goods received book?
   (b) the cellar stock book or bin cards?
8 What is the purpose of a cellar transfer book?
9 What are the main reasons why you should maintain a constant level of stock in the cellar?
10 Why is it important to keep storage areas secure at all times?

ELEMENT 3: Return unsaleable items and containers

What you need to do

- Prepare the area from which goods are dispatched before they are collected.
- Pack and store items to be returned in the correct manner.
- Keep the dispatch area clean, tidy and free from rubbish.
- Prevent any person who does not have your employer's permission from entering the area.
- Deal appropriately with any unexpected situations that might arise and inform the appropriate people where necessary.
- Carry out your work in an organised and efficient manner taking account of priorities, organisational procedures and safe and hygienic working practices.

What you need to know

- Which drinks items and containers are returnable.
- How to pack and store correctly unsaleable drink items and containers.
- What form of record you should keep of returns.
- Why dispatch areas should be kept clean, tidy and free from rubbish.
- Why dispatch areas should be kept secure and you should supervise goods being removed.
- How to deal effectively with unexpected situations
- How to organise your time in order to complete the work safely and efficiently.

RETURNABLE GOODS

The value of the goods in the cellar is not only the contents of each bottle, keg or cask. The actual containers such as the wooden or plastic crates, some bottles, the kegs and the gas cylinders also have a cash value. This is because suppliers charge the licensee a deposit for some items.

Crates and containers often have high deposit charges, so it is important to control and check all empties to be returned.

Ullages

The term 'ullage' refers to any drink product which is not fit to be served. Typical examples are:
● bottled beverages and minerals which are flat, infected or have an off taste or odour when poured
● draught beers which are sour or infected, unfit for service or have passed their 'sell-by' date.

All ullages should be re-sealed as well as possible and kept. When these are returned to the supplier, the licensee can in most cases have the goods replaced free of charge. If ullages are poured away, the licensee will lose the value of the drink.

Equipment

Some items of equipment used in the bar are supplied either on loan or hire from the brewery or other supplier. Examples of these are the dispense taps, in-line coolers and chill cabinets.

Equipment on loan or hire should be returned to the supplier when it is no longer being used. The lending company should be informed if faults occur so that the equipment can be repaired.

Non-returnable goods

Not all goods carry a deposit charge. Those that do not should be disposed of safely outside the cellar area.

Generally, bottles which come in plastic or wooden cases are returnable. Those which are delivered shrink-wrapped on a cardboard tray are not. The bottles of most imported premium beers are also non-returnable.

PACKING AND STORING RETURNABLE GOODS

After the bar has been restocked, most of the empty crates and cases are returned to the cellar. After each service session, the empty bottles are returned to the cellar, usually in a skip, if a bottle chute is not used.
● Empty crates and cases should be stored either in or as close as possible to the collection point.
● Each skip should be unpacked and the empty bottles placed in the appropriate crate or case or set aside to be disposed of later.
● Make sure you put the correct size of bottle in the appropriate supplier's crate.

Full cases

Most suppliers will only accept full crates or cases of empties. The reason for this is because it would be too time-consuming for them to count individual bottles in part-filled cases.
● After placing the empties into their crates, all full crates should be removed to the collection area and stored.
● Part-filled cases should be kept in the cellar to await the next supply of empties from the bars.
● As the cost of most ullages is to be claimed back in full from the supplier, it is important that these are kept separate from the normal empties. These should either be pointed out to the draymen and recorded on the delivery note or given to the appropriate sales representative when she or he calls.
● If more than one brewery supplies goods to the premises, it is important that you keep the empties and ullages of each supplier in separate sections of the storage area.

MEMORY JOGGER

What are the main practices you should follow when packing and storing returnable goods?

Essential knowledge	It is important that returnable items are packed correctly:

- because suppliers will only accept cases or crates filled with the correct bottles
- because the licensee can claim back the cost of some ullages
- to prevent returnable goods being damaged in storage.

It is important that they are stored correctly:
- so that brewery staff only collect their own empties and ullages
- to comply with Food Safety and Food Hygiene Regulations
- to prevent deliberate or accidental damage to the goods
- because they are valuable and could be stolen.

RECORDING RETURNED GOODS

Returnable goods are normally collected at the same time as new stock is being delivered. Details of returns and ullages will be recorded on the delivery note in a separate section. This can act as a record of returns. However, you should:

- count the number of empties to be returned before the goods are collected and keep a note of the amounts of each item. You may use a returns book for this purpose. See below
- accompany the draymen and make sure that they only collect their own brewery's goods

Returns Note 19th June 19 9 –

From: Dog and Duck

V.A.T. Regd. No.

To: Wetley's Brewery

			Amount exclusive of V.A.T.		V.A.T. Rate	V.A.T. NET
			£		%	£
4	Case (24) Guinness ½ pts		9	60		
2	Case (24) Kaliber		4	80		
10	Case (24) N. Brown		24	00		
2	Case (48) 7 Up Split		4	80		
8	Case (48) Coca Cola 7oz		38	40		
6	Key Harp		30	00		
8	Key Best Bitter		40	00		
			151	60		

Re Invoice No.

Date of Invoice _____ 19

V.A.T. _____

TOTAL £151·60

A completed returns note

An example of a returns section on a delivery note (courtesy of Guinness (NI) Ltd)

- compare your own note of the amounts to be returned with what is written on the delivery note and query any differences. If you do not agree with the delivery person's entries, contact your supervisor or employer immediately before the goods leave the premises.

Look at the example of a returns section on a delivery note above. Note the section for empties left on the premises. This would be filled in if the storage area was locked and the draymen could not collect the empties or were not able to remove them during a delivery.

If goods awaiting dispatch are not collected, you should inform your supervisor so that the necessary arrangements for collection can be made. If returnable goods are allowed to accumulate, they may overflow storage areas and you may not be able to store them securely.

Essential knowledge	It is important that any returns documentation is completed correctly:
	• because some returnable items are valuable and the licensee will be credited with their value
	• so that accurate records can be kept of stock leaving the premises and being returned to suppliers and stolen or missing stock identified.

MAINTAINING THE DISPATCH AREA

MEMORY JOGGER

What safe and hygienic working practices should you follow in areas where goods are being stored before dispatch?

The area where goods are left for collection will vary between establishments. Where there is a separate bottle store, empty bottles can be stored along with full bottles.

As ullages will be stored with empties, the dispatch area is considered to be a food storage area by the Environmental Health Department of the local authority and high standards of hygiene are required to be maintained.

Cleanliness and tidiness

● The storage area for returnable goods should be included in the routine cleaning work of the cellar. It should be kept clean and dry.
● Where outside stores are used, doors should be well-fitting and there should not be holes which would allow the entry of dirt, pests or vermin such as rats or mice.
● After goods have been removed, you should sweep the area and mop it down with an appropriate cleaning agent.
● The methods of storing crates, kegs and gas cylinders in the dispatch area should be the same as in the cellar.
● Rubbish, such as broken or damaged crates, should not be allowed to gather up in the dispatch area.

SECURITY IN THE DISPATCH AREA

Returnable items have a cash value, so you should:
● prevent people entering the dispatch area who do not have your employer's or supervisor's permission
● keep the area locked when not in use.

When the goods are being collected, you should:
● supervise their removal from the stores
● not allow other staff or customers into the area while goods are being collected, in order to prevent theft or accidents
● stand where you can see and count the goods being removed and do not allow yourself to be distracted during the collection.

Essential knowledge

The main reasons why you should keep dispatch areas secure at all times are:
● to prevent goods being stolen by dishonest staff, tradesmen or customers
● to make sure that only the correct goods are taken from the store when they are being collected
● to prevent deliberate damage to the goods by vandals
● to prevent accidental damage to the goods by inexperienced staff or members of the public.

Case study

The manager of a city centre pub was visited by an Environmental Health Officer who wished to inspect his premises. When he visited the cellar and storage areas where new stock, empties and ullages were stored together, he found moulds and slime on the floors and walls. Dirt and dusty cobwebs were found on kegs and crates. Dirty and discarded equipment was stored in a corner along with broken glass, parts of crates and cigarette butts discarded by staff who obviously used the area for smoking on duty. He was fined a total of £12 500 for breaches of the Food Safety and Food Hygiene Regulations.
1 Identify as many faults as you can in:
  (a) how the cellar and storage areas were arranged
  (b) the general maintenance of the cellar and storage areas.
2 What procedures should the manager have operated?

Do this

1 Make a list of all returnable containers that you find in the cellar.
2 Make a list of all the non-returnable containers that you find in the cellar.
3 Find out where the following empties are stored:
   (a) kegs and gas cylinders
   (b) beer bottles
   (c) mineral bottles
   (d) returnable equipment.
4 Find out what record is kept of goods to be returned. Make a copy of the headings on any record you find.

What have you learned

1 Give two examples of ullages. How should they be treated differently from empties?
2 What should you do if a fault occurs in equipment which is on loan or hire?
3 What should you check when you are sorting empties into crates?
4 Why are high standards of hygiene required in areas where empty bottles and ullages are stored?
5 What are the main reasons why you should keep the dispatch area secure at all times?
6 Why is it important that you should be present when draymen are collecting the empties from the storage area?

Get ahead

1 Find out from your employer how the Manual Handling Operations Regulations affect work in the cellar. Has any assessment of risks been made?
2 Find out the establishment's procedures for:
   (a) reporting accidents
   (b) reporting defects in the cellar and stores.
   Are there any written records kept?
3 Ask your employer how frequently he checks the stock in the cellar and how often a stock taker visits to take a complete inventory of the stock. Find out what records the stock taker uses to do his or her job.
4 If your establishment uses an electronic point-of-sale computer system, find out how it operates and ask if you can see a copy of the print-out.
5 Find out how the Food Safety and Food Hygiene Regulations affect the storage of empties and the disposal of waste and rubbish in your establishment.
6 Ask your employer about what action you should take if you suspect that goods have been stolen during a delivery/collection or when strangers are on the premises.

Maintain cellars, kegs and drink dispense lines

This unit covers:
ELEMENT 1: **Maintain cellars**
ELEMENT 2: **Prepare kegs and gas cylinders for use**
ELEMENT 3: **Clean drink dispense lines**

ELEMENT 1: **Maintain cellars**

What you need to do

- Make sure that floors are clean, tidy and free from rubbish.
- Keep cellar drainage systems clean and free from blockages.
- Keep walls and ceilings clean and free from mould.
- Make sure cellar equipment is kept clean and in good working order.
- Use the correct cleaning materials for each type of work and store them safely after use.
- Control the environmental conditions in the cellar to comply with all legal requirements and establishment procedures.
- Make sure that no one enters the cellar without your employer's permission.
- Deal effectively with any unexpected situations which might arise and inform the appropriate people where necessary.
- Carry out your duties in an organised and efficient manner taking into account any priorities, organisational procedures and legal requirements.

What you need to know

- Why it is important to keep all parts of the cellar structure clean, tidy and free from rubbish.
- How frequently cellar areas and equipment need to be cleaned and checked.
- What cleaning equipment and materials you should use, and how these should be stored.
- What the ideal environmental conditions are – humidity, ventilation, lighting and temperature – and how these should be maintained at the required levels.
- Why you should not allow people into the cellar without your employer's permission.
- How to deal effectively with unexpected situations.
- How to carry out your duties in an organised and efficient manner.

INTRODUCTION

One of the most important factors governing the state of the cellar area is cleanliness. Because the cellar and any bottle stores are 'food' areas, they must be kept as clean and sterile as possible.

THE CELLAR STRUCTURE

The cellar structure includes floors, walls, ceilings and the drainage system. Where cask-conditioned beers are kept, the stillaging equipment (stillion, thrawls) would be included if this is of a solid construction.

With the introduction of new laws and the enforcement of others, work methods are changing and new surfaces and varieties of cleaning materials have been introduced.

THE CELLAR MAN AND THE LAW

There are several laws which relate to the maintenance of the cellar.

Food Safety Act and Food Safety (General Food Hygiene) Regulations

These laws require the cellar to be kept scrupulously clean at all times. The same level of cleanliness and hygiene is required in areas where beverages are stored as in kitchens and other food stores.
● There should be regular and systematic cleaning of all food areas and, in most cases, records should be kept of cleaning operations.
● All equipment which comes into contact with food or drink should be clean, sterile and free from damage.

The Health and Safety at Work Act

This Act lays down the duties of both the employer and employee to provide a safe and healthy working environment.
● The cellar must be kept tidy and free from rubbish.
● All mechanical and electrical equipment must be free from damage and in good working order.

Control of Substances Hazardous to Health Regulations (COSHH)

These regulations require employers to protect employees and others who may be exposed to substances hazardous to health, to assess the health risks involved and to prevent or control an employee's exposure to such substances.

Many of the cleaning materials used in licensed premises, such as those used for beer lines, floors, drains, glass- and dish-washers are toxic, corrosive or irritant and must be handled carefully.

Personal Protective Equipment at Work Regulations

These regulations are related to the COSHH regulations.
● Employers must provide personal protective equipment such as goggles, gloves and face masks to employees who handle hazardous substances.
● Employees should practise high standards of safety. Do not take short cuts like leaving off gloves and goggles if these are provided for your work.

Manual Handling Operations Regulations

Injuries caused by mishandling heavy loads can occur quite easily. Employers should assess potential problems and train staff in the safe approach to manual handling tasks.

MEMORY JOGGER

What are the main points that you should remember so that you will handle chemicals and cleaning materials safely in the cellar?

| *Essential knowledge* | Handling and using chemicals and cleaning materials in the cellar need not be dangerous if you follow these general guidelines. |

Storage
- Do not store detergents, poisons, pesticides, corrosive or flammable substances in the cellar, bottle stores or bar. Always store them in the designated cupboard or area.
- Keep these materials in a separate store which is cool and dry and can be locked. Some of these substances may need to be stored apart from each other. Chlorides should not be stored with acids like descalers and toilet cleaners.
- Always store these materials out of the reach of animals and children. However, caustic substances should not be stored above eye level.

Containers
- Keep cleaning agents and other materials in their original containers. Do not store them in containers designed for other products in case they are used for the wrong type of work, or even drunk by mistake.
- Do not put detergents into aluminium containers.

Use
- Always wear the correct protective equipment – gloves, masks, goggles – when handling chemicals.
- Always follow the manufacturer's instructions when using chemicals.
  - Don't exceed the recommended concentration or temperature.
  - Don't use the agent for any work other than the type it was supplied for.
  - Don't mix substances together as this can release poisonous fumes.
- Don't measure out chemicals into containers like half-pint glasses or bottles where it could be mistaken for a drink.

Accidents
- Any information or safety sheets should be kept in a safe place in case they need to be referred to quickly if an accident happens. Instruction sheets should be displayed prominently.
- Find out the appropriate first aid treatment for all substances that are used on the premises.

Do this

1 Make a note of any notices displayed in the cellar areas which are related to the Food Safety, Food Hygiene, Health and Safety or COSHH laws or regulations.
2 Larger establishments should have a written statement of their Health and Safety policy. Try to obtain a copy of the statement.
3 Find out where the information sheets for chemical and cleaning agents are kept. Who should you go to in the event of an accident?

MAINTAINING FLOORS

A dirty floor leads to dirt and bacteria in the air which can infect beer in casks and any equipment used in the cellar.
- The cellar floor must be kept clean at all times. It must be cleaned each day, and thoroughly scrubbed and cleaned at least once each week.

Assemble your equipment
You will need:
- a sweeping brush
- a mop
- a plastic or galvanised steel bucket
- a suitable cleaning agent
- 'Wet Floor' signs.

Procedure
1 Sweep the floor thoroughly and remove any litter.
2 Make up the cleaning solution in a bucket. Use the correct concentration of detergent and the recommended water temperature. Switch off and unplug any electrical equipment which sits on the cellar floor.
3 Mop the floor thoroughly. Move items like kegs on tap and clean the surfaces beneath them. Mop into corners.
4 Mop up any excess water. Check that there are no greasy or oily patches that have not been cleaned thoroughly.
5 Erect 'Wet Floor' signs at the entrances to the cellar and inform other members of staff that the floor is wet.
6 Allow the floor to dry before you begin other work in the cellar.

● Report any holes, cracks or crevices in the floor which may provide entry or a hiding place for pests such as mice and insects.
● Spillages should be cleaned up immediately.

MAINTAINING WALLS AND CEILINGS

Wall fittings such as those holding a gas ring main or wash main should be treated as part of the wall and cleaned at the same time. Doors and wall-mounted electrical fittings should also be cleaned.

The frequency of cleaning will depend on establishment procedures.
● A thorough cleaning of walls and ceilings should be completed at least every three months.
● Daily or weekly cleaning of some parts may be required.

Assemble your equipment
You will need:
● sponge cloths
● buckets
● possibly a sprayer
● a suitable detergent.

As you may be working above head height, you may also require rubber gloves and goggles. Always use a ladder. Do not stand on kegs or crates.

Procedure
1 Make up the cleaning agent in a bucket or sprayer according to the manufacturer's instructions. Fill another bucket with warm water.
2 Switch off and unplug any wall-mounted electrical equipment.
3 Spread or spray the solution evenly on to the surface.
4 Wipe with a damp sponge cloth.
5 Rinse a sponge cloth in clean warm water and wipe the surface again.
6 Allow the surface to air dry.

● Check the surfaces for dirt smears or splash marks and any holes, cracks or crevices.
● Some detergent-sterilants are only effective if they are used after dirt has been removed and they are allowed to air-dry on the surface.

MAINTAINING THE DRAINING SYSTEM

The floors of some cellars often have a slight downward slope leading to a channel or gully. The gully is frequently tiled and covered with metal grids/gratings.

The gully leads to a drain or sump, depending on whether or not the cellar is connected to the main drainage system. If the cellar is below the main drainage level, a pump may be fitted to the sump.
● A thorough cleaning should be done once each week.

Assemble your equipment
You will need:
● a stiff brush or scrubbing brush
● a mop and bucket
● a suitable cleaning agent.

Procedure
1 Make up a quantity of the cleaning agent in the bucket.
2 Remove the gratings covering the gullies and turn them upside down. Scrub the gratings thoroughly. Turn the gratings over and repeat the process on the upper surface.
3 Mop down the gullies ensuring thorough cleaning of sides and base.
4 Examine drains to check if deposits have built up on the surfaces. If necessary, scrape the drains to remove any build-up.
5 After cleaning, replace all gratings and rinse down all areas with clean hot water.
6 Clean all equipment and store cleaning agents and equipment in the appropriate stores.

● If there is a sump, it must be cleaned out at least once each week. Scrub it out thoroughly with a suitable detergent.
● Where a sump pump is fitted, you should make sure that the sump pump filter and grating are kept clean and in position.

CLEARING UP AFTER STRUCTURAL CLEANING

● The equipment and materials used for cleaning structural surfaces and solid stillages should be stored away after use.
● Make sure that the equipment is kept apart from equipment used for cleaning any part of the beer dispense system or ice-making equipment.
● Remove any cleaning agents from the cellar immediately after use and lock them away safely.
● Clean and rinse any equipment used and store it in the correct location.

Job cards and hygiene schedules

Some large detergent companies provide establishments with task or job cards which give details of the type of cleaning agent to be used, the level of dilution, the cleaning procedure and the standard of cleanliness required. These also recommend the frequency of cleaning operations. See opposite for an example of a task/job card.
● Establishments involved with food preparation and service must keep a record of cleaning operations in the form of a hygiene schedule.
● In an establishment where a hygiene schedule is kept, you must complete the record after each cleaning operation. An example is given below.

Hygiene Schedule										
Name	Item	Product	Frequency	M	T	W	T	F	S	S
Paul	Floor	EPI	Daily	X	X	X	X	X		
John	Cold Room	DBX	Weekly		X					
Paul	Shelves	DBX	Weekly	X						
John	Ice machine	D4A	Weekly			X				

An example of part of a hygiene schedule

PRODUCT	EQUIPMENT	CLEANING METHOD	STANDARD
EPI	Sweeping brush	1. Sweep floor to remove litter.	No loose litter
4B	Mop	2. Make up EPI solution in hot water $\frac{1}{2}$ cup per bucket (1–2oz/gal, 6–12g/l).	No grease patches
Yellow Powder	Bucket	3. Mop thoroughly, taking care around legs and underneath units.	Floor must be dry before being in regular use again
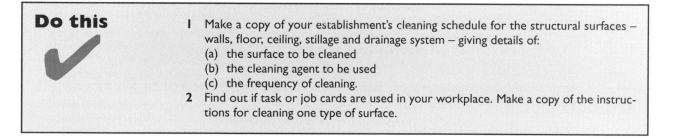		4. Mop up excess water.	
		5. Erect "Wet Floor" signs.	
		6. Allow to dry. Make sure your workmates know the floor is wet.	
Daily		QUARRY TILE FLOOR	Diversey Limited
CT/11			

Job/task card for floor cleaning (courtesy of Diversey Ltd)

Do this

1 Make a copy of your establishment's cleaning schedule for the structural surfaces – walls, floor, ceiling, stillage and drainage system – giving details of:
   (a) the surface to be cleaned
   (b) the cleaning agent to be used
   (c) the frequency of cleaning.
2 Find out if task or job cards are used in your workplace. Make a copy of the instructions for cleaning one type of surface.

CELLAR EQUIPMENT AND MACHINERY

All items of equipment and machinery should be kept clean and monitored to check that they are operating properly.

From the Food Safety and Food Hygiene viewpoint, the cleanliness of areas where food and drink are stored such as cold rooms and any racks or shelves is extremely important. Also, as ice is served as an accompaniment to many drinks, any ice-making equipment must be scrupulously clean and sterile.

Maintaining ice-making equipment

Most modern cellars will have some form of ice-making machine (see page 132). As there are many different models available, you should read carefully any instructions regarding cleaning supplied by the manufacturer.

The parts of the ice-making equipment that should be cleaned include the storage bin and water reservoir, the tilting pan and evaporator, the water filter, condenser and the cabinet exterior.

Ask your supervisor to demonstrate the cleaning operations required for the model of ice-maker in your establishment.

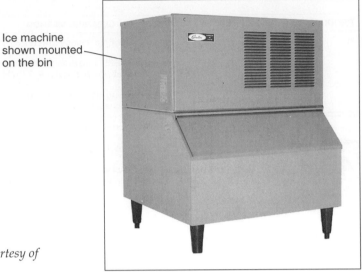

Ice machine shown mounted on the bin

An ice-making machine (courtesy of IMI Cornelius)

General maintenance

Apart from the cleaning operations, there are other checks to perform to ensure the machine is in good working order.

● Check the water inlet and outlet tubes have no leakages.
● Check that the amount of ice being produced is neither too little nor too excessive. Adjust the bin thermostat accordingly or advise your supervisor or employer.
● Check frequently the quality of the ice produced. If cubes are hollow or too full, adjust the evaporator thermostat.

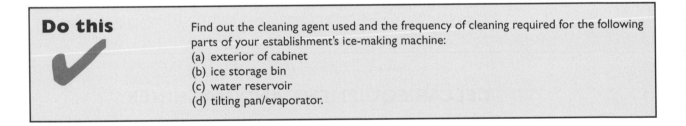

Do this

Find out the cleaning agent used and the frequency of cleaning required for the following parts of your establishment's ice-making machine:
(a) exterior of cabinet
(b) ice storage bin
(c) water reservoir
(d) tilting pan/evaporator.

MAINTAINING RACKS AND SHELVES

Shelves and racks are used in the cellar to store bottled goods like spirits and wines and also some items of cellar equipment. All surfaces should be cleaned with an appropriate detergent-sterilant. As several types of surface may be involved, check the type of cleaning agent to be used.

Assemble your equipment
You will need:
● a duster
● sponge cloths
● a bucket or sprayer
● the appropriate cleaning agents for the surfaces to be cleaned.

Procedure
1 Remove any goods stored on the shelves or racks. Place items of equipment or

bottles on a clean surface when removing them from shelves or racks. Keep them in the original order.

2   Make up the cleaning agent in a bucket or sprayer as appropriate.
3   Dust down shelves or racks with a dry duster to remove any superficial dust and dirt.
4   Apply the solution to the surface and wipe down until no dirt is visible. Clean well into any angles or corners.
5   Rinse down the area with clean warm water, if appropriate.
6   Allow the surface to air dry before replacing stock or equipment.

● Check shelves or racks for damage or loose fittings. Report any damage to your supervisor and tighten up loose nuts and bolts as required.
● Shelves and racks are normally cleaned on a weekly basis.

Do this

Make a list of the types of surface of any shelves and racks you find in the cellar. Against each type of surface make a note of the cleaning agent you should use and the frequency of the cleaning operation.

CELLAR REFRIGERATION

Cellar refrigeration has become more complicated and sophisticated. Depending on the mix of draught products, you may find more than one temperature-controlled area in the cellar and a variety of equipment.

The main forms of cellar refrigeration units include:
● air conditioning units
● cold rooms
● multi-line coolers.

A 'python' system may be used.

Maintaining air-conditioning units

There is little routine cleaning and maintenance with these units which can be performed by the cellar man. However, it is important that the fan unit is kept as clean and sterile as possible.

Assemble your equipment
You will need:
● a sponge cloth
● a sprayer
● a suitable cleaning agent.

If the unit is wall-mounted, you will also need a set of steps.

Procedure
1   Switch off the unit and unplug it.
2   Make up the cleaning solution in the sprayer and spray evenly over the surface. Make sure that the vents covering the fan unit are evenly sprayed.
3   Wipe down the surface with a damp sponge cloth.
4   Rinse the cloth in clean, warm water and wipe the surfaces again. Allow to air dry.

● This operation should be performed each week.

Internal cleaning

The fans inside the unit may need to be cleaned on a monthly basis. This involves removing the ventilation grille after the unit has been switched off. The fans may be cleaned with a suitable detergent-sterilant. Interior parts may be cleaned using a soft non-metallic brush or vacuum cleaner.

General maintenance
- The thermostat should be checked daily to make sure that it is set at the correct temperature.
- Check the fan unit for signs of over-icing.
- If the unit has a water outlet pipe, this may need to be cleared periodically by pouring hot water down it.

Check the cellar temperature each day to make sure that the refrigeration unit is working properly. If the thermostat is at the correct setting, but the cellar temperature is too high or too low, you should inform your supervisor or contact the refrigeration contractor.

A temperature record card should be kept in the establishment and you may be required to complete a daily record.

Do this

1 Find out which types of refrigeration unit are used in the cellar of your workplace.
(a) What are the recommended thermostat settings?
(b) How frequently are the units serviced by the company that installed the system?
2 Discuss with your supervisor what you should do if you find that the cellar temperature is too high or too low.

Maintaining cold rooms

The cold room is an efficient system of providing a good storage temperature for beers which are served cool.

The room is kept cold by the use of a fan-assisted air-conditioning unit and this should be maintained and cleaned as described above. If the floor of the cold room is the same as the cellar floor, it should be cleaned in the same way and with the same frequency.

The best time to clean the cold room is at a time during the week when stock levels are reasonably low.

Assemble your equipment
You will need:
- a non-abrasive detergent-sterilant
- a bucket or sprayer
- a sponge cloth
- a set of steps (if necessary).

Procedure
1 Move any free-standing units, such as racks for white wine or crates, away from the walls. Remove any stock from shelves.
2 Make up the cleaning agent into the correct concentration in the bucket or sprayer.
3 Rinse the sponge cloth in the solution and wash all wall surfaces, shelves, wall-mounted fixtures such as boards holding the gas ring and wash mains and ventilation grids.

4 Rinse with clean water, if appropriate, and allow to air dry.
5 Replace any stock on shelves. Replace free-standing units.

General management of cold rooms
To keep the cold room operating efficiently, you should:
● check the temperature daily – it should normally be in the range between 8–10°C
● keep the door closed after entering and leaving
● keep the cold room tidy.

Maintaining multi-line coolers

Multi-line coolers are designed to be used in establishments which do not have space for a cold room. However, in large establishments they are often used in conjunction with a cold room whenever extra chilling is required (see below). Cleaning is confined to the surface of the unit. The air inlet and outlet grids should be cleaned frequently. The interior of these grids may be cleaned with a vacuum cleaner or soft brush every three months.

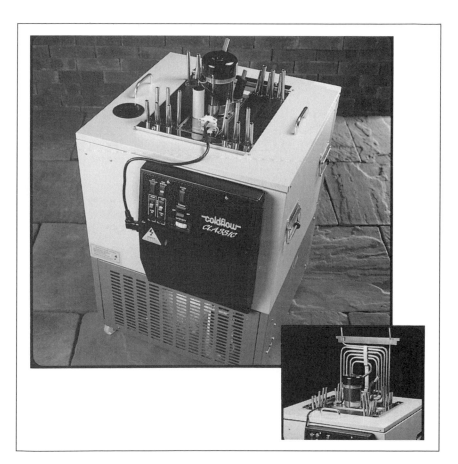

A multi-line cooler (courtesy of IMI Cornelius)

General maintenance
● Check the temperature of the water re-circulation unit each day. It should usually be below 5°C.
● Some models have alarm systems/warning lights fitted to indicate if the temperature control has failed or if there is some form of electrical failure. These should be checked at regular intervals each day.
● Keep air inlet and outlet grids clear of any obstructions.

Do this

✔

1 Visit the cold room if your establishment has one. Make a note of the surfaces (walls, floor, ceiling), any shelving or racking and wall-mounted fixtures. Identify:
   (a) what each surface is made of
   (b) the type of cleaning agent appropriate to the surface
   (c) the frequency of cleaning the surfaces required by your supervisor.
2 If you have a multi-line cooler for draught products installed in the cellar, find out:
   (a) how many lines are attached to the cooler.
   (b) how to read the thermostatic control and how to check for temperature or electrical failure.

MEMORY JOGGER

Why is it important that the cellar temperature should be carefully controlled and monitored regularly?

MAINTAINING THE CELLAR ENVIRONMENT

Apart from the routine cleaning of surfaces and equipment and making sure that equipment is operating efficiently, you must also pay attention to controlling the cellar environment.

Temperature

One of the most important aspects of cellar management is to maintain the temperature at a constant level. Draught and bottled beers, wines and some spirits can deteriorate quite rapidly if exposed to sudden changes of temperature.

The different products stored in the cellar and other storage areas are stored ideally at a variety of temperatures. The storage temperatures are recommended by the brewery supplying the products and these should be maintained as far as possible.

Procedure
The procedures you should follow will depend upon the type of temperature control (if any) that is operated in your workplace.
● A large, easy-to-read thermometer should be hung in the cellar and cold room away from walls or draughts. You should check each thermometer regularly, at least several times each day.
● Where refrigeration units are installed with automatic temperature control:
   1 Regularly check the temperature gauge/thermostat to ensure it is operating correctly. Check the reading with the cellar thermometers. Thermostats can fail.
   2 Never tamper with the thermostat.
   3 Contact the installer/refrigeration contractor or inform your supervisor if the temperature is too high or too low.
   4 Open the cellar doors and flaps for a short time once each week to allow a change of air.
● Where refrigeration units are not installed, the cellar may need to be cooled during the summer months and heated during the winter months to maintain a steady temperature. A wall-mounted fan heater with a thermostatic control or central heating radiators will provide adequate indirect heat.

Humidity

Warm, moist conditions provide the ideal environment for yeasts, moulds, bacteria and insect pests to develop and thrive.
● The level of humidity (dampness) in the cellar should be kept as low as possible.
● After routine cleaning operations, all areas should be left as dry as possible to avoid pools of water forming on floors and in gullies which can become stagnant and add moisture to the air.

● Ventilate the cellar regularly to change the air and reduce any dampness in the air.

Ventilation

Effective, regular ventilation is necessary to maintain a fresh atmosphere in the cellar and keep it free from contamination.
● Check any air shafts or ventilation bricks. Make sure that these are cleaned regularly and do not become blocked.
● It may be necessary to increase ventilation by opening cellar doors and windows early in the morning during the summer months. In the winter, ventilation should be reduced to maintain cellar temperature.
● Prevent draughts when ventilating the cellar. Draughts can produce sudden changes in temperature which can disturb sediment beers and cause beer and other products to deteriorate.

Remember, if a cellar thermometer is exposed to a draught, it will give a false reading.

Lighting

All areas should be adequately lit in order for routine work to be carried out safely and to prevent dirt building up in unlit areas.
● As lights and light fittings attract dust and dirt they should be cleaned on a regular basis.
● Any light that fails or is broken should be replaced as soon as possible. Remember to replace the safety cage securely.
● Broken light fittings, exposed or worn wiring, damaged switches and any other electrical faults should be reported to your supervisor immediately.

Do this ✔

1　Find out from the drayman or brewery what the ideal storage temperature is for their draught and bottled beers and ciders. Make a list of the brands stocked in your cellar and the ideal temperature for each brand.

2　Keep a record of any changes in temperature in the cellar for each day of the week. Read the cellar thermometer three times each day, at say 10 a.m., 2 p.m., and after closing. Make a note each time you do it. Repeat this each day for one week. Are there any variations? What might be the causes?

MAINTAINING SECURITY IN THE CELLAR

Ideally, access to the cellar should be limited to:
● persons on brewery business, such as draymen, delivery men or service men
● persons on your employer's business, such as staff drawing stock or a stock taker
● persons who have a right of entry under the laws governing licensed premises (see page 138).

General procedure
● Whenever the cellar or storage area is open, you should not leave it.
● When work has been completed in the cellar, all entrances should be securely locked.
● Do not leave keys in locks or in places where other people can get hold of them without your knowledge. Report to your supervisor immediately any signs of tampering with locks or if keys are lost.
● If other people are in the cellar, stay with them in order to watch their movements and activities in the cellar.

Right of entry

Certain officials have a legal right of entry to licensed premises at any time. These include Police Officers, Environmental Health Officers, Weights and Measures Inspectors, Customs and Excise Officers, Fire Officers and Licensing Magistrates.

If a person claiming to be one of these officials enters the premises, you should:
- greet them politely, ask them for their name and to show you their official identification
- contact your supervisor or employer immediately. Ask the person(s) to wait until your supervisor or employer arrives and do not leave them unsupervised.

Essential knowledge

It is important that you should prevent any person from entering the cellar without your employer's permission because:
- a dishonest tradesman or member of staff may steal from the cellar stock
- a person who is unfamiliar with cellar organisation or procedures may accidentally damage the stock or equipment in the cellar
- an inexperienced person may have an accident or may cause another member of staff to have an accident.

Case study

A licensee had purchased a new range of cleaning materials after having the cellar and storage areas refurbished to meet the Food Safety (General Food Hygiene) Regulations. Before training the staff to use the new cleaning agents, he told them to use up any old stock. Two members of staff were cleaning the cellar when the agent used for wall cleaning ran out. One of them decided to use some of the new cleaning agent to finish the job. Ignoring the instructions on the label regarding the concentration and the use of goggles and gloves, he began to clean the walls. While he was cleaning above his head, some of the solution splashed into his eye.

He rinsed his eye thoroughly with water according to the instructions, but refused to go to the Accident and Emergency Unit of the local hospital as instructed on the label. Several hours later his vision became blurred. When he eventually went to hospital, it was too late. The solution was corrosive and he lost the sight in his eye.

1 Who was responsible for this accident?
2 What actions should the licensee have taken with the new cleaning agents?
3 How were the employee's actions partly responsible for the accident?
4 How would you have behaved in this situation?

What have you learned

1 Which law deals specifically with the handling of cleaning agents and detergents?
2 Why should you keep chemicals and cleaning agents in their original containers?
3 How often should you clean:
   (a) cellar floors?
   (b) walls and ceilings?
   (c) the drainage system?
4 Why is it important that ice-making machines should be regularly cleaned?
5 Why should you check the thermostatic settings of refrigeration units with the cellar thermometer?
6 Why should you prevent people entering the cellar without your employer's permission?

ELEMENT 2:   Prepare kegs and gas cylinders for use

**What you need
to do**

- Recognise when a keg or gas cylinder needs to be changed.
- Safely disconnect and correctly remove a keg or gas cylinder following organisational procedures.
- Prepare and safely connect a new keg or gas cylinder so that service can resume.
- Remove empty kegs and gas cylinders from the cellar and store them correctly ready for collection.

- Deal effectively with leakages in kegs and gas cylinders and inform the appropriate people when necessary.
- Carry out your duties in an organised and efficient manner taking account of priorities, organisational procedures and any legal requirements related to safe and hygienic working practices.

**What you need
to know**

- The main components of draught dispense systems.
- How to disconnect empty kegs and gas cylinders and prepare and connect replacements.
- How to store empty gas cylinders and kegs ready for collection.

- How to perform these operations safely to avoid accidents or injuries.
- How to deal effectively with leakages in kegs and gas cylinders.
- How to organise your time to complete these operations efficiently.

THE DISPENSE SYSTEM

Dispense systems vary in their degree of complexity from one establishment to another. See the diagram on page 140.

Kegs

Kegs are made in a range of sizes and may contain between 5 and 36 gallons (22 to 164 litres) of beer or other beverage. They are of a sturdy metal construction with protective rims at both top and bottom.
- Kegs are used in an upright position.
- The connector valve, called the extractor, closure or spear, is situated at the top of the keg and is normally covered with a coloured protective, tamper-proof seal, when it leaves the brewery.
- A keg may be either single- or two-part. Both types hold the product under a top pressure.
    - Single-part kegs have one chamber and are pressurised at between 10 and 38 psig (pounds per square inch [measured by] gauge).
    - Two-part kegs have an internal gas chamber containing the gas required to dispense the product stored under high pressure (between 90 and 120 psig).

**Essential
knowledge**

- Under no circumstances should you attempt to remove the spear from the top of the keg. Even empty kegs contain gas under pressure.
- The Food Safety and Food Hygiene Regulations forbid the return of waste beer or other products to kegs.
- Returning waste beer or beer from drip trays to kegs can result in prosecution of the establishment by the trading standards or environmental health authorities.

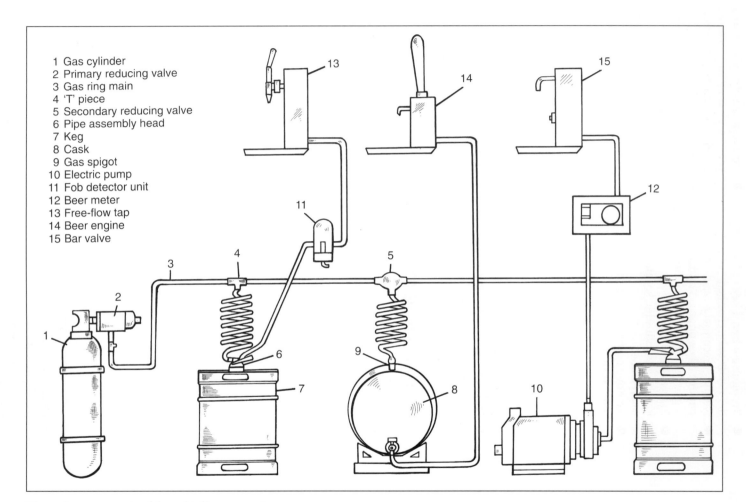

1 Gas cylinder
2 Primary reducing valve
3 Gas ring main
4 'T' piece
5 Secondary reducing valve
6 Pipe assembly head
7 Keg
8 Cask
9 Gas spigot
10 Electric pump
11 Fob detector unit
12 Beer meter
13 Free-flow tap
14 Beer engine
15 Bar valve

The main components of draught dispense systems

Pipe assembly head

There are various names for this piece of equipment. It may also be known as the dispense head, connector head, keg coupler or tapping head.

The pipe assembly head has two pipes made of food grade PVC, nylon or medium density polythene tubing attached to it. One pipe (gas line) is attached to the gas system to supply gas to the keg; the other carries the draught liquid under pressure to the dispense tap in the bar. An ON-OFF gas switch in the form of a handle is found on most modern heads (see below).

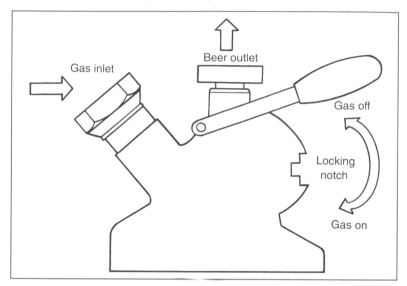

Pipe assembly head (keg coupler)

Do this

1 Make a list of the elements of the dispense system from the figure given opposite. Examine the system in your work situation and tick off each element that you find.
2 Make a list of the draught keg brands that are sold in your workplace. When these products are being delivered, ask the delivery person (the drayman) about:
    (a) the size of kegs available (in gallons/litres)
    (b) the total weight (liquid and container) of a full keg.
3 Identify the colour of the protective seal for each brand above.

Gas cylinders

Gas cylinders also come in different sizes. The standard weights are currently 3.2, 6.5 and 12.7 kg, but can be much higher in bulk systems.
- Carbon dioxide cylinders are always painted black and contain the liquid and gas under a pressure of between 600 to 900 psig.
- Mixed gas cylinders containing a mixture of nitrogen and carbon dioxide, are painted grey with a black collar and contain the gas mixture at a much higher pressure than pure carbon dioxide.

The valve assembly at the head of the cylinder has an outlet valve to connect to the gas system, a safety disc, known as a bursting disc, to release excess pressure and, usually, an ON-OFF valve which can be moved by hand.

Gas cylinders can be stored in either a horizontal position secured by wedges or in an upright position attached to the wall with clamps or chains.
- Gas cylinders in use must be in the upright position and firmly attached to the cellar wall. Cylinders not in use, whether full or empty, should not be stored in the cellar.
- Gas cylinders can be dangerous. You must handle them carefully at all times (see page 142).

Essential knowledge

Carbon dioxide (CO_2) cylinders
- Carbon dioxide is colourless and has no noticeable smell which makes it difficult to detect in the air.
- It is heavier than air and tends to concentrate at floor level and build up towards the cellar ceiling. However, cooling fans in the cellar will mix it into the air quite rapidly.

Obvious signs of leakage
- 'Frosting' upwards from the bottom of the cylinder.
- A sudden and noisy release of gas if the bursting disc ruptures. If a cylinder is not secured, this can propel it round the cellar.

If either of these events occur, you should leave the cellar immediately and report the problem to your supervisor so that the appropriate action can be taken.

The effects of inhaling carbon dioxide
Anyone inhaling a high concentration of carbon dioxide will experience shortness of breath, increased heart and breathing rate, slight tingling of the eyes and, maybe, a desire to cough. A headache, sleepy feeling and ringing in the ears may follow and the person can rapidly lose consciousness.

What should you do?
If you experience any of these symptoms or a cylinder bursting disc has ruptured, you should:
1. Leave the area at once. Inform your supervisor and do not enter it again for at least one hour.
2. Open all doors and cellar flaps from the outside, if possible.
3. Before attempting to re-enter the area, make sure there is another person watching from a safe position.
4. Fine water spraying will help to absorb carbon dioxide gas.
5. Notify the brewery or Fire Service, if you are in doubt about the safety of returning to the cellar.

Routine precautions
- Check regularly for gas leaks from cylinders and lines. Report any problems to your supervisor immediately.
- Ventilate the cellar by opening all doors for a short time each morning and evening.

MEMORY JOGGER

What actions should you take if there is a major leakage of gas in the cellar?

Gas pressure reducing valve

The pressure in the cylinder is much higher than the pressure needed to dispense the liquid in the keg. Reducing valves are essential. Two types are commonly used in cellars:
- primary reducing valves, which reduce the pressure in the cylinder down to the level required for dispensing highly-carbonated products (usually between 30 and 40 psig)
- secondary reducing valves, which are fitted into the gas ring main to lower the pressure from 30 to 40 psig to that required for low carbonated products or cleaning operations, usually 0 to 25 psig.

- Never interfere with a reducing valve as they are preset to give the correct pressure and have bursting discs which will break if the valve develops a fault.
- A faulty reducing valve should be reported to the Technical Services/Support Section of the brewery for repair or replacement. Never attempt to repair one yourself.

Essential knowledge	Working with kegs and gas cylinders need not be dangerous if they are handled properly. The main dangers that can arise from incorrect handling and storage are:

Working with kegs and gas cylinders need not be dangerous if they are handled properly. The main dangers that can arise from incorrect handling and storage are:

- handling heavy objects in the wrong way, which can lead to bruises, muscle strains and other more serious injuries
- kegs may have protective rims broken or damaged by mishandling making them difficult or unsafe to handle or they may be pierced or have seams or seals damaged causing them to leak
- throwing or dropping a gas cylinder may damage the head valve and lead to a sudden or slow leakage of gas into the cellar
- placing a gas cylinder next to a source of heat may raise the pressure in the cylinder and cause the bursting disc to rupture and gas to be released suddenly.

Beers or other draught beverage lines

Draught dispense lines lead from the pipe assembly head to the dispense tap in the bar. Kinked lines, sharp edges, dirt or yeast growth, which can prevent the liquid flowing at a steady rate, will create problems like fobbing at the dispense tap.

Gas ring main and 'T' pieces

In most establishments, gas is supplied from the cylinder to the kegs through a single main pipe, the gas ring main, which will have junctions leading to the individual kegs. (See the diagram on page 140.) The main pipe is attached to the primary reducing valve. The junctions in the main leading to individual kegs are made using either:

- a 'T' piece, often fitted with an ON-OFF switch, if the pressure required for dispense is the same as in the main
- a secondary reducing valve which may be fitted with an isolation switch to shut off the gas supply to the keg.

Electric impeller pump

Electric impeller pumps are commonly used in the cellar to lift beer from the keg to the dispense point and with bar valves.

Pumps are also commonly used where a product is dispensed from a single keg to several taps in bars and lounges. In this situation a two- or three-branched fitting is attached on or close to the outlet valve of the electric pump.

Fob detector units

Keg products are likely to 'fob' (foam up), both when the keg is running out and when a new keg is being fitted, as the line will fill with gas. This creates a lot of wastage.

A fob detector unit shuts off the flow of beer when too much gas is detected in the line. See the photographs on page 144. As some beer is held in the line, it enables a smooth flow of the product to be maintained after a keg has been changed.

Beer dispense meter

This equipment is designed to deliver a fixed amount of a draught product to a dispense tap each time it is operated.

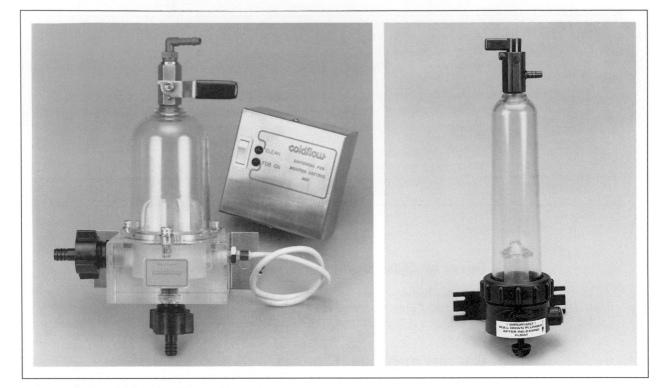

Fob detection units
(courtesy of IMI Cornelius
Ltd)

Cellar refrigeration or cooling system

Beers and other keg products are normally stored in the cellar between 10 and 14.5 °C (50–58 °F). However, the dispensing temperature required may be lower than this.

Cooling may take place in the cellar, using a cold room, through a multi-cooler and 'python' system (see Element 1 of this Unit) or, using an in-line cooler, under the bar counter.
● If the dispensing temperature is too cold, this may result in a poor head being formed.
● If the temperature is too high, the product may fob and too high a head may be formed.

Dispensing equipment

The dispensing equipment mounted on the bar counter is normally provided by the brewery. Although the general appearance of the taps may differ, they are essentially similar for all pressure dispense systems. They are called free-flow taps.

The two main components of the free-flow tap are:
● an ON-OFF valve in the form of a handle moving backwards and forwards
● a flow control which controls the speed at which the product flows into the glass. This is not always fitted.

Some taps also have a creaming facility to improve the tightness and quality of the head. Apart from free-flow taps, you may also find:
● electric push-button taps (bar valve dispensers)
● manual beer engines if your establishment offers cask-conditioned beer to its customers.

<table>
<tr>
<td>

Do this

✔

</td>
<td>

1   Find out the sizes of gas cylinders available for use by your local licensed trade. You should find out:
    (a) the height of the cylinders
    (b) the total weight of full cylinders
    (c) the internal pressure of a full cylinder in psig.
2   Create a list of the brands of keg beers, lagers and ciders available locally. Try to find out the ideal dispense pressure for each brand. Are there any differences?
3   Where are the reducing valves located in the cellar? How are they connected to the cylinder and gas ring main? Draw a rough sketch.
4   Follow the gas line from the primary reducing valve to the kegs. Locate any 'T' pieces. How do you switch off the gas supply to the keg?
5   Locate the fob detectors in the dispense system. How do you reset them?

</td>
</tr>
</table>

REPLACING AN EMPTY OR FAULTY KEG

When should you change a keg?

The signs will vary depending on whether or not a fob detector is fitted to the line.
● **No fob detector fitted** – The product will pour high and become difficult to serve. The tap will begin to splutter and flow will cease. The hiss of gas will be heard when the tap valve is in the ON position.
● **Fob detector fitted** – As the fob detector prevents the product becoming too high and the line filling with gas, flow at the dispense tap will stop suddenly. No sound of escaping gas will be heard.

Faults in draught products

You should also replace kegs when faults appear in the product – if the product is cloudy, sour or has an off-odour.
● Remember to draw off any of the faulty product remaining in the line before resuming service.
● Lines should be cleaned as soon as possible if these faults appear.

Procedure for replacing kegs

Disconnecting a keg
1   Switch off the gas supply to the keg.
2   Move the handle (if fitted) on the pipe assembly head to the OFF position.
3   Turn the head until the release position is reached. (This is usually in an anti-clockwise direction.)
4   Lift the head from the keg closure.

When the head is not connected, it should be kept clean and free from dirt or other debris.

<table>
<tr>
<td>

Essential knowledge

</td>
<td>

You should switch off the gas before disconnecting the pipe assembly head from the keg:
● to prevent beer escaping as the head is released and spraying around the cellar
● to prevent gas escaping into the cellar while the head is disconnected.

</td>
</tr>
</table>

Connecting a keg

1 Check that the replacement keg is the correct brand and type.
2 Manoeuvre it into position, if necessary. Use safe handling techniques such as rolling the keg at an angle on its lower rim, and wear protective equipment such as gloves.
3 Place the keg close to the head to avoid stretching or twisting lines.
4 Remove the protective tamper-proof seal from the keg closure.
5 With gentle downward pressure, insert the head into the closure and turn the head to the service position (usually clockwise). Do not over-tighten.
6 Move the handle on the head into the ON position.
7 Switch on the gas supply to the keg.

Empty kegs should be removed from the work area and stored ready for collection in a secure area as soon as possible.

Essential knowledge	● If a keg is found to be leaking, it should be removed from the cellar and stored in a way which prevents the liquid leaking from it. ● Report leaking kegs to your supervisor as it may be possible to recover the value of the keg and its contents from the supplier.

Quick fault finding

If the product will not flow after a keg has been changed, you should check the following:
● the handle at the pipe assembly head is in the ON position.
● the gas shut-off valve is in the ON position or connected.
● the float release lever on the fob detector is in the correct position.
● the line is not kinked or obstructed.
● the flow control valve on the dispense tap is in the OPEN position.
● the gas cylinder is connected and not empty.

REPLACING AN EMPTY GAS CYLINDER

When should you change a gas cylinder?

There will be signs that a cylinder needs to be replaced in both cellar and bar.
● Most gas systems have a dial or gauge between the cylinder valve and the primary reducing valve which indicates the amount of gas in the cylinder. A needle pointer indicates the appropriate level.
● In the bar, the signs that a cylinder is running out are:
   – the pouring speed will become slower and cannot be adjusted using the flow control (if fitted) on the tap
   – the product will begin to pour flat, making it difficult to form a head.

Duplex installations

Some cellar gas systems have two cylinders set side-by-side, both of which are connected to the system. One cylinder will be in use and the other acts as a reserve. When one cylinder becomes empty, the other can be brought into use by simply moving a change-over switch. The empty cylinder should then be replaced as soon as possible.

MEMORY JOGGER

What procedures should you follow to change a gas cylinder safely?

Procedure for changing gas cylinders

There are three basic types of fitting used: hexagonal nuts, wing nuts and bayonet fittings. See the diagram below.

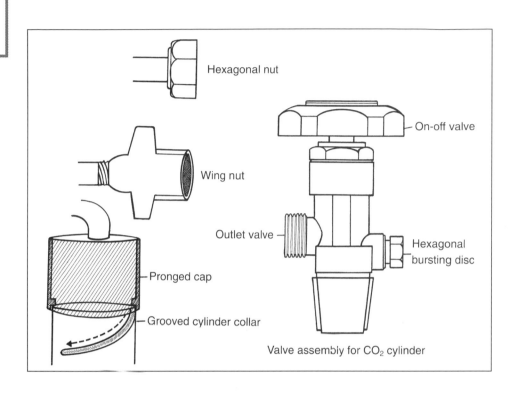

The three types of gas cylinder fitting

Hexagonal nut

Wing nut

Pronged cap

Grooved cylinder collar

On-off valve

Outlet valve

Hexagonal bursting disc

Valve assembly for CO_2 cylinder

Disconnecting a gas cylinder
1 Shut off the cylinder valve at the head of the cylinder.
2 Loosen the fitting joining the head valve to the cellar pressure system. A spanner will be required for hexagonal nuts.
3 Release the cylinder by loosening the restraining clamps attaching the cylinder to the wall.
4 Mark the empty cylinder with an 'E' and, as soon as possible, remove the cylinder to the area where empty cylinders are stored. Use the appropriate equipment and secure the cylinder.

Connecting a gas cylinder
1 Place the new cylinder in an upright position in the restraining clamps and secure it.
2 Remove the protective cover from the cylinder valve and quickly open and close the ON-OFF valve on the cylinder to expel any dirt or moisture that may have lodged in the valve. This should not be done in the direction of your eyes – tilt cylinders with bayonet fittings away from you when performing this operation.
3 If the ON-OFF valve is jammed, do not attempt to loosen it with a wrench. Mark it as defective and use another cylinder.
4 Connect the fitting to the cylinder valve using the reverse procedure to disconnecting the cylinder.
5 Open the ON-OFF valve fully.

Essential knowledge

It is important that gas cylinders should be safely secured with clamps or chains to a wall or in a safety cage. An unsecured cylinder might fall and:
- damage the dispense system causing gas to leak into the cellar
- hurt any person standing close to it
- damage any stock stored close to it
- if the head valve has been damaged, either leak or be propelled around the cellar causing damage to staff or goods.

Safety precautions

There are a few general rules that you should always observe when working with gas pressure systems in the cellar.
- Always shut off cylinder valves between serving hours. Apart from the safety aspects, it prevents the product becoming over-carbonated and fobbing when service is resumed.
- Do not connect up equipment supplied by one brewery to that supplied by another. It may not operate in the same way and create a safety hazard.
- Do not attempt to alter or adapt equipment.

Essential knowledge

When handling kegs and gas cylinders, it is important that you use safe and correct handling techniques.
- Wear strong shoes and gloves for personal protection.
- Always maintain your balance and move smoothly avoiding jerking movements.
- Move your feet as you move the keg or cylinder and avoid twisting your body.
- Make sure that you have adequate space to manoeuvre the keg or cylinder.

Using safe handling techniques can:
- help prevent serious injuries to your back or other parts of your body
- prevent unnecessary damage to equipment or stock.

Do this

1 Find out how many kegs of each different brand your workplace uses in an average week. Find out on which days of the week the kegs are changed most frequently.
2 Using your answers to the activity above, construct a chart for one week showing the number of kegs required in the working area of the cellar for each day. For example:

Monday   1 ABC lager
              2 DEF lager
              1 GHI stout.
3 Warning notices are quite often placed close to where gas cylinders are connected. If there is a notice in the cellar, copy down the statements.
4 Make a note of the type of fittings used to connect up with the female valve on the gas cylinders. Are they hexagonal, wing nuts or bayonet fittings? Do all cylinders have an ON-OFF valve?

ORGANISING YOUR WORK

As you learn the pattern of trade in your workplace, you will become aware of the days and times when demand is high. You can prepare for these times by bringing additional stock into the cellar. If you are well prepared, you can replace empty kegs and cylinders quickly. Your customers will not have to wait too long or select an unwanted alternative.

Each morning
- Make sure that sufficient stocks of kegs and cylinders are available to be changed as quickly as possible during service.
- As gas cylinders are not usually stored in the cellar, you should check the gauge each day and bring in a replacement cylinder only when necessary.
- If the area where kegs are put in service is a cold room, kegs should be stored there for three days before being put in service.
- Remove empty kegs and cylinders to the appropriate storage areas as soon as possible to leave the cellar clean and tidy. Remember, kegs and gas cylinders are valuable and are liable to be stolen if they are not locked away in a secure area.

You should report all faults with the dispense system or keg products to your supervisor or contact the Technical Services/Support Section of the brewery which has supplied the equipment or products.

Case study

One Saturday evening during a busy service session, the gas ran out and all the taps were out of action. A young barman was sent down to replace the cylinder. He followed the correct procedure, but as he was leaving the cellar he heard a loud noise behind him. The cylinder he had just fitted had fallen and had torn the high pressure line that connected the cylinder to the primary reducing valve. Carbon dioxide was leaking rapidly from the cylinder which was revolving and moving around the cellar floor. Afraid of reporting the problem to his supervisor, he attempted to trap the cylinder and turn the valve off at the cylinder head. However, the protective guard had been damaged when the cylinder fell and the head valve was jammed.

While looking for a wrench, he noticed that he was beginning to develop a headache and to feel sleepy. He began to cough and breathing became difficult. Fortunately, his supervisor came down shortly afterwards to find out why the gas had not been restored, found him unconscious and carried him out of the cellar.

1 *What was the cause of the accident?*
2 *What action should the barman have taken immediately the cylinder fell and it was obvious that the gas was escaping very rapidly?*
3 *Why did he lose consciousness?*

What have you learned

1 What are the two main types of container used for draught products?
2 Why should you not return waste draught products to kegs?
3 How is the size of gas cylinders usually expressed?
4 How can you tell the difference between a pure CO_2 and a mixed gas cylinder?
5 What are the obvious signs of gas leakage?
6 What are the symptoms which follow inhaling a high concentration of CO_2?
7 What are the main dangers that can arise from the incorrect storage and handling of kegs and gas cylinders?
8 What is the purpose of a fob detector unit?
9 How does a duplex system for gas cylinders work?
10 What checks should you make each morning?

ELEMENT 3: Clean drink dispense lines

What you need to do

- Assemble the equipment you will need to clean the lines at the appropriate time.
- Prepare the lines correctly for the cleaning operation.
- Use the cleaning agent at the correct concentration and temperature.
- Perform the necessary checks of lines and taps after completing line-cleaning operations.
- Check the quality of the draught products before service is resumed.
- Deal effectively with any unexpected situations and inform the appropriate people where necessary.
- Carry out your work in an organised and efficient manner taking account of priorities, organisational procedures and legal requirements.

What you need to know

- How to prepare drink dispense lines for cleaning.
- How to clean a variety of drink dispense line systems using the correct cleaning agents, equipment and methods.
- What checks you should perform after completing line-cleaning operations.
- How to deal effectively with unexpected situations.
- How to carry out your work in an organised and efficient manner.

CLEANING DRINK DISPENSE LINES

Why should you clean dispense lines?

In order to be able to dispense draught products easily and to your customers' satisfaction, your dispense equipment must be clean at all times.

Spoilage organisms tend to grow quite quickly in beer dispense lines and to be absorbed into the tubing and other surfaces of the dispensing equipment. If dispense lines are not clean, you could experience one or more of the following problems: blockages, product pouring high, off-flavours or off-odours.

Lines which are not cleaned frequently may become blocked and require specialised cleaning by the supplier's technical staff or complete replacement of the lines.

When should you clean?
Ideally, beer lines should be cleaned each week. Post-mix syrup dispense lines do not need such frequent cleaning. Line cleaning will normally take place when the establishment is closed and a record or chart should be kept in the cellar showing the dates when lines have been cleaned.

Draught line cleaning systems

The type of cleaning system you will use will vary with the size of the establishment and the draught products that are offered to customers.

Essential knowledge

Line cleaning detergents
- All line cleaning methods require a detergent to clean lines efficiently. They often contain caustic and corrosive chemicals which can cause serious injuries or kill if they are misused.
- Warning notices should be fitted to the taps or the system being cleaned informing staff not to use them. This prevents the possibility of people being served a drink contaminated with cleaning fluid.

See Element 1 of this Unit for detailed instructions about the use of detergents.

CLEANING BEER, LAGER AND CIDER DISPENSE LINES

Cleaning a manual draught line

Manual draught lines are used almost exclusively with cask-conditioned beer.

Assemble your equipment
You will need:
- three sterilised plastic or stainless steel buckets
- a quantity of line cleaner
- a container for collecting fluid in the bar.

Procedure
1 **Disconnect and drain the line**
   - Turn off the cask tap and disconnect the beer line from it. (See Unit 2NC11 for details of this procedure.)
   - Drain off any beer in the line into a clean, sterilised bucket. Follow establishment procedure in disposing of this beer.
2 **Rinse out the line**
   - Transfer the end of the line into a bucket of clean, cold water.
   - Using the bar pump ('beer engine'), draw the water up through the line and catch it in the container.
3 **Clean the line**
   - Mix the correct quantity of line cleaner and cold water in a bucket. Always use the correct type of detergent for the type of line to be cleaned. If you do not have enough of the correct detergent, do not add or use others which may not be suitable for the job. Delay the cleaning and report the problem to your supervisor or employer.
   - Transfer the end of the beer line into the bucket of cleaning fluid and draw it up through the line until it appears through the bar tap.
   - Leave the fluid to stand in the line according to the manufacturer's instructions.
   - Draw a little fluid off once or twice to move any deposits loosened by the fluid and allow the fluid to penetrate more effectively.
4 **Rinse out the line**
   - After the required time, transfer the line end into a bucket of clean, cold water and draw it through the line until the detergent is flushed out of the system.
   - Continue until the water runs clear and there is no trace of cleaning fluid left in the line. A minimum of two gallons of clean water should be drawn through the system.

Essential knowledge

It is very important that the lines carrying any draught product should be thoroughly rinsed with clean water after a line-cleaning detergent has been used:
- to remove all traces of detergent which could contaminate the product
- to provide the customer with a safe product in the best condition possible
- to comply with the Food Safety legislation.
Detergent left in a line which is not being used can damage the line or other fittings.
Always draw off and dispose of any cleaning fluid.

5 **Drain and reconnect the line**
   - Drain the water from the beer line and reconnect it to the cask tap. Open the cask tap.
   - Draw up any remaining water and beer through the line until the beer flows correctly.

6 **Dealing with blockages**

If lines have not been cleaned for some time, they can become blocked by dirt and debris during the cleaning process. If this happens, you should report the matter to your supervisor immediately. Removing blockages from beer lines requires specialised cleaning which may involve extremely strong detergents or sending a pellet through the line.

7 **Tidy up**

- Safely dispose of the cleaning fluid and any liquids which may have been contaminated with it.
- Wash out and clean all equipment and store it away securely until it is needed again.

8 **Check for contamination**

After every line cleaning operation, three aspects of the product should be checked carefully.

- **Appearance** Is the product clean and bright? Is it properly conditioned with a good colour, body and head?
- **Aroma** Does the product smell clean? Are there untypical or off-odours?
- **Taste** Does the product have the correct taste? Is there any sourness or off-flavours? Does it have the correct strength?

If the product is clear, in good condition and has the correct aroma and flavour, it is ready to serve. If it does not pass any one of these checks, inform your supervisor immediately.

Do this ✔

1 Find out when draught lines are cleaned in your establishment. Are they all cleaned at the same time? Is a written record kept of line cleaning operations?
2 How long should the line-cleaning agent be left in the line? Is a maximum or minimum time given in the instructions?

Cleaning a pressurised draught line

Because gas pressure is involved, this requires great care and attention. While you will find several different systems, depending on the type and complexity of the dispense system involved, the process can be illustrated by using a single line as an example.

Single line cleaning

Ideally, two bottles (one for water, one for detergent) are used. These are usually made of reinforced plastic and have a closure at the top which matches up to the pipe assembly head for a particular brewery's products.

- Cleaning bottles and the correct type of line cleaning fluid are usually supplied by the brewery, often free of charge, and may only be suitable for use with their equipment.
- As pressure is involved, these bottles are fitted with a pressure release valve on the closure.

Assemble your equipment

You will need:

- two bottles (water and cleaning)
- a quantity of line cleaning detergent
- a measuring container
- a container to catch the liquids drawn up through the dispense tap.

Procedure

1 **Prepare the water bottle**

- Fill the bottle to the marked height with clean, cold water, assemble it and connect the head. Always follow the supplier's instructions regarding safe working pressure and water temperature.

- Always keep within the safe working pressure of the bottle. A bottle provided by one brewery for a low pressure system may be dangerous if used for another brewery's high pressure system.
- Hot water should not be used, but you should observe the instructions printed on the side of the bottle and containers of line cleaner.

2 Disconnect the head

Switch off the gas supply to the keg and move the handle on the head into the OFF position. Release the head from the keg closure.

3 Flush out the line

- Connect the head to the closure on the cleaning bottle.
- Move the handle on the head into the ON position and switch on the gas supply.
- Draw up the beer and water by opening the dispense tap. Catch the liquid in a container. Continue drawing until the water runs clear.

4 Disconnect the water bottle

- Switch off the gas supply and release the head from the water bottle.
- Remember to release the pressure from the water bottle through the neck valve before refilling it.

5 Clean the line

- Fill the cleaning bottle to the marked level with correctly diluted line cleaning detergent.
- Connect the head to the cleaning bottle and switch on the gas supply.
- Open the dispense tap and keep pouring until the water is pumped out and the cleaning fluid appears.
- Leave the cleaning fluid in the line for the time recommended by the manufacturer. Draw off small amounts every now and again to move any deposits and allow the fluid to penetrate more effectively.

6 Rinse out the line

- Switch off the gas supply, disconnect the head from the cleaning bottle and connect it to the freshly-filled water bottle. Remember to release the pressure from the cleaning bottle using the neck valve, and safely dispose of any remaining fluid in the cleaning bottle immediately. Rinse it thoroughly.
- If you do not switch off the gas or release the pressure from the bottle, any remaining cleaning fluid may spray over you, possibly into your eyes, and around the cellar. Remember, the fluid may be caustic or corrosive.
- Switch on the gas supply and draw out the cleaning fluid from the line by operating the dispense tap. Keep pouring until the water runs clear and there is no sign of the cleaning fluid left. Two gallons of clean water is the recommended amount to be drawn through a line.

7 Reconnect the line

- Switch off the gas supply and disconnect the head from the water bottle.
- Connect the head to the keg closure and switch on the gas supply. The line will be full of water so you must draw it off until the beverage flows normally.

8 Tidy up

- Safely dispose of the cleaning fluid and all liquids which have been contaminated with it.
- All equipment which has been used during the cleaning operation should be thoroughly cleaned and stored in a secure area until needed.

9 Check for contamination

You should carry out the three checks described on page 152 for each line you clean.

MEMORY JOGGER

Why is it very important that you should switch off the gas before you detach the head and release the pressure from the cleaning bottle before opening it?

Single bottle cleaning operations

Some breweries recommend using a single bottle for both cleaning and rinsing the lines, rather than the use of two bottles, and no initial rinsing operation.

The advantages are:
- a two-step process is less time-consuming
- as the cleaning bottle is emptied and rinsed out before the line is flushed, this prevents any detergent being left in the cleaning bottle and is an additional safety factor.

The main disadvantage of using this method is the difficulty of completely removing all traces of detergent from the cleaning bottle before flushing out the lines.

Essential knowledge	The main reasons why draught beverages should be checked after lines have been cleaned are as follows: ● If draught lines are not thoroughly rinsed and cleared of cleaning fluid, small amounts will remain in the lines and contaminate the product. ● As the cleaning fluid is often toxic, containing caustic and corrosive chemicals, any customers served a contaminated drink may become ill. ● Serving a contaminated product is an offence under the Food Hygiene Regulations and the management may be prosecuted by the Environmental Health Department of the local authority. A customer made ill by the product may claim compensation. ● Even a small amount of cleaning fluid in the lines may make the product lose condition quickly in the glass and become flat. This will make the customer dissatisfied with the product and create a poor reputation for the product and the establishment.

Multi-line cleaning

MEMORY JOGGER

What is a wash main and how is it used for line cleaning?

Medium- and large-sized establishments may have a 'wash main', that is a special circuit attached to the cellar wall so that all lines can be cleaned at the same time. In a typical system, the pipe assembly heads or lines attached to cask taps are disconnected and attached to valves in the wash main. These valves are identical to those on the top of each keg or the thread of the cask tap. A separate pipe assembly head is connected to the wash main and is only used for connecting up to the cleaning bottle. See the diagram opposite.

The cleaning process is the same as that described for single line cleaning above, using the special head attached to the wash main. Each dispense tap connected to the wash main has to be opened and closed, as in the single line cleaning example, to draw off water and cleaning fluid when necessary.

When the cleaning process is finished, the heads or lines are disconnected from the wash main and reconnected to the appropriate kegs, or cask taps. Each product should be drawn off and checked for contamination after the cleaning operation is finished.

Automatic cleaning

Some larger establishments may have automatic line cleaning equipment. You should follow carefully the procedures laid down by the manufacturer for using such equipment.

- Always check the products for contamination. Machines do not always work perfectly.

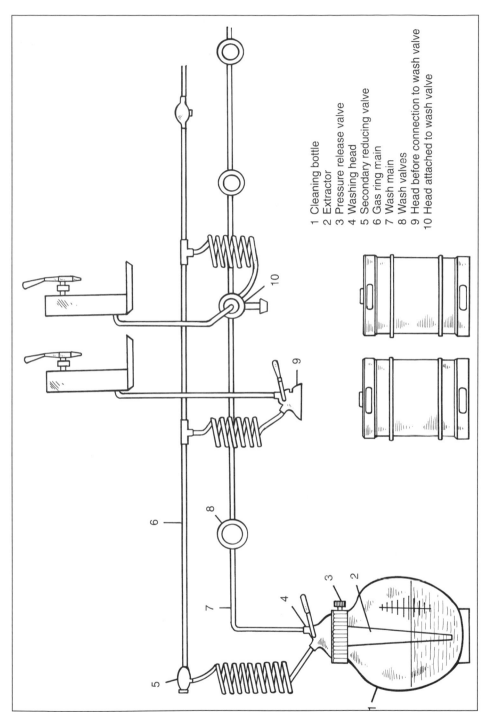

1 Cleaning bottle
2 Extractor
3 Pressure release valve
4 Washing head
5 Secondary reducing valve
6 Gas ring main
7 Wash main
8 Wash valves
9 Head before connection to wash valve
10 Head attached to wash valve

The wash main for multi-line cleaning

CLEANING POST-MIX DISPENSE LINES

The cleaning method for post-mix dispense lines will depend on which type of bulk syrup system is used in your establishment. Generally, bulk syrup will be supplied either as a bag-in-a-box or in a lined cylinder which may be sealed to prevent tampering. Unlike beer, lager or cider which are 'live', syrups are inert and sterile. The major reason for cleaning the system regularly is to prevent the build-up of sugar deposits in the lines and taps.

Cleaning bag-in-a-box systems

Procedure

Follow the normal procedure of water-detergent-water as with beer line cleaning. Place a warning notice on the dispenser to prevent anyone drinking contaminated liquid.

1   Fill a sterilised plastic or stainless steel bucket with clean water. Prepare a second bucket with the correctly diluted cleaning solution. Follow the manufacturer's instructions regarding the correct water temperature and concentration of the detergent.

2   Disconnect the syrup line from the valve on the box and attach the appropriate sterilised cleaning valve. These are usually identical to the box valve and are available from either the syrup supplier or the manufacturer. In an emergency, a valve cut from an empty box could be used. However, this could be difficult to sterilise.

3   Place the line in the clean water and draw the liquid up through the line by operating the dispense tap. When the water runs clear, close the tap and transfer the line into the bucket containing the cleaning solution.

4   Draw up the cleaning solution by operating the tap and collect it in an appropriate container. Remember, you should not use a glass or any other container which people can drink from in case of an accident. Leave the cleaning fluid in the line for the time recommended by the manufacturer.

5   Transfer the syrup line back into the bucket of water and draw enough water through to remove all traces of detergent from the line.

6   Remove the line from the bucket and the cleaning valve from the line. Reconnect the syrup line to the valve on the box. Draw up the syrup until the mixture from the dispense tap is of the correct consistency.

7   Check the mixture for off-tastes or odours. If it has the correct consistency, appearance, smell and aroma, it is ready for dispense.

8   After all lines have been cleaned, you should dispose of all contaminated fluid in the recommended way and clean and sterilise all equipment. Store all equipment in the appropriate areas.

Several lines can be cleaned at the same time using this method.

Cleaning cylinder systems

The cleaning method used with these systems will vary. Some suppliers may provide the user with cleaning cylinders with the appropriate detergent and rinse inside. In other cases, the supplier's technical services staff will be responsible for cleaning the lines. On the other hand, you may be required to mix the detergent with water and seal the container. Another variation may be related to the number of lines that can be cleaned at one time. Some cylinders may have more than one outlet valve to allow for multi-line cleaning.

The procedure below is based on using two cylinders (sometimes called 'transfer tanks') one for cleaning and the other for rinsing. However, you should learn to clean the system used in your establishment using the relevant equipment.

Procedure

Place a warning notice on the dispenser before you start the cleaning operation.

1   Switch off and disconnect the electricity supply.

2   Disconnect all syrup and gas lines from the cylinders and turn off the water supply to the carbonator.

3   Connect the tank containing the cleaner-sanitiser to the CO_2 system by attaching one of the gas lines to the inlet valve and raise the pressure up to around 50 psi (3.5 kg/cm).

4   Connect the syrup lines to the outlet valves on the head of this tank (there are usually five or six to allow multi-line cleaning) and flush each line with the

cleaner-sanitiser solution by opening each dispense valve. Catch the solution in an appropriate container. When the solution runs correctly, close the dispense valves and allow the solution to stand in the lines for 5 to 10 minutes.

5 Disconnect the cleaner-sanitiser tank. Connect the tank containing the rinsing solution. This is often soda water if a bleach-based cleaning agent has been used. Flush the system to remove all traces of the sanitising solution by opening the dispense valves. Catch the cleaning solution in an appropriate container.

6 If a chlorine-based cleaner has been used, test the rinse water from the dispenser using a litmus stick to check that the water is chlorine-free.

7 Disconnect the tank containing the soda water. Use the special adaptor, usually a combination of a gas tank and liquid tank fitting, to link the CO_2 line to the syrup lines and blow out all traces of water from the product lines. Close all the dispense valves.

8 Switch on the water supply to the carbonator, reconnect the dispenser to the power supply and switch on.

9 Reconnect the syrup and gas lines to the appropriate containers and draw up the syrup until the correct mixture is obtained. Check the appearance, taste and aroma to ensure that all traces of the detergent have been removed from the line(s).

10 Clean and sterilise all equipment and store it away safely in the correct location.

Post-mix dispense lines are normally cleaned every three months. At the same time as cleaning the lines, it is also usual to remove all water and ice from the water bath compartment, sanitise it and refill it with water to which a solution is added to prevent the growth of algae.

CLEANING AND MAINTENANCE OF EQUIPMENT

Apart from performing the line cleaning operations described above, you should also:
- clean and sterilise all items of equipment such as taps, buckets, containers and reusable cleaning bottles immediately after use
- after cleaning, check all gas and beverage lines for signs of damage or wear especially at joints with valves and other equipment
- check that all clips are properly tightened and there are no leaks in the system
- check that lines are not kinked or twisted as a result of movement during the cleaning operation
- correct any faults with the equipment that you can do within your own competence. Report any serious defects that you cannot correct to your supervisor immediately.

Do this ✔

1 Watch an experienced member of staff cleaning the lines. Make a list of all the equipment and materials used in the cleaning operation.

2 Carefully read the directions for use on the container of line cleaning fluid used in your establishment. Make a copy of the instructions related to:
 (a) how to dilute the cleaning fluid
 (b) what safety precautions (e.g. clothing, spillages) you should take
 (c) what to do in the event of accidents.

3 Most cleaning bottles have instructions printed on them regarding how they should be used. Make a copy of them. Is the maximum fill height clearly marked on the bottles?

4 Find out if your establishment has a wash (cleaning) main. If it has, locate the following:
 (a) the pipe assembly head connecting the wash main to the cleaning bottle
 (b) the secondary reducing valve, if one is fitted to the gas ring main.

Case study

A new licensee had taken over a pub and found that the previous owner had neglected to clean the beer lines for a long period. The lines were clogged and filthy. In conversation with the brewery, he found out that a powerful, concentrated line cleaner was available, but was considered so dangerous to handle that only trained brewery staff were allowed to use it. He talked one of the Technical Staff into giving him a small supply and began to clean the lines. He measured out the cleaner in a Slim Jim glass before diluting it. A small amount was left in the glass. While the licensee was upstairs drawing the cleaning fluid through the lines, one of his young children went into the cellar and saw the fluid in the glass. Thinking it was lemonade, the child drank it. Several days later the child died, her mouth, throat and stomach so badly burned by the corrosive substance that nothing could be done.

1 *What mistakes were made in this case?*
2 *What are the appropriate safety precautions that should be taken with line cleaning detergents when cleaning beer lines?*

What have you learned

1 What problems could be experienced with beer if dispense lines are not regularly cleaned?
2 Why should warning notices be placed on taps in the bar when lines are being cleaned?
3 What action can you take to help cleaning fluid penetrate more effectively?
4 What actions should you perform when tidying up after a line cleaning operation?
5 What aspects of the product should be checked after every line cleaning operation?
6 What are the main reasons why draught beverages should be checked after lines have been cleaned?

Get ahead

1 Ask your supervisor or employer if an assessment of the risks involved in staff handling cleaning agents has been made. Find out if any staff training has been done by either the supplier of the cleaning agents or the employer.
2 Find out which company(ies) supply your establishment with its cleaning agents. Ask your supervisor if job/task cards were supplied with the products. Try to examine them and find out which products are general purpose detergent-sterilants and which are specific to a single operation or material.
3 Most ice-making machines are supplied with a manual giving instructions about installation and maintenance. Ask your supervisor if you can read the manual to make yourself familiar with the controls and maintenance operations.
4 Discuss with your supervisor the effect of too high and too low temperatures in the cellar on draught products, especially any problems with dispensing them.
5 Find out from your employer or brewery staff, such as the drayman, about the effects of the Manual Handling Regulations on handling kegs and gas cylinders.
6 If your establishment has a mixed gas system, find out:
   (a) the proportions of nitrogen and carbon dioxide in the mixture
   (b) the pressure the mixture is stored under in the cylinder.
7 As carbon dioxide gas is potentially dangerous if released into the cellar, find out if your employer has made a risk assessment as required by the Control of Substances Hazardous to Health Regulations.
8 Ask your employer or supervisor if there are any data sheets or other documents related to the line cleaning agent used in your establishment. Find out if there is a telephone number you can contact in case of emergencies for further information.

Provide a drinks service for licensed premises

This unit covers:
ELEMENT 1: **Prepare and serve alcoholic and non-alcoholic drinks**
ELEMENT 2: **Maintain customer and service areas during drink service**

ELEMENT 1: **Prepare and serve alcoholic and non-alcoholic drinks**

What you need to do

- Deal with customers in a polite and helpful way at all times.
- Serve alcoholic drinks only to those people whom you are permitted to serve by law.
- Give customers accurate information about any drink that you are serving.
- Promote certain drinks to customers at the appropriate times.
- Make sure that all your service equipment is clean and free from damage before you start serving.
- Make sure that you take down customers' orders clearly and accurately to avoid misunderstandings.
- Dispense a variety of drinks using the correct equipment, at the correct temperature, and with the appropriate accompaniments.
- Deal effectively with unexpected situations and inform the appropriate people where necessary.
- Carry out your duties in an organised and efficient manner, taking account of priorities, organisational procedures and legal requirements.

What you need to know

- What the appropriate ways are for dealing with customers.
- Who you may and may not serve with alcoholic drinks.
- Why legal measures must be used to serve some alcoholic drinks.
- Why customers must be given accurate information about the drinks being served.
- How and when to promote certain types of drinks.
- Why your service equipment should be clean and free from damage.
- Why it is important that you correctly identify the drinks your customers require.
- How to dispense and serve a range of alcoholic and non-alcoholic drinks either at the bar or at the table.
- How to deal effectively with unexpected situations.
- How to carry out your work in an organised and efficient manner.

DEALING WITH CUSTOMERS

To be able to deal successfully with customers, you must understand what they expect from the bar person when they enter the bar.

Customer expectations

When customers enter licensed premises, they pay not only for the products you sell them but for a 'total experience'. They are paying for the atmosphere of the bar, the lighting and heating and, among other things, the wages of the staff. In return for their money, the customers not only expect a good quality of drink, but also a good quality of service.

In order to meet the customers' expectations, three aspects of the bar person are very important. These are your:
● appearance
● attitude
● social and professional skills.

Appearance

It is important that you present yourself well to your customers. This means that you must pay particular attention to personal hygiene and cleanliness. As you will be handling glasses and, possibly, food and will be working in close contact with customers, any neglect on your part can affect the health and comfort of your customers.

Remember, you are to some extent responsible for the health of your customers. If you do not pay close attention to your personal hygiene and cleanliness, you may spread infection to glasses, cloths and food and cause illness or food poisoning.

Re-read Unit NG1, Element 1 to refresh your memory, if necessary.

Attitude

It is important that you have a positive attitude and approach towards your customers. Remember that part of the profit from the drinks you sell to them will pay your wages and those of other staff.
● Try to see serving your customers as a personal challenge. If you create a good impression with the professionalism of the service you give them, they will stay in the bar. More importantly, they will be happy to come back again.
● A good bar person shows that he or she is interested in the customer. Avoid any behaviour which suggests to the customer you are not interested, such as arguing or chatting with other staff, reading behind the bar or leaving the bar unattended.
● Don't treat customers as if you are doing them a favour by serving them. Remember, they are the most important people in the establishment. They are doing you a favour by being there and giving you the opportunity to serve them.

There is always plenty of work for the bar person to do. Quiet times can be filled by replacing stock, polishing glasses and maintaining the appearance and cleanliness of the customer and service areas.

Do this ✔

1 Locate the nearest wash-hand basin that can be used by the staff. Is a nail brush provided? What type of soap and towels are provided?
2 Observe the regular staff during the morning cleaning operations. Do they wear different clothing (protective clothing) than they wear for service?
3 Find out the procedure used in your workplace for:
   (a) dealing with cuts or other wounds which occur during working hours.
   (b) reporting infectious illnesses, such as flu and gastro-enteritis.
4 Ask your supervisor or employer about how they think staff should appear to the customer in relation to how they dress and their attitudes.

Social and professional skills

The professional barman or woman must possess a wide range of both social and professional skills in order to satisfy the customers' needs and expectations. Re-read Unit 2NG3, if necessary.

THE BAR PERSON AND THE LAW

There are a number of laws related to serving alcoholic drinks that you should be aware of. The main ones are the:

- Licensing Acts
- Weights and Measures Acts
- Trade Descriptions Act and other consumer protection Acts
- Food Safety Act and Food Hygiene Regulations
- Health and Safety at Work Act.

It is not possible to deal with all the relevant laws in detail, but the main points of each are given below.

MEMORY JOGGER

What are the major laws related to serving alcoholic beverages on licensed premises?

Licensing laws

The licensing laws state who may or may not be served alcoholic drinks and the hours of opening allowed under the law (called 'permitted hours'). You may not serve alcoholic drinks to:

- **young persons under 18 years of age** in a bar to be drunk either on or off the premises. It is also an offence to sell drink to an older person if you know it is to be drunk on the premises by a person under 18 years. This information is summarised in the table below.

Age	Permitted	Not permitted
Under 5 years		To be in a bar that does not have a Children's Certificate To consume alcohol unless under a doctor's orders
Between 5 and 14 years	To consume alcohol if purchased by an adult in an area set aside for meals, but not in a bar	To be in a bar without a Children's Certificate unless (a) they are children of the licensee, (b) they are children of hotel residents, or (c) they have to pass through to reach another area
Between 14 and 16 years	To be in a bar To consume alcohol if purchased by an adult as part of a meal	To consume alcohol in a bar To purchase alcohol anywhere
Between 16 and 18 years	To purchase beer, stout, cider, perry (and wine in Scotland) for consumption at a meal, but not in a bar	To purchase or consume alcohol in a bar

A summary of the licensing laws related to the age of the customer in premises not covered by a Children's Certificate

- **persons who are drunk.** It is also an offence to sell alcoholic drink to another person if you know it is to be given to a person who is already drunk and is to be consumed on the premises.
- **persons acting in a violent or disorderly manner.** It is an offence under the licensing laws for a licensee or his staff to allow people acting in a violent or disorderly manner to remain on licensed premises. Obviously, such people should not be served drinks or encouraged in any way to stay.
- **Persons under an exclusion order.**
  - A licensee can refuse to serve any customer without having to give a reason. He or she also has the right to forbid a person from entering the premises.
  - Some people who have appeared in court frequently for offences which have taken place while they are drunk may be placed under an order by the court which forbids them entering licensed premises.
  - Any person known to be under a court order or forbidden by the licensee from entering the premises should not be served.

Permitted hours

- Licensed premises are only allowed to sell alcoholic drinks to be drunk either on or off the premises during certain hours each day.
- Different types of licence may vary permitted hours. For example, residents in a hotel which holds a residential licence may purchase alcoholic drinks at any time for themselves or their guests.
- It is an offence to sell alcoholic drinks for consumption either on or off the premises outside the permitted hours.

Essential knowledge	To make sure that you do not commit an offence against the current licensing laws, you should not sell alcoholic drinks to:

To make sure that you do not commit an offence against the current licensing laws, you should not sell alcoholic drinks to:
- any person in the bar that you suspect is under 18 years of age or any person attempting to buy a drink for them
- any person in a restaurant or area put aside for taking meals who you suspect is under 16 years of age
- a customer who is obviously drunk or any person attempting to buy more drink for that customer to drink on the premises
- any customer behaving in a violent or disorderly manner or who is under an exclusion order.

You should also not sell alcoholic drinks to be drunk either on or off the premises unless it is within the permitted hours of opening of the licence.

If you do serve any of the customers described above or serve alcoholic drink outside the permitted hours, your employer (the licensee) can be prosecuted and have their licence endorsed as well as having to pay a substantial fine.

Drinking-up time

Drinks supplied during permitted hours can be drunk on the premises during the first 20 minutes (15 minutes in Scotland) after the hours have ended.

If drinks are supplied for consumption with a meal, drinking-up time is extended to 30 minutes after the permitted hours have ended. This mainly applies to hotels and restaurants, but can also apply to licensed premises where substantial bar food meals are served.

Essential knowledge

Dealing with customer incidents

The majority of customers you serve will comply with the law. However, in some cases you may be required to deal with customers who you are not permitted to serve under the licensing laws or who may be dishonest. There are a few general rules you should follow and some simple precautions you can take.

- Inexperienced bar staff should not attempt to handle difficult customers alone. If you are in doubt about whether you should serve a customer, always contact your supervisor, employer or a more experienced member of staff immediately.
- You should not serve a customer who you suspect is under age or who comes in drunk. Contact your bar manager or employer.
- If a customer becomes drunk on the premises, try to avoid them and inform other members of staff and your employer about the situation so that the appropriate action can be taken.
- Do not allow other customers to get involved in dealing with difficult customers, even if they are trying to help you. This can lead to fights and injuries.
- Be alert for early signs of trouble such as raised voices or customers showing signs of becoming drunk and inform your supervisor.
- Not all customers are honest. You should watch for:
  - customers who remove drinks from the bar and then claim you have not served them
  - customers who claim they have given you a larger note (£10 instead of £5, and so on) than they have.

You should keep a count of the drinks you serve and name them to the customer as you serve them. Do not put any bank note into the till until you have given the customer their change. It also helps if you name the note as you take it from the customer: 'A £10 note, sir. I'll get your change.'

All customer incidents should be reported to your supervisor so that appropriate action can be taken. It is far easier to prevent trouble developing by taking early action than it will be to stop it after it has started.

Also see Unit 2NG3, Element 3 for other information related to customer incidents.

Do this

1 Ask an experienced member of staff or your employer/supervisor what you should do and what you should say if:
   (a) you suspect a customer is under age
   (b) you suspect a customer is drunk
   (c) an argument or fight starts
   (d) a customer complains that you have not served a drink which you know you have
   (e) a customer complains you have not given him or her the correct change.
2 Find out what type of licence your establishment has. Is it:
   (a) a Full On-Licence?
   (b) Restaurant Licence?
   (c) Residential Licence?
   What are your permitted hours?
3 Find out if your establishment has any of the following:
   (a) a Supper-Hour Certificate
   (b) an Extended Hours Order
   (c) a Special Hours Certificate
   (d) a Children's Certificate.

Weights and measures laws

The Weights and Measures Acts set out the legal measures that must be used when selling draught beers and cider, some spirits and wine by the glass. The legal measures are as follows.

- Draught beers and ciders must be sold in quantities of one-third of a pint (rarely used now), half a pint or a multiple of half a pint like the pint itself.
- Gin, rum, vodka and whisky must be sold in a metric measure of either 25 or 35 millilitres or in multiples, such as doubles or trebles.
- The sale of wine by the glass is also covered by weights and measures laws that require still table wine to be sold in quantities of either 125 or 175 millilitres or in multiples of these amounts.
  - The quantity must be one of those given above and must be displayed where customers can see it.
  - An optic, lined glass or thimble which bears a government or manufacturer's stamp must be used to dispense the wine.
  - The Weights and Measures Act, Trade Descriptions Act and price marking laws have to be complied with.
  - No laws apply to the quantities to be sold if the wine is sparkling, fortified or aromatised.

Exceptions

You should be aware of the following exceptions.

- The laws do not apply to alcoholic drinks which are pre-packaged, such as those sold in bottles, cans or boxes, although their contents must be expressed in centilitres (cl) or millilitres (ml).
- If beer or cider is sold as part of a mixture of two or more liquids (for example, a shandy or lager and lime), a legal measure is not necessary, but the measures cannot be described as a half-pint or pint. Although they can be served in such glasses, they can only be described as 'small' or 'large'.
- You do not have to use legal measures for spirits if:
  - the customer requests a different quantity
  - the drink is a mixture of three or more liquids, such as a cocktail.

However, apart from acting as the laws require, there are other advantages in using legal measures to dispense alcoholic drinks using government stamped glasses, meters, measures and optics. These are:

- the customer is not given short- or over-measure of any drink
- the price at which the drink is sold is based on the size of the measure used and so customers are neither over-charged nor under-charged when a standard measure is used
- the licensee can keep better control of his/her stock because he/she can estimate the number of measures that can be obtained from any container such as a keg, cask or bottle of spirits.

Essential knowledge	The main reasons why you should use legal measures when serving alcoholic drinks are as follows.

The main reasons why you should use legal measures when serving alcoholic drinks are as follows.
- You are required by law to use legal measures when serving certain types of alcoholic drinks.
- The price charged for a particular alcoholic drink may have been calculated on the basis of the legal measure used to serve it.
- Stock control procedures are often based on the number of legal measures that can be obtained from a particular size of container like a keg or a 70 or 75 cl bottle.
- It prevents staff giving short- or over-measures of alcoholic drinks and over- or under-charging customers, both of which are illegal and will also make customers dissatisfied with your establishment.
- Failure to comply with the laws can result in the licensee being prosecuted and fined.

Trade Descriptions Act and other consumer protection laws

The Trade Descriptions Act operates alongside other laws such as the Weights and Measures Acts and the Price Marking Order.

Essentially, there should be a price list displayed in any place where food or drink is sold for consumption on the premises. There should also be a notice stating the measures used for serving alcoholic drinks.
- The prices indicated by a price list should be for the quantity (measure) of liquid being sold.
- It is an offence to give less than the advertised quantity of any drink or to suggest that the price is lower than it actually is.

Any description of drinks offered for sale should be written carefully so as not to be misleading or ambiguous.

Essential knowledge	It is important that you give customers accurate information about any drinks that you serve, especially about the price, strength and quantity served: ● to comply with the Trade Descriptions Act and other consumer laws ● to prevent customers becoming dissatisfied and feeling cheated or mis-led ● to prevent customers consuming a larger amount of alcohol than they wish, especially when drinking cocktails, 'light' or low-alcohol products ● to ensure that customers receive an efficient and high quality service. However, you should not reveal any 'trade secrets' related to any speciality products offered by the establishment or details such as trade or cost prices of drinks or profit margins. This type of information should be kept confidential.

Food Safety Act and Food Hygiene Regulations

The Food Safety Act defines food as any article used for food or drink for human consumption and the regulations cover a wide range of activities. The main points of concern to the bar person are as follows.
- It is an offence to sell any food or drink that is unfit for human consumption, contaminated or not of the nature or quality demanded by the customer. This includes:
  - waste beer ('slops') being returned to a keg or cask
  - diluting beer or spirits with water.
- Any article or equipment likely to come into contact with food or drink must be in good condition and clean. This includes counters and other surfaces as well as all the equipment for drink dispense and service.

Health and Safety at Work Act

This Act requires employers to provide a safe and healthy working environment for their employees as far as possible. At the same time, it is the duty of every employee to take reasonable care for the health and safety of him/herself, other members of staff and the customer.

Bar staff should use safe working practices such as:
- clearing up spillages straightaway
- not obstructing stairs or passageways
- reporting faulty equipment and other hazards
- reporting situations which could be dangerous
- reporting accidents at work
- reporting diseases which could lead to food poisoning if the person continues working.

Re-read Unit 1, Elements 1 and 3 to refresh your memory, if necessary.

Establishment procedures

As well as acting in ways which enable you to obey the laws and regulations outlined above, you should also follow any rules or regulations regarding working practices laid down by your employer.

Essential knowledge

The main laws related to the sale and service of alcoholic drinks and their relevance to the operation of licensed premises are the:
- Licensing Acts, which regulate general aspects of the operation of licensed premises including who may be served and the permitted hours of opening
- Weights and Measures Acts, which outline the quantities (measures) which can lawfully be used to dispense draught beers and cider, some spirits and wine by the glass
- Trade Descriptions Act and other consumer protection laws, which require that any description of a drink should be written accurately including details of its price, contents and the quantities it is sold in
- Price Marking (Food and Drink on Premises) Order, which requires prices of both food and drink to be consumed on the premises to be prominently displayed.

It is important that licensees and their employees comply with these and other laws as failure to do so can result in prosecution, heavy fines and can even lead to the withdrawal of the licence and closure of the premises.

Do this

1 Find out the legal measures used in your establishment for:
(a) spirits
(b) draught beers and ciders.

Also find out what quantities the following drinks are sold in:
(a) wine by the glass
(b) liqueurs
(c) sherry.
2 Give details of any notices that are displayed in the bar area. Which laws are they related to?
3 Make a copy of six entries on the establishment's price list. Try to choose different types of drinks.

PROVIDING CUSTOMERS WITH ACCURATE INFORMATION

The Trade Descriptions Act makes it an offence to give a false or misleading description of any drink you serve (including both the measure and the price) and the Food Safety Act makes it an offence to sell any drink which is not of the nature or quality required by the customer.

Obviously, it is important that you give customers the correct information when you are selling them any beverage. If you have a good knowledge of the products you sell, there are usually few problems.

Prices and promotions/special offers

- Be familiar with the price for each of the drinks you sell. The price of mixed drinks such as lager and lime, shandy or brandy and soda should be calculated by adding together the cost of each part, unless a separate price is displayed on the price list.

- Find out before service starts about any special offers such as reduced prices, free goods or promotions of particular brands.
- If a customer questions the price charged for a particular drink (and you haven't mis-calculated), refer them to your supervisor or employer.

Ingredients of drinks

If your establishment serves cocktails or drinks such as speciality coffees or punches, find out their ingredients so that you can answer customers' enquiries about them. If you don't know something, tell the customer that you will find out for them.

Relative strength

Many customers are now more conscious of the amount of alcohol they drink, especially if they are driving. Be able to advise them of the alcoholic strength of the drinks you serve, if the customer asks for this type of information.

There are several points you should be aware of when advising your customers.
- There is approximately the same amount of alcohol in a glass of wine, a half pint of normal strength beer, a 25 ml measure of a spirit and a small glass of sherry or port.
- While it would not be possible to drink enough alcohol-free beer to be over the legal limit for driving, it is possible to exceed the limit by drinking a sufficient quantity of low-alcohol beer.
- If you have any doubts about the strength of an alcoholic drink, check the label or consult your supervisor.

The Food Labelling Regulations require that the alcoholic strength of drinks above 1.2 per cent alcohol by volume should be stated on all pre-packaged drinks, such as those in bottles, cans and boxes.

They also require that strength markings should be given for a representative sample of dispensed drinks sold in bars and restaurants. The strength marking can be indicated along with the prices of drinks on a price list.

Recommending substitutes or alternatives

It is not possible or practical for any licensed premises to stock every brand of alcoholic drink which is available. Even a well-stocked bar will not be able to supply every drink that is likely to be requested.

If you are asked by a customer for a brand that you do not stock, suggest a suitable substitute. However, do not suggest that the substitute is in some way of lesser quality by using phrases like 'We only stock Brand X.'

If a customer requests a drink for which you have no substitute brand available, suggest an alternative.

The ability to offer substitutes and alternatives to your customers highlights the need for the skilled bar person to have a thorough knowledge of the products he or she sells and of other products which are available.

Never attempt to pass off a substitute or alternative as the brand or drink a customer has requested. Always consult the customer.

Do this ✔

Over a period of a week, make a note of any drinks that you are asked for which you do not stock. Discuss the situation with your supervisor. What action could be taken?

PROMOTING AND SELLING DRINKS

The skilled bar person is a salesman/woman who is selling the customer products, like drinks and food, and a service. Remember, a satisfied customer will stay in the bar and, more importantly, will come back again.

Like a salesperson in any other type of business, you must have a positive approach to selling your products and be alert for opportunities to promote and sell drinks.

Use promotional materials

Any materials used to promote products must be accurate, clean and helpful.
- Drink lists should be kept up-to-date. If a drink is not available, the customers should be informed before they order.
- Table-top items such as tent cards, drip mats and coasters should be clean and unmarked. Soiled items should not be re-used.
- Posters recommending certain brands or new products should be displayed in a prominent position, but not on the bar counter.
- Limit the amount of material displayed. Too much material has little or no impact.

Display your products

The bar area is your 'shop window' in which you display the food and drink you sell.
- Make sure the bottles are well-polished and placed where they are within the bar lighting.
- Display any products that you are promoting in a prominent position and place them in groups or clusters.
- Vary the position of the goods you display. Regular customers will notice changes and their attention will be drawn to the products.

Use a positive selling approach

Positive selling requires you to take the initiative when dealing with the customer. Remember, the main aim of the positive approach is to encourage customers to buy at times when they might not have intended to or to buy a better quality (and more expensive) product.

Promote selected drinks at appropriate times

Some customers refuse to change their drinking habit and order the same drink every time. Other customers are open to new ideas. At the same time, some drinks are more suitable at one time than at others. Part of positive selling is to recommend drinks to your customers.

Aperitifs are taken before a meal. You can recommend/suggest:
- wine or wine-based cocktails
- sparkling wines like champagne
- sherry or chilled white port.

After a meal you can recommend/suggest:
- liqueurs or cognac
- certain cocktails, some based on brandy (see Unit 2NC10) or frappés
- speciality coffees like Irish or Gaelic coffee.

In cold weather you can recommend/suggest:
- drinks like hot whisky and other toddies
- mulled wine or punches.

In hot weather you can recommend/suggest:
- well-chilled premium beers, like Budweiser, Sol, Rolling Rock
- long mixed drinks, like Slings, Juleps and Pimms
- spritzers.

Promotions and special offers

Occasionally, suppliers will run promotions on a certain brand for a limited period, either when launching a new brand or trying to increase sales of a particular product.
- Make sure that all promotional materials are displayed in the bar area.
- Display the product in a prominent position.
- Watch for 'buying signals' in your customers, such as reading the promotional material or asking questions about the product.
- Tell your customers about reduced prices or any offers available to them if they purchase the product, such as competition prizes or free gifts.

Buying signals

Be aware of openings to offer customers another drink.
- Look for customers who have almost finished. A polite 'May I freshen your drink, sir?' often brings a repeat order.
- A casual question to a customer about a drink you have served them such as, 'Was there enough lime (or soda or tonic water) in your drink?' may also lead to a repeat order.

Do this ✔

1   Find out how drinks are promoted in your establishment. Look for:
   (a) tent cards
   (b) wall/back bar displays
   (c) sections on wine lists, menu holders or cards
   (d) drip mats, coasters and drink decorations.
2   Ask an experienced bar person about the buying signals they look for in customers.
3   Find out from your supervisor/employer if the establishment has a policy for promoting certain types of drinks and what you should do to help promote them.

PREPARING FOR SERVICE

It is important that all the service equipment you use is clean and in good condition.

Check your glassware

It is essential that you check all glassware that you intend to use. Look carefully for lipstick, fingerprints and other grease smears. Check carefully for cracks in glasses and examine the rim for signs of chipping.

Polish the glassware using a dry lint-free glass cloth. Small glasses used to serve spirits can be polished by holding the base with one end of a clean, dry glass cloth over a bowl of hot water until the steam condenses on the glass. You can then polish the bowl with the other end of the cloth. Use a new dry cloth when the first one becomes damp. Your bare hands should not come into contact with the glass when you are drying or polishing it, otherwise you will leave fingerprints on the glass.

(See the section on cleaning glassware in Element 2 of this Unit and the illustration of popular types of glass on page 170.)

| Dimple | Nonic | Tulip | Sleeve |

Draught beer glasses (half pint and pint, lined or unlined)

| 12 oz Worthington (33–35 cl) | 14 oz Pilsner or lager (38–40 cl) | 12 oz Wellington | 12 oz Waterloo |

Bottled beer glasses

  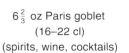 

Flute (wine)   Hock (wine) $6\frac{2}{3}$ oz Paris goblet (16–22 cl) (spirits, wine, cocktails)   Balloon (brandy)

Elgin (liqueurs, sherry)   Elgin schooner (sherry)

Popular shapes of glasses

Check your measures

Optics

Make sure that all optics are clean and in working order. Some establishments leave the spirit bottles with the optics in place overnight; other establishments remove the bottles from the optic brackets and stand them upright overnight.

An optic on a full or part-filled bottle which is left on its bracket overnight will not deliver a correct measure when used again for the first time on the following day. In order to get the optic to produce the correct measure:

1 Remove each bottle from its optic bracket and stand it upright.
2 Allow the spirit to flow back into the bottle.
3 Press down the bar on the optic to its full extent. Do not use your fingers. When you place the bottle back on the bracket, the spirit will fill the optic so that the correct measure can be dispensed.

Where the bottles have been allowed to stand upright overnight, perform action **3** above and replace each bottle on its bracket.

Optics should be cleaned regularly This can be done either:

● by filling an empty bottle with a cleaning agent and attaching and filling the optic with the fluid. You should allow the fluid to remain in the optic for the recommended time and then empty and remove the optic and rinse it thoroughly before re-using it
● by washing out the optic using hot water with an added sterilising agent and rinsing thoroughly in clean water.

When optics are being cleaned, check the condition of the cork or ribbed seal. A damaged cork/seal may allow liquid to seep out of the joint between the optic and the bottle.

Ideally, separate optics should be kept for different types of drink.

● Free-flow optics used for serving strongly-flavoured drinks, such as some cordials, should not be used to serve other liquids like wine.
● Remember, whisky, gin, rum and vodka must be served using a government-stamped optic measure which is sealed. You should not attempt to dismantle the optic. If the seal is broken, it is illegal to continue using the optic as a measure.

Thimble measures

These are also government-stamped measures. In order to serve a legal measure they should be free from damage.

Check that these measures are clean and dry before using them. If they have been left overnight with the remainder of a spirit in them, they will be both sticky and unhygienic.

Bottle openers and corkscrews

Check that bottle openers, either hand-held or fixed to the counter with a crown cork catcher below, and corkscrews are clean before service starts. As beer and soft drinks will frequently foam on opening, bottle openers can become sticky and bacteria can thrive on them.

Pourers

Stainless steel and plastic pourers are commonly used on bottles of spirits, liqueurs and cordials, especially where cocktails are regularly offered.

Make sure that pourers are clean and in good condition. Soak them in a detergent-sterilant before service, if necessary.

Chopping boards, knives and fruit tongs

Any equipment used for the preparation and service of food garnishes should be clean and sterile before service. Check their condition before service starts and clean and sterilise them if necessary.

Ice buckets, scoops and tongs

Check that counter-top ice buckets are clean both inside and outside. If water from melted ice has been left in them overnight, wash the inside of the bucket with a detergent-sterilant and rinse thoroughly before filling. Ensure ice scoops and tongs are also clean and undamaged.

Trays or salvers

Circular trays or salvers should be cleaned prior to service. Plastic and stainless steel trays should be washed with the appropriate detergent and polished with a dry glass cloth. Silver salvers should be cleaned regularly with a silver cleaner and treated like plastic or stainless steel trays between thorough cleaning.

Coasters and drip mats

Before service starts, check that there is an adequate supply of clean coasters and drip mats to last through the service session. Discard any that are damaged or stained.

If any service equipment is missing or damaged, you should report the matter to your supervisor immediately if you cannot resolve the problem yourself.

Prepare your accompaniments

Ice
- Make sure you have a good supply of ice cubes available well in advance.
- Make sure the ice is clean and clear.
- If you are serving cocktails, prepare a supply of cracked and crushed ice and store it in the freezer compartment of a refrigerator.

Water
Fill water jugs and place them on coasters or drip mats on the bar counter. It is important that you use a tap connected to a mains supply for drinking water. Run the tap for a short while to remove water standing in the pipes overnight before filling jugs.

Cordials, minerals and juices
- Check that you have an adequate supply of these accompaniments and requisition any additional stock you require.
- Clean any bottles brought up from the cellar and place them on the shelves behind older stock.
- If you require freshly-squeezed juices from oranges and lemons for making cocktails, soak some of the fruit in hot water for a short time before squeezing them. Store the fresh juice in small jugs in the refrigerator. Cover jugs with cling film.

Food garnishes
- Prepare a small supply of lemon and orange slices and wedges on the chopping board. Store them in covered containers to keep them fresh.
- Check that you have an adequate supply of bottled fruit, such as maraschino cherries and olives.
- If you offer cocktails, obtain a supply of fresh fruit and vegetables (see Unit 2NC10).

● Keep a supply of white and brown sugar and spices such as cloves for serving hot drinks.

Decorative items
Check that you have an adequate supply of decorative items for drinks such as straws, stirrers, cocktail sticks/swords and plastic decorations. Re-stock as required.

Check your equipment
Check all manual and electric equipment such as kettles, blenders, refrigerators, chill cabinets and ice crushers. If you find any faults, mark the equipment as out of order or place a warning notice on the equipment and report the problem to your supervisor immediately.

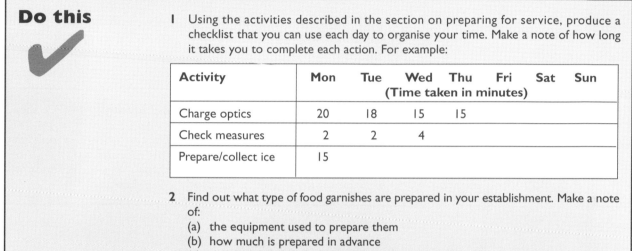

Do this

1 Using the activities described in the section on preparing for service, produce a checklist that you can use each day to organise your time. Make a note of how long it takes you to complete each action. For example:

Activity	Mon	Tue	Wed	Thu	Fri	Sat	Sun
			(Time taken in minutes)				
Charge optics	20	18	15	15			
Check measures	2	2	4				
Prepare/collect ice	15						

2 Find out what type of food garnishes are prepared in your establishment. Make a note of:
   (a) the equipment used to prepare them
   (b) how much is prepared in advance
   (c) the method of preparing wedges, slices, zests and twists.

TAKING CUSTOMERS' ORDERS

Taking customers' orders can be either simple and straightforward or quite complicated.

When an order is complicated:
● make a note of the drinks ordered. If you are taking orders at a table, try to write the order by using the seating arrangement. A diagram on the pad can help
● if a particular drink is not available, inform the customer and offer a substitute or alternative
● repeat the order to the customer to check if all the drinks have been included.

It is also important that you check which accompaniments your customers require with their drinks.
● As some customers prefer their spirits and liqueurs served chilled, ask the customer if they would like ice with their drink.
● Do not add fruit decorations such as lemon slices to a drink without asking the customer if they want them added. (See the section on accompaniments served with spirits on page 179).
● If the customer asks for a drink using a name you are unfamiliar with, ask them politely to describe it to you. It is not possible to know all the odd names for drinks that customers can use and the customer is often pleased to show off his knowledge.

Taking orders for cocktails can be more complicated. You should read the relevant section of Unit 2NC10.

MEMORY JOGGER

Why is it important that you should check which accompaniments customers require and take down their orders accurately?

There are several reasons why you must make sure that you take down customers' orders accurately.

- The customer will not be happy if they are given the wrong drink. Some may suffer in silence, others may complain after tasting the drink and ask for the correct drink.
- It may not be possible to recover any part of the incorrect drink if the customer has drunk from the glass or you have already added a second liquid like a mineral or cordial to the drink.
- More time will be lost in replacing the incorrect drink and having to give a refund or charge the customer more.

Details of any drink that cannot be recovered either because the customer has drunk from the glass, the drink has been mixed or because of a fault in the drink, such as a flat beer or mineral, should be entered into the bar spillages or wastage book.

Normally, you would enter the date, the drink, the price and the reason for the wastage along with your name. Find out and follow the establishment's procedures regarding wastages or spillages.

Do this ✔

1 Find out from an experienced bar person how they take down large orders. Do they use a shorthand like G/T for a gin and tonic?
2 Find out how experienced staff take orders at tables. Do they take orders from left to right? How do they remember what each customer has ordered?
3 Ask your supervisor/employer what you should do if you pour an incorrect drink or spill a drink while serving it. Ask about a wastage or spillage book.

DISPENSING ALCOHOLIC AND NON-ALCOHOLIC DRINKS

The laws that a bar person should be aware of have been mentioned in a previous section. So too was the bar person's responsibility for providing a good quality of service to the customer. The importance of these two aspects can be seen in the practical activity of pouring and presenting drinks to your customers.

Dispensing draught beers and ciders

Pumps and taps
Draught beers and ciders are dispensed by several different types of pump or tap. These include beer engines, free-flow taps and bar valves. A mixture of types is commonly found in many bars.

Glasses
The beer or cider is dispensed into a glass which must have a government stamp indicating that it is of the correct capacity (half-pint or pint). There are basically two types of glass:

- the brim-measure glass, which holds the correct legal measure when filled to the brim – the most widely-used type
- the lined glass, which holds the correct legal measure when filled to the line around the neck of the glass – sometimes called an 'over-sized' glass.

Under-measures and over-measures
The Weights and Measures Acts and the Trade Descriptions Act make it illegal to serve an under-measure of beer. It is also an offence to serve a customer an over-measure, although this is currently under review.

The main problem of draught beer dispense relates to the head on the beer, which is a mixture of gas and beer.

Serving beer in a brim-measure glass

When you serve beer in this type of glass, the head must reach the brim or be above it. When the head collapses, the amount of beer may be less than the legal measure. If the customer requests that you top-up the glass, you should do so. Avoid any spillage, if possible.

Serving beer in a lined glass

If you are not using a tap which dispenses a measured amount, fill the glass to the point where the liquid will reach the line when the head has fully collapsed.

If you fill the glass with liquid to the line, you will have served an over-measure as the level of beer will be above the line when the head collapses.

General points

- Handle the glass by the base, at the centre or by the handle. Do not handle it near the rim where the customer may place his mouth while drinking.
- A clean glass should be used for each drink you serve. Re-filling a customer's empty glass could spread infection if the beer comes into contact with the tap nozzle or outlet.
- No part of the tap should come into contact with the beer or cider in the glass. An exception is the 'swan-necked' dispenser described below.

Using a manual pump (beer engine)

1 Hold the glass by the base or centre and bring it up towards the nozzle of the tap without touching it.
2 Tilt the glass away from you at an angle of about 45°.
3 Pull the pump handle towards you with a smooth, steady motion allowing the beer to run down the side of the glass.
4 As the glass fills, gradually tilt it towards you until it is upright.
5 To top up the glass move the handle back to the half-way position and pull it forwards until the glass is full.

If the drink is pouring slightly flat, you can lower the glass and, if necessary, move it up and down. Some taps have a 'sparkler' built into the nozzle which can be adjusted to increase or decrease the size of head on the beer.

'Swan-necked' dispensers

Some beer engines, often known as swan-necked dispensers, have a curved neck and a long vertical spout with a 'creamer' at the bottom. During dispense the creamer rests at the bottom of the glass and the spout is immersed in the beer as it is poured. This type of dispense generates an extremely large head on the beer.

When using this type of dispenser, it is extremely important that you use a clean glass every time to avoid contaminating the spout.

Using a free-flow tap

1 Follow the procedures described in steps 1 and 2 for a manual pump above.
2 Pull the handle of the tap towards you, allowing the drink to run down the side of the glass.
3 As the glass fills, gradually tilt it into an upright position. You may need to 'rest' the drink to allow all the gas to form a head when the glass is between two-thirds and three-quarters full.
4 Top up the glass to the correct fill height.

Some free-flow taps can be adjusted to control the amount of gas in the drink (see Unit 2NC7). Some also have a 'creaming' device (to create a thick head on the beer) which is operated by pushing the tap handle backwards away from you.

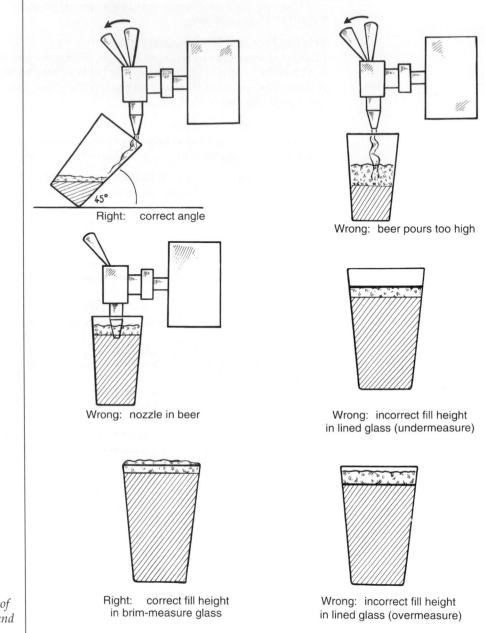

Right: correct angle

Wrong: beer pours too high

Wrong: nozzle in beer

Wrong: incorrect fill height
in lined glass (undermeasure)

Right: correct fill height
in brim-measure glass

Wrong: incorrect fill height
in lined glass (overmeasure)

*Right and wrong methods of
dispensing draught beers and
ciders*

Using a measured dispenser (bar valve)

This type of dispenser usually has a measuring vessel which has been tested and
stamped. A lined glass should be used with this type of system.

● After pressing the button or switch on the tap mounting, gradually tilt the glass
from 45° into an upright position as it fills.
● The drink dispensed by this method will have the liquid level below the line. It
should reach the line when the head collapses.

Serving temperatures

The serving temperature for draught drinks varies with the type of product. As a
rule you should follow the brewery's recommendations. General guidelines are:
● ales like bitter and mild: 12–15.5°C (55–60°F)

- stouts: 8–10°C (47–50°F)
- lagers: 7–9°C (45–49°F)
- chilled beers (like Budweiser): 4–6°C (40–43°F)

A modern trend is to serve many draught beers and lagers highly chilled at around 3°C.

Cold and chilled beers should be served on a drip mat as condensation develops on the outside of the glass.

Do this

✔

1 Make a list of the draught products you sell. Against each product, state the type of dispense tap that is used.
2 Find out what types of half-pint and pint glasses are used in your establishment. Are they government stamped?
3 Find out the ideal serving temperature for the draught products you listed in the first activity. Ask your supervisor if you can test the dispense temperature:
  (a) before service starts in the morning
  (b) during a busy service time or immediately afterwards.
Note any differences you find.

Dispensing bottled beers and ciders

1 Choose a glass which will hold a larger amount than the bottle capacity to allow space for the head. For example, if you are pouring from a 28 cl bottle, you will need a glass which holds about 34 cl. Bottles containing 33 cl require a glass which holds about 38 cl.
2 Take the glass in one hand, raise it and check it is clean and undamaged.
3 Take the bottle in the other hand with the label facing outwards and remove the crown cork using the bar opener. The label should be visible to the customer.
4 Holding the glass and bottle at shoulder height, hold the glass at a 45° angle. Keeping the bottle neck about half an inch above the glass, start to pour the beer gently down the side. Keep tilting the bottom of the glass downwards as you pour.
5 Do not touch the glass with the neck of the bottle or allow the neck of the bottle to enter the drink in the glass.
6 If the head is too high, either slow down the speed of pouring or stop pouring and let the head settle in the glass. If only a slight head is formed, lower the glass away from the bottle and speed up the flow from the bottle.
7 When you have finished pouring, place the empty bottle in the skip.

Sediment beers are poured using a different technique. Having chosen a suitable glass:
1 Lift the bottle carefully from the shelf without shaking or tilting it. Stand it on a level surface and open it with a hand opener.
2 Hold the glass in one hand at eye level and tilt it at a 45° angle from the horizontal.
3 Tilt the bottle slowly with the other hand and gently pour the beer, gradually straightening the glass as it fills up.
4 Watch the sediment as it moves from the bottom of the bottle and stop pouring when it is held by the shoulder of the bottle.

Ordinary bottled ciders are poured in the same way as bottled beers. Sparkling ciders and perries, such as Babycham, are usually served in a flute or saucer-shaped champagne glass.

Serving temperatures
● Bottled beers are normally served at 12–15°C (55–60°F).
● Lagers are ideally served at lower temperatures from refrigerated shelves or chill cabinets. They are served using a Pilsener glass at about 7°C (45°F) using a drip mat to catch the condensation.
● Many premium beers are served highly chilled at around 3°C and this trend has been extended to some traditional beers and stouts.

Essential knowledge	**Dispensing mixed beers**
	Some customers like various combinations of draught and bottled beers to be served in a pint glass.
	The Weights and Measures Acts state that you must serve a measured amount of draught beer and when asked for a mixed beer/cider drink:
	● dispense the draught beer through a measured pump (if available) into a pint glass or pour the beer into a stamped half-pint glass and then transfer it to a pint glass
	● pour the bottled beer (or cider) on top of the draught beer until the head reaches the top of the glass
	● leave any remaining beer in the bottle and place it beside the glass to be added by the customer.
	If a customer requests that the bottled drink be placed in the pint glass first, you should fill a stamped half-pint glass with the correct measure of draught and add it slowly to the bottled beer. Do not fill the pint glass from the tap. If you do, you may not serve a correct legal measure.

Dispensing spirits and wines through optics

There are two types of optic:
● those that deliver legal measures which are always used to dispense spirits
● free-flow optics which can be used to serve drinks such as cordials which are not necessarily served in quantities laid down in law.

When dispensing drinks from optics:
1 Use a clean glass each time to prevent contaminating the bar of the optic. Your customer's mouth will have been in contact with a used glass.
2 Place it beneath the optic so that the centre of the glass is below the central point of the optic and the rim of the glass just touches the bar.
3 Check that the chamber of the optic is full.
4 Push the glass upwards slowly and evenly against the bar and hold it there until the chamber is empty. Remove the glass.

Dispensing wine by the glass

Wine may be dispensed using a measured optic as described above. Where a quantity is advertised and no measured optic is available, wine may be served in a government-stamped lined glass, or a 125 ml or 175 ml thimble measure may be used.

Serving temperatures
Spirits and red wines are served at normal room temperature. White wines are served either cool at about 13°C or lightly chilled at 9–10°C.

Using a thimble measure
The majority of the most frequently-used spirits will be available on the optic. However, some spirits and liqueurs will have to be poured using a thimble measure. The measure used will depend on the quantity that the establishment has chosen to offer. The legal measure used for other spirits is commonly used.

1 Place the glass on the counter or back bar where the customer can see it. This is good practice, but it is also a legal requirement in some parts of the UK that spirits and liqueurs poured with a thimble measure must be dispensed in full view of the customer.

2 Pick up the thimble measure by the base or handle with one hand and the bottle with the other hand.

3 Hold the measure over the centre of the glass.

4 Hold the bottle neck or pourer about half an inch above the centre of the measure. Make sure the label of the bottle is uppermost so that drips or runs will not smear the label.

5 Pour the liquid slowly into the measure until it is filled to the brim.

6 Tilt the measure sharply over the glass and let all the liquid drain from the measure.

7 Rinse the measure thoroughly and leave it to drain before re-using it.

If a customer complains about receiving a short measure, offer to re-pour the drink or call your supervisor to re-measure the drink.

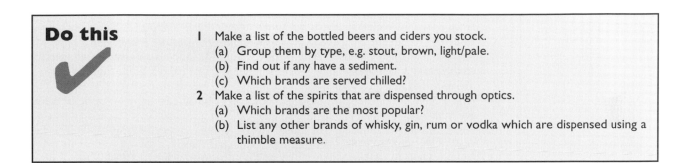

Do this

1 Make a list of the bottled beers and ciders you stock.
   (a) Group them by type, e.g. stout, brown, light/pale.
   (b) Find out if any have a sediment.
   (c) Which brands are served chilled?
2 Make a list of the spirits that are dispensed through optics.
   (a) Which brands are the most popular?
   (b) List any other brands of whisky, gin, rum or vodka which are dispensed using a thimble measure.

Accompaniments served with spirits

When you are taking orders for or serving spirits, ask your customer which accompaniments he or she would like to be added.

Gin, vodka, white rum, tequila
● Offer ice and a slice of lemon or lime. Salt is often served with tequila.
● Select a larger-sized glass (17.5 or 25 cl) if the customer requests a mineral, such as a cola.
● Offer to pour in any mineral, like lemonade or tonic water, or place the bottle to the right of the drink for the customer to pour for him/herself.

Whiskies
These are usually served in a 15 or 17.5 cl goblet either with or without a mixer. A double with a mixer is often served in a 25 cl goblet or Slim Jim glass.
● Offer ice.
● If the customer has not asked, offer water or soda and place the jug or syphon beside the glass.
● Offer to pour in any mineral as above.

Rum
The accompaniments offered with rum will vary with the style of rum your customer requests.
● Golden and dark rums are often served neat or with a measure of cordial like blackcurrant or peppermint.
● Offer ice if a mineral has been ordered.

Brandy
In the bar, brandy is usually served in the same way as whiskies. If brandy is served after a meal, it is usually served in a balloon glass.

Cocktails and other mixed drinks
When serving cocktails and other drinks containing a mixture of liquids, it is customary to decorate the drinks with food garnishes and use decorative items like cocktail swords, umbrellas and stirrers. For more detailed information, see Unit 2NC10.

Dispensing hot drinks

As hot drinks are often prepared by bar staff for restaurants or areas where meals are taken, you should know how to prepare them.

Preparing toddies
A toddy can be made using any spirit. Scotch or Irish whiskies, dark rum and, occasionally, brandy are most commonly used.

1 Warm a stemmed or handled spirit glass (15 or 17.5 cl) by pouring in hot water from a freshly-boiled kettle or hot water boiler. Place a spoon in the glass before pouring to prevent the glass from cracking. Empty out the water.
2 Ask the customer how much sugar they would like and add the required amount to the glass with the bar spoon. Check what spices – cloves, cinnamon, nutmeg – are required.
3 Add a measure of the spirit requested on top of the sugar using an optic or thimble measure.
4 Place a wedge of lemon in the glass. Two or three cloves can be pressed into the peel of the lemon, if the customer has requested them.
5 Fill the glass to within between $\frac{1}{4}$ and $\frac{1}{2}$ inch from the brim with freshly-boiled water, leaving the spoon in the glass to absorb the heat.
6 If the customer has requested cinnamon or grated nutmeg, these can be sprinkled on top of the liquid.
7 Serve the drink on a coaster or drip mat to protect wooden or polished surfaces. A stirrer should be provided to allow the customer to stir the drink.

Preparing speciality coffees
Speciality coffees consist of sugar, a spirit or liqueur, black coffee and cream. They are properly served in handled glasses, but may also be served in a medium- to large-sized (15 or 17.5 cl) goblet. They are usually served after a meal, either at the table or in a lounge.

Almost any spirit or liqueur can be used and the name given to the drink varies with the spirit/liqueur used. The best-known are:
● Irish coffee – Irish whiskey
● Gaelic/Highland coffee – Scotch whisky
● Caribbean coffee – Jamaican rum
● Calypso coffee – Tia Maria
● Cafe Royale – Cognac brandy
● Balalaika coffee – Vodka
● Gaucho's coffee – Tequila
● Witch's coffee – Strega
● Monk's coffee – Benedictine
● Bonnie Prince Charlie's coffee – Drambuie

1 Warm the glass by adding hot water to it. Place a spoon in the glass if the water is very hot to prevent the glass from cracking.

2 Pour out the hot water. Add a teaspoon of white or brown sugar (according to your customer's preference) to the glass and a measure of the spirit or liqueur. Leave the teaspoon in the glass.

3 Pour hot black coffee into the glass until it reaches between $\frac{1}{4}$ and $\frac{1}{2}$ of an inch beneath the rim. Stir the liquid well.

4 When the surface of the coffee is still, gently pour double cream over the back of the bowl of the teaspoon which should just be touching the surface of the coffee. The cream should be about $\frac{1}{4}$ of an inch in thickness. Dust the cream with a little cinnamon.

5 Place the glass on a doily set on a small side plate. Place a teaspoon alongside the glass.

If you are serving the drink away from the dining area, provide your customer with a napkin as the cream tends to stick to the customer's upper lip when they take their first sips from the glass.

Dispensing soft drinks

These drinks are often referred to as 'minerals' or 'mixers'. They include a range of still and sparkling (carbonated) drinks, including:
● mineral waters, such as Perrier, Ballygowan, Vichy, Evian and Volvic
● mixers, such as soda water, tonic water, lemonade, dry ginger ale, bitter lemon and colas
● fruit juices, such as tomato, orange, pineapple, grapefruit and apple
● squashes and crushes, such as orange, lemon, lemon barley and grapefruit
● cordials and syrups, such as blackcurrant, peppermint, lime, ginger and orange.

The majority of these drinks are packaged in sealed bottles. However, many bars have installed counter-top dispensers for branded products like Coca Cola, Pepsi Cola and Seven-Up which are dispensed either using a similar system to keg beers or through a 'gun'.

Presentation of soft drinks
Good presentation is a necessary part of dispensing soft drinks.
● Use an interesting shape of glass like a Slim Jim, Highball or Old Fashioned glass.
● Offer ice in the drink. Fizzy drinks keep their sparkle longer if they are served chilled.
● Add orange slices to colas and lemon slices to tonic water and bitter lemon.
● Add wedges of orange or lemon to the rim of glasses containing fruit drinks.
● Frost the rim of the glass by rubbing it with a slice of lemon and dipping it into a shallow bowl of loose caster sugar.

Offer interesting combinations, such as a St Clements – a combination of bitter lemon and pure orange juice.

As well as fruit garnishes, you can decorate soft drinks with swords, stirrers and miniature umbrellas to give them a cocktail appearance. Straws may also be provided, especially if children are being served.

Do this

1 Find out what types of hot drink are regularly served in your workplace.
   (a) Which toddies are most frequently requested?
   (b) Are speciality coffees offered? If so, which are most frequently requested?
2 Using the list of the various types of soft drinks commonly found in licensed premises, check which ones are available in your workplace.
3 Ask an experienced member of staff about the glasses they use to serve soft drinks and which food garnishes and decorative items they use when presenting the drink.

Case study

The licensee of a city-centre establishment had employed a young local girl as a part-time bar person for the Christmas period. One evening, two minutes before closing time, a young man who was obviously quite drunk left a large, noisy group sitting at tables and came to the bar to order a round of drinks. By the time she had finished serving another customer, it was after closing time. The young man began to argue when he was refused service saying that he had been at the bar before time was called. Hoping to avoid any problems, she began to dispense the drinks and, while doing so, saw in the mirror on the back bar that the customer was passing down drinks from the counter to his friends and was sipping from a glass of spirits. When she had finished dispensing the order, the young man claimed that he hadn't received all the drinks and that he had been given short measure.

She began to argue with the customer and asked other customers sitting close by to support her that drinks had been passed down. Another group of young men, some of whom were friends of her family, came across and she told them what had happened and how she was being wrongly accused. A violent argument began and punches and glasses began to be thrown. The fight erupted out into the street and the police had to be called. Several people were injured and several hundred pounds worth of damage was done to the premises.

1 *How did the bar person act outside the licensing laws?*
2 *How did the bar person fail to observe good practice in dealing with the situation?*
3 *How would you have dealt with the situation?*

What have you learned?

1 What three aspects of the bar person are important to meet the customers' expectations about a good quality of service?
2 What types of alcoholic drinks can a 16–18-year-old person purchase and where?
3 Who are you not allowed to serve alcoholic drinks to in a bar?
4 Not all customers are honest. State two problems you might have with dishonest customers.
5 What are the legal measures for:
  (a) beer?
  (b) most spirits?
6 What are the main reasons why you should use legal measures when selling alcoholic drinks?
7 Give as many examples as you can of safe working practices in the bar.
8 Give three actions you can take to display your products well.
9 How can you polish small glasses?
10 What should you do before serving a drink if a spirit bottle has been left on its optic bracket overnight?
11 Why is it important that you take down customers' orders accurately?
12 Why is it important to put the draught beer into the glass first when serving a mixed beer drink?

ELEMENT 2: Maintain customer and service areas during drink service

---

What you need to do

● Deal with customers in a polite and helpful manner at all times.
● Keep drink stocks and accompaniments at the level required to provide an efficient service.

● Correctly store, arrange and rotate drink stocks and accompaniments.
● Keep all the equipment used for drink service clean, tidy and ready for use.

- Keep the customer and service areas clean, tidy and free from rubbish.
- Make sure that the environmental control systems are maintained at the level required for customer comfort.
- Deal effectively with unexpected situations and inform the appropriate people where necessary.
- Carry out your duties in an organised and efficient manner taking account of priorities, organisational procedures and legal requirements.

What you need to know

- What procedures you should follow in order to maintain a constant supply of drink stocks and accompaniments.
- How to store, arrange and rotate drink stocks.
- What procedures you should follow to make sure that all drink service equipment is kept clean, tidy and ready for use.
- How to make sure that customer and service areas are kept clean, tidy and free from rubbish.
- What actions you should take to maintain the environmental control systems at the required level.
- Why you should prevent any person entering the service area without your employer's permission.
- How to deal effectively with unexpected situations within your responsibility.
- How to carry out your work in an organised and efficient manner.

INTRODUCTION

Having completed all the pre-service activities and prepared the service areas and the customer areas for opening, it is necessary to keep these areas up to a standard which will:
- allow a high quality of service to be maintained
- provide a clean and comfortable environment for your customers.

While the bar is open, you should always be occupied either:
- serving your customers, or
- preparing for future customers.

Much of the work that has to be done is routine and requires you to use your time in an efficient manner and to develop a methodical approach to your duties. Even when the bar is not busy, there is always something to be done.

THE BAR PERSON AND THE LAW

Hygiene

Because the service area is a food area (remember, beverages are classed as 'food'), it must be maintained to a high standard of cleanliness. At the start of service, make sure:
- all areas of the bar counter – top, undershelves, front – are clean and polished where required
- storage areas like shelving are clean or lined with plastic glass mats
- any containers like the bottle skips and waste bins are clean, empty and in place
- there is an adequate supply of glass washing sterilant and cleaning agents available
- any food offered for sale – sandwiches, salads and so on – is correctly covered and stored at the right temperature.

Health and safety

It is your responsibility as far as possible to take all reasonable precautions to protect the health and safety of yourself and other staff working with you. At the start of service, make sure:

● all areas where staff will work are dry and free of any obstruction
● any equipment, especially electrical equipment, is free of damage (for example, frayed leads, faulty switches) and in good working order
● any hazards have been reported to your supervisor and appropriate notices (for example, Out of Order) have been placed or staff warned.

Other legal requirements

Some of the laws related to licensed premises require certain notices to be displayed. Other notices are also displayed which relate to these laws. Before service starts, check that all the necessary notices are clearly visible and not hidden behind bottles and other promotional material. These may include:

● the price list
● the measures used for alcoholic drinks, especially spirits
● the notice stating that persons under 18 years are not allowed to buy or consume alcohol on the premises
● a notice informing customers of the length of drinking-up time
● any notices related to the extension of permitted hours
● any notices related to liability for loss or theft of customers' belongings.

It is important that standards are maintained as far as possible during service. The last customer entering the bar is entitled to the same standards of service, hygiene and comfort as the first customer.

Do this ✔

1 Use the information in the section above to perform a pre-service check of your workplace.
2 Make a list of any notices you find displayed in your workplace. Ask your supervisor which ones you are legally required to display. Note that there may be differences if you work in a hotel or restaurant.
3 Find out what action you should take if you notice that any of the legal requirements above are not being observed.

DEALING WITH CUSTOMERS

This area has been dealt with in detail in Unit 2NG3. During service a situation may arise where another person may wish to contact one of your customers by telephone. If this happens, follow this procedure:

1 Ask the caller for his or her name.
2 Tell the caller that you will go and see whether the customer is in the bar or that you will have the customer paged.
3 Approach the customer if he is in the bar, give him the name of the caller and ask him if he wants to take the call.
4 If you do not know if the customer is in the bar, call out 'Telephone call for Mr/Mrs/Miss ____'
5 If the customer wishes to take the call, direct him or her to the telephone.
6 If the customer does not wish to take the call, tell the caller, 'Mr/Mrs/Miss ____ does not seem to be in the bar.'
7 Ask the caller if they wish to leave a message in case the customer comes in.

The main points to remember in this situation are:
- Do not say that a customer is on the premises without the customer's permission.
- Some customers may not want it to be known that they are in your premises or may not want to be disturbed if they are taking a meal or having a meeting.

MAINTAINING A CONSTANT SUPPLY OF DRINK STOCKS

As stock is sold during service, it will need to be replaced. This can involve:
- requisitioning new stock from the cellar
- replacing new stock on shelves or optics.

Requisitioning additional stock

The method for obtaining stock from the cellar will depend on the procedures which operate in your workplace.

Requisition book
Each bar may have its own requisition book. This is normally a numbered duplicate book where, when an order is written on one page, a copy is automatically made on the following page. When using this book:
- write out your requisition on the top page
- draw a line under the last item to prevent anyone adding extra items later
- have the order signed by the head barman/woman or sign it yourself (Follow establishment procedures.)
- take the requisition book to the cellar man and obtain the stock required
- the cellar man should sign the requisition and keep the top copy for his records.

An example of a completed requisition is shown below.

MEMORY JOGGER

Why should you always keep a record of stock that is brought up from the cellar? What types of record are usually kept?

Completed requisition/order form

```
ORDER No. 0917

Bar    Lounge              Date    23.01.97

1 × 1.5 l Smirnoff vodka
1 × crate Harp lager
1 × case soda water

Signature   B. Armanager    Signature   C. Ellarman
```

Imprest System
Some establishments will only issue replacement stock for certain beverages, especially spirits, when the empty bottles are returned to the cellar or store.

Cellar transfer book
Where no full-time cellar man is employed, you may be required to enter details of any stock taken up from the cellar into a cellar transfer book. (See Unit 2NC6.) Whichever system is in operation:
- always follow the establishment's procedure
- complete any written records at the time you draw stock, even if you are busy.

When should you re-stock?

While there are no hard and fast rules, there are several points you must bear in mind.

Beers, wines, spirits and soft drinks

- It will take several hours for drinks like bottled beers or red wine to reach room temperature after leaving a cool cellar or store.
- Beers and soft drinks which are served chilled will require several hours to cool down on a refrigerated shelf or in a chill cabinet.
- A 70 cl bottle of spirits contains approximately twenty-eight 25 ml measures. If the bottle on the optic is one-third full, two or three large rounds could empty it.
- Some stocks, for example the most popular drinks, are used very quickly; other stock may be used more slowly. A larger reserve stock of the most popular drinks is necessary.

As a general rule, it would be wise to re-stock:

- when the stock of popular bottled drinks remaining on the shelf equals one case or crate (usually 24 or 48 bottles)
- when the stock of less popular bottled drinks equals half of one case or crate
- if the last bottle of a spirit, wine or cordial is placed on the optic.

Hot drinks

If hot drinks like coffee, speciality coffees and toddies are offered:

- make sure you have an adequate supply of filter papers, coffee grounds or coffee granules
- make sure that at least one full jug of filtered coffee is available on the hot plate if you are using a Cona type machine which uses a filter or percolation method.

Other items

An adequate supply of other drink items should be available such as:

- Angostura bitters, used in cocktails and pink gin
- sauces, such as Worcestershire and Tabasco, for drinks containing tomato juice
- cream for cocktails and speciality coffees
- egg white for cocktails and salt or sugar rims on glasses
- freshly squeezed orange and lemon juice for cocktails
- bar snacks like crisps or nuts.

Ideally, used stock is replaced during service breaks. This may not always be possible, especially during busy service periods, and you may have to use any quiet periods that occur during service sessions.

- You should not leave the bar unattended while replacing stock. Always make sure another member of staff is present to deal with customers and prevent any theft from or damage to the stock or bar.
- Good teamwork between bar staff is essential in order to maintain a high quality of service. Before leaving the bar to obtain new stock, you should inform the other staff and make sure they can deal efficiently with the customers during your absence.

Do this ✔

Find out by talking to your supervisor or experienced bar staff:
(a) What drinks are most popular?
(b) What are the minimum stock levels held in the bar for:
   - popular bottled beer?
   - popular spirits and liqueurs?
(c) If the amount of stock kept on the shelves is constant, or whether more stock is brought up for busy periods like weekends.

MAINTAINING A CONSTANT STOCK OF ACCOMPANIMENTS

It is not the responsibility of any single member of the bar staff to make sure that a constant supply of accompaniments is available. It is the responsibility of every member of staff to replace these items when necessary.

Ice and water

- Ice should be obtained from the ice-making machine in the cellar. If ice is taken from trays in an ice-making compartment of a refrigerator, refill the trays with water whenever the ice is removed.
- If the ice in a bucket becomes watery, empty out the bucket and obtain a new supply.
- When water jugs are almost empty, refill them with clean, cold water drawn from a tap connected to the mains supply.

Food garnishes

- Use quiet times during service to prepare slices, wedges, zests and twists for use during busy periods. These can be stored in sealed containers in the refrigerator or on a plate/tray covered with plastic film shortly before a busy service time.
- Freshly-cut fruit is always best. Fruit cut a long time before use may discolour drinks.
- Bottled items like cherries, olives and pearl onions should be replaced when stock levels are low.
- Fresh food garnishes should be prepared on a chopping board using a sharp knife.

Cordials, minerals and juices

These items should be replaced in the same way as bottled beers and spirits, i.e. when the last bottle of cordial is opened or the stock on the shelf is less than one case or one half case.

Decorative items

An adequate supply of cocktail sticks/swords, muddlers, plastic figures and miniature umbrellas should normally be available before service starts. New stock should be drawn as required.

Essential knowledge	**Stock levels**
	It is important that you keep replacing your stock of drinks and accompaniments to the required level. The quality of service and customer satisfaction will be low if:
	● customers have to wait while new stock is obtained from the cellar or stores
	● drinks are served at the wrong temperature, for example warm lager
	● drinks are served without the proper accompaniments, for example without a cordial or ice and lemon
	● customers have to accept an unwanted alternative.

MEMORY JOGGER

What are the main rules you should remember when restocking shelves and chill cabinets?

STORING AND ARRANGING REPLACEMENT STOCKS

Stock rotation

An important principle to observe when bringing new stock into the bar is the 'first in, first out' principle.

Canned and bottled beers, ciders, soft drinks and mixers have a limited shelf life. The bottles or cans usually have a 'best before' or 'sell by' date stamped or punched on them. It is important that stock with the earliest 'best before' date is used before stock with later dates.

Canned and bottled beers, ciders, soft drinks, minerals and juices
These are stored on normal or refrigerated shelving in the bar. When re-stocking with these drinks:
● pull forward the stock remaining on the shelf and position it at the front
● if the new bottles have not been cleaned in the cellar, wipe them with a damp cloth to remove any dust or dirt
● place the new stock on the shelves behind the old stock with the label facing forwards
● do not store bottled beer in direct sunlight or near a heat source.

The same system should be used when re-stocking refrigerated shelving and chill cabinets.

As it can take several hours to chill a drink down to the required serving temperature, the ideal situation is to regularly replace these items and keep a constant level of stock on the shelf or in the cabinet.

Wines, spirits and liqueurs
These drinks are stored either on optics or standing on the back bar above the shelving for other bottled drinks.

Wines sold by the glass
White wine is usually served lightly chilled and is normally stored either in a chill cabinet with other cold drinks or in a special wall-mounted chill cabinet where it is dispensed by optic. Red wine is stored at room temperature on the back bar or optic. (See the diagram opposite for the method of opening bottled wine.)
● Wines stored in screw-top bottles or boxes are usually stamped with a 'best before' and should be used on the 'first in, first out' principle.
● New stock brought from the cellar should be cleaned, stored either in a chill cabinet/wine fridge or shelf behind older stock and with the label facing forwards.

Essential knowledge

After a bottle of wine has been opened it will begin to deteriorate. To prevent serving bad wine to your customers:
● make a note on the label of the date on which the bottle was opened or attach a label to the bottle giving the opening date
● seal opened bottles not placed on optics using a vacuum seal or inert gas method
● don't open more wine than can be used within two to three days of opening.

Spirits and liqueurs
Spirits and liqueurs are used on a 'first in, first out' basis. Bottles should be stored upright on the back bar with the label facing to the front.
● Store spirit bottles beneath the optics they are to be placed on whenever possible.

● Do not accept bottles of spirits or other drinks from the cellar if the metal or plastic seal has been broken. The drink in the bottle may have been tampered with or diluted. Inform your supervisor as it is an offence to serve diluted beer or spirits.

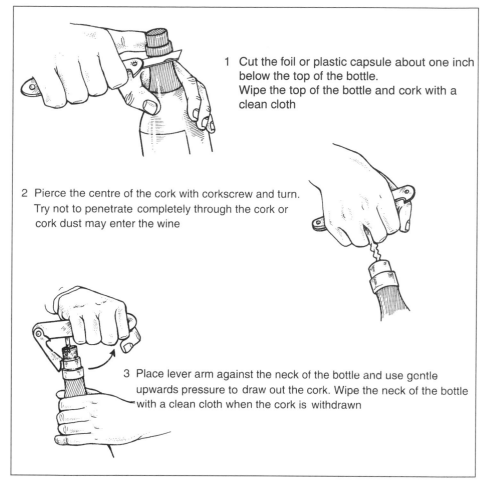

1 Cut the foil or plastic capsule about one inch below the top of the bottle.
Wipe the top of the bottle and cork with a clean cloth

2 Pierce the centre of the cork with corkscrew and turn. Try not to penetrate completely through the cork or cork dust may enter the wine

3 Place lever arm against the neck of the bottle and use gentle upwards pressure to draw out the cork. Wipe the neck of the bottle with a clean cloth when the cork is withdrawn

Opening a wine bottle with a 'waiter's friend'

Do this ✔

1 Discuss with your supervisor or an experienced bar person, how many slices, wedges, twists and zests should be prepared before busy service periods.
2 Find out the minimum level of stock you should keep for:
  (a) cordials
  (b) minerals like tonic water, soda, lemonade and dry ginger
  (c) bottled fruit juices.
3 Make a list of the products which are stored on refrigerated shelving or in chill cabinets in your workplace. Find out the ideal serving temperature for these chilled products.
4 Make a list of the products dispensed through optics in your workplace. Against each product note:
  (a) the type of optic, i.e. measured or free-flow
  (b) the quantity dispensed by measured optics.

Replacing drinks on optics

A bottle on an optic should be changed when the last complete measure has been dispensed. The procedure is as follows:

1 Take hold of both the optic and bottle neck with one hand.
2 With the other hand, release the mechanism (usually a spring button) which attaches the optic to the bracket.
3 Pull the optic from the bracket and grip the upper part of the bottle with the other hand.
4 Stand the bottle upright with the optic attached to allow any remaining liquid to run back into the bottle. Remove the optic.
5 Open the new bottle and pour in any liquid remaining in the old bottle.
6 Place the optic in the new bottle with the fastening bracket pointing to the back of the bottle.
7 Depress the bar of the optic.
8 Holding the base of the full bottle in one hand and the optic and bottle neck in the other, turn the bottle upside down and replace it on the bracket. Make sure the bottle label faces the front.

Other items

Bitters and sauces are stored on the back bar as they require no special storage conditions. Bottles should be kept sealed when not in use.

Containers for items such as cream, egg white and yolks, which can easily become sour or contaminated in a warm atmosphere, must be covered with plastic film and stored in a refrigerator.

Freshly-squeezed fruit juices will also retain their freshness longer if they are kept chilled.

Do not keep more than one day's supply of egg whites/yolks, cream or freshly squeezed fruit juices and dispose of any remaining stock at the end of each day. Obtain or make fresh supplies each day.

STORING AND ARRANGING DRINK ACCOMPANIMENTS

Ice

A plentiful supply of clear, clean ice is essential for service. The commonest form is ice-cubes made in an ice-making machine.

Ice cubes are stored in insulated containers called 'buckets' which are usually placed on the bar counter. Cubed ice is served using metal tongs or an ice scoop. Ice on the point of melting is of little use as it will dilute any drink in which it is placed.

A supply of crushed ice for cocktails and frappés can be kept in a plastic container in the ice compartment of a refrigerator.

Water

A supply of clean drinking water should be available in small jugs placed on drip mats on the bar counter. Ideally, the jugs should be kept covered to prevent dust and other particles settling on the surface.

Replace the water in jugs frequently.

Food garnishes

Food garnishes must be prepared fresh each day. Lemon and orange slices, twists and zests can be cut freshly each time when service is not too busy. Fresh fruit should be thoroughly washed before being used.

● Food garnishes should be handled as little as possible. Ideally, fruit tongs should be used.
● Dispose of unused garnishes at the end of each day.

Bottled fruits should be kept sealed with their juices when not in use. They should not be used after their 'best before' or 'sell by' date has passed.

Cordials, minerals and juices

Cordials

Cordials should be used following the 'first in, first out' principle as they will deteriorate over time. They are usually stored together in a group on the back bar with their labels facing forwards.

Cordials are often dispensed by using a pourer. This should be made of plastic as some cordials will react with metal to produce a poisonous substance. Some establishments put frequently-requested cordials like lime and orange on either a measured or free-flow optic for dispense.

Minerals and bottled fruit juices

These items are stored on shelving in the same way as bottled beers and you should follow the procedures already described in that section.

Decorative items

These items are delivered in large quantities (often 1000 per box) and it is not practical to keep these quantities stored in the bar.

A common practice is to store a small supply of items like cocktail swords/sticks and stirrers in appropriately-sized glasses (Paris goblet or highball) on the back bar next to the supply of food garnishes. They can then be used to lift or secure the garnishes in the drinks.

Essential knowledge	You should follow the correct storage and rotation procedures for drink stocks and accompaniments because: ● some bottled drinks have a limited shelf life and must be used before their 'best before' date ● drinks like bottled beer and white wine will deteriorate rapidly if they are stored in the wrong conditions (sunlight, heat) ● items like cream, egg whites and yolks and fresh fruit juices can become sour or contaminated if kept in a warm atmosphere ● food items which are not kept covered can be contaminated by dust, cigarette ash or airborne bacteria and may cause illness or infection.

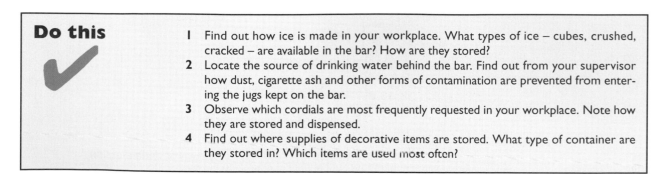

Do this

1 Find out how ice is made in your workplace. What types of ice – cubes, crushed, cracked – are available in the bar? How are they stored?
2 Locate the source of drinking water behind the bar. Find out from your supervisor how dust, cigarette ash and other forms of contamination are prevented from entering the jugs kept on the bar.
3 Observe which cordials are most frequently requested in your workplace. Note how they are stored and dispensed.
4 Find out where supplies of decorative items are stored. What type of container are they stored in? Which items are used most often?

MAINTAINING DRINK SERVICE EQUIPMENT

Part of teamwork among bar staff depends on each member of the team acting with consideration towards the others. The effect of bad working practices is to reduce the establishment's standards as well as the speed and efficiency of service.

All equipment used during drink service must be kept clean, tidy and ready for use.
● The Food Hygiene and Food Safety laws require you to keep all items of equipment that are used in the preparation and service of food clean and sterile to avoid contamination.
● After cleaning, each item should be returned to its normal storage position. Everything should be kept in its place as far as possible.
● Inform other staff and your employer of any equipment failure as soon as possible, especially if electrical equipment is involved.
● If you notice any faults with equipment which can be easily corrected, take any appropriate action required.

Bottle openers

Two types are commonly found in the bar:
● the small hand-held type
● the counter model with a container below to catch the bottle caps.

● Rinse hand-held openers in hot water with an appropriate sterilant after use to prevent them becoming sticky and contaminated.
● Empty counter-mounted bottle openers frequently to prevent bottle caps overflowing onto the floor and creating a hazard for staff. Clean them thoroughly at the end of service.

Corkscrews

There are several types of corkscrew available (see the diagram below). Ideally, they should be stored close to the point of use. Clean immediately after use.

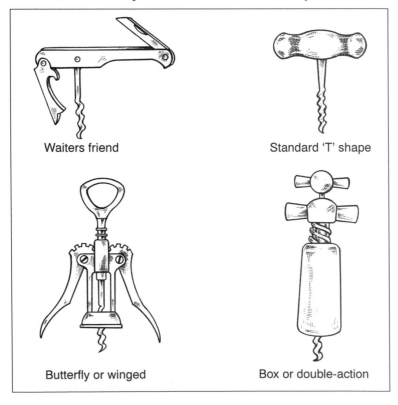

Waiters friend

Standard 'T' shape

Butterfly or winged

Box or double-action

Types of corkscrew

Optics and measures

Important points to remember are:
● never tamper with sealed optics
● wash measures immediately after use and leave them to drain on a drip tray.

Pourers

As pourers are used for liquids like syrups with a high sugar content they can become sticky. If they are not cleaned regularly, dirt and dust can easily become attached to the outer and inner parts.

Both metal and plastic pourers should be cleaned at least once each week by soaking in warm water with a suitable sterilant. A small, flexible brush should be used to clear any deposits inside the pourer.

Knives and chopping boards

These items are normally kept on the back bar. (See Unit 2NC10, pages 231–2.)

The board and tray should be cleaned frequently during service as fruit juice will quickly become sour and infected. Clean knives in hot water and detergent immediately after use.

Ice buckets and tongs

Both the outer and inner surfaces of ice buckets should be clean. Tongs should be cleaned at the end of each service or if they come into contact with any drink being served.

Do this

✔

1 Find out where the following items of bar equipment should be kept:
   (a) hand-held bottle openers
   (b) corkscrews
   (c) spirit measures
   (d) chopping board and fruit knife
   (e) ice buckets.
2 List:
   (a) the types of corkscrews used
   (b) the sizes of measures used for spirits and wine by the glass
   (c) which products have metal pourers and which have plastic pourers.

Glassware

While all items of equipment should be kept clean, it is especially important that glasses are cleaned and stored correctly.
● As glass comes into contact with the customer's mouth, hygiene is extremely important.
● If you serve a customer a drink in a dirty glass, apart from being in breach of the hygiene laws, you may lose the person's custom and create a bad reputation for the establishment.

Cleaning glasses by hand
When cleaning glasses by hand you will need a plentiful supply of hot water, a suitable detergent/sterilising agent and clean, dry glass cloths.
● For effective sterilisation of glasses, the washing bowl of the sink, the draining

MEMORY JOGGER

What are the major steps you should follow when cleaning glasses by hand?

board and glass cloths must be clean and sterile.
● Empty all waste from glasses before washing.

Procedure

1 Fill the sink with a sufficient supply of hot water. Do not use boiling water which may crack the glasses and scald your hands.
2 Add the correct amount of detergent-sterilant according to the manufacturer's instructions printed on the label. Check the exact amount with your supervisor if you are not sure.
    ● Too much sterilant may cause beer to lose its head; too little may reduce its effectiveness in killing bacteria.
    ● Too much sterilant may cause skin problems on your hands.
3 Check each glass for cracks, chips or lipstick smears before washing them. Safely dispose of cracked or chipped glasses.
    ● Clean off lipstick before washing the glass or a thin layer of grease will form on the water and then get on to each glass being washed. A greasy glass will make beer go flat quickly.
4 Immerse each glass completely in the solution.
    ● Hold glasses by the base and make sure all parts of the glass are in contact with the sterilising solution. Any part which is not immersed will still be contaminated.
    ● Rinse the glasses in a second sink filled with hot water at a minimum temperature of 65°C.
5 Change the cleaning water frequently.
    ● The cleaning solution quickly becomes contaminated by waste from the glasses and loses its effectiveness.
6 Place the freshly-washed glasses upside down on the draining board to dry.
7 Store the polished glasses on clip mats on the appropriate shelves.

After washing the glasses, wash down the sink and draining board with a swab which has been soaked in a double-strength solution of sterilant. It is important that the swab used for this purpose is not used for any other form of cleaning. Separate swabs should be used for cleaning the counter top and tables.

Cleaning glasses by machine
General guidelines
● Check that there is sufficient sterilant and rinse aid before operating the machine.
● Empty glasses and remove all food garnishes before you place them in the machine.
● Always follow the manufacturer's instructions regarding the operation and cleaning of the machine.
● Report any faults with the machine to your supervisor immediately. Faulty electrical equipment is a safety hazard and special care needs to be taken where water is involved.

Do this

✔

1 Find out what type of sterilant is used to wash glasses in your establishment. Read the instructions and make a copy of any information related to:
    (a) the level of dilution
    (b) how frequently you should change the washing solution if you are washing by hand.
2 Ask your supervisor or employer to show you:
    (a) how to check if there is sufficient sterilant and rinse aid in the glass washing machine
    (b) how to operate the machine
    (c) how to clean the machine and when you should do it.

Trays, coasters and drip mats

Trays
During service, clean any dirty trays (or salvers). Wipe them with a clean, damp cloth which has been soaked in a sterilant, dry them and return them to their storage position.

Coasters
● Metal and wooden coasters should be wiped clean after use.
● Paper coasters should be disposed of when soiled or damaged.

Drip mats
Drip mats should also be disposed of when soiled or damaged.

Electrical equipment for drink service

A variety of electrical equipment is used behind the bar.

General guidelines
● Most types of refrigeration equipment like in-line coolers and cold shelves use fans to assist cooling. Any vents on this type of equipment should not be covered or used to dry cloths.
● Cold shelves and chill cabinets must be kept clean and defrosted regularly. Both operate better if they are kept well stocked.
● The outer surfaces of all equipment must be cleaned regularly using the appropriate cleaning agents for metal, glass and plastics. Keep air intakes or outlets clean either by wiping with a cloth or using the nozzle attachment of a vacuum cleaner.

Observe the necessary safety guidelines when cleaning electrical equipment:
1 Always switch off the appliance and remove the plug from the socket before beginning cleaning operations.
2 Read and follow the manufacturer's instructions when operating and cleaning electrical equipment.
3 Report any faults to your supervisor as soon as possible. Place a warning notice securely on the equipment.

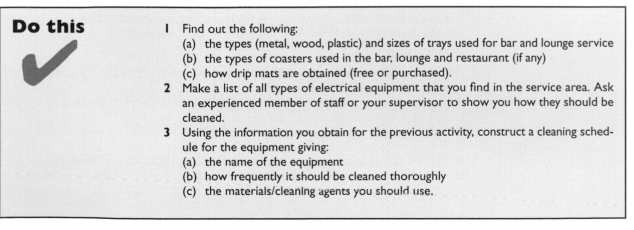

Do this

1 Find out the following:
  (a) the types (metal, wood, plastic) and sizes of trays used for bar and lounge service
  (b) the types of coasters used in the bar, lounge and restaurant (if any)
  (c) how drip mats are obtained (free or purchased).
2 Make a list of all types of electrical equipment that you find in the service area. Ask an experienced member of staff or your supervisor to show you how they should be cleaned.
3 Using the information you obtain for the previous activity, construct a cleaning schedule for the equipment giving:
  (a) the name of the equipment
  (b) how frequently it should be cleaned thoroughly
  (c) the materials/cleaning agents you should use.

MAINTAINING CUSTOMER AND SERVICE AREAS

Maintaining customer areas

The Hygiene and Health and Safety laws require you to keep the customer areas clean, tidy and free from rubbish. In addition, few customers will be satisfied with tables containing dirty glasses, overflowing ashtrays and empty crisp packets and bottles.

Floors
Occasionally, situations will occur where you must respond immediately and leave your other duties for a while. The two commonest occasions requiring immediate response are:
- when a glass or bottle has been broken
- when drink has been spilled.

Dealing with broken glass
- Use a brush and pan to sweep all the pieces from the outside towards the centre. Check carefully in a wide circle.
- Do not use your hands to pick up pieces as small splinters can easily penetrate your skin.
- Sweep all the pieces into the pan, hold them in position with the brush and take them away for disposal.
- Broken glass should be carefully wrapped in thick kitchen paper or several pages of a newspaper and disposed of in a rigid metal or plastic bin, preferably outside the premises. Even when wrapped, it should not be carried in your hand, but placed on a tray or in a dust pan.

MEMORY JOGGER

How should you deal with customer incidents such as broken glasses and spillages?

Cleaning up spillages
- Spillages on vinyl floors should be mopped up immediately using hot water and detergent. A squeegee mop is best suited for this purpose. The floor should be left as dry as possible. Erect a 'Wet Floor' sign, if necessary.
- Spillages on carpets should be sponged down with warm water and detergent to remove as much of the spilled liquid as possible and avoid stains and off-smells.

It is important that you deal with these types of incident as soon as possible to prevent:
- customers or staff being cut or slipping
- broken glass or spillages damaging customers' belongings
- claims for compensation for injury from staff or customers arising from negligence on your part.

Routine floor cleaning
Be alert for opportunities to sweep the floor in front of the bar and around tables when customers are not present. An accumulation of rubbish can be a fire hazard and creates a poor impression with customers entering the establishment.

It is important that floors are swept at the end of service sessions in case lit cigarettes have been dropped onto the floor and may be smouldering.

Clearing tables
Tables should be cleared of bottles and glasses and ashtrays changed regularly. If you do not clear tables frequently:
- customers may begin to place glasses inside one another which can lead to damage and/or breakages
- empty glasses and bottles may be placed on the floor beneath tables and chairs where they can be kicked over or broken and become safety hazards
- bottles and glasses can be knocked over causing spillages and breakages
- ashtrays will become full and create off-smells or become a fire hazard if tissues or paper bags are placed in them.

Clearing glasses and bottles from tables

The procedure is:

1 Collect a large tray or salver (45 to 60 cm) from the bar.
2 If the customers are still sitting at the table, ask them if they have finished with the glasses.
3 Remove the empty glasses and bottles. Do not put your fingers inside the glasses, place glasses inside one another or lift glasses by placing your hand over the top of the glass.
   ● Lift straight-sided glasses by the base and stemmed glasses by the stem. See the diagram below.
4 When loading the tray, try to keep the tray in balance by spreading glasses around the tray evenly.
5 If the tray is resting on a table, pull it towards you with one hand and place the other hand with fingers spread out under the centre of the tray and lift it carefully.
6 Take the tray back to the bar counter and unload the glasses as close as possible to where they will be washed. Empty bottles should be placed in the bar skip or bottle chute.

Wrong methods of putting down or collecting glasses

Right methods of placing and collecting glasses

Right and wrong methods of placing and collecting glasses

Clearing ashtrays

The procedure is:

1 Take a clean ashtray on a tray to the table.
2 Place the clean ashtray upside down over the dirty one and lift both at the same time onto the tray.
3 Pick up any loose material (empty crisp bags or cigarette packets) and place it on the tray.
4 When you are clear of the table, lift the clean ashtray from the top of the dirty one and place it on the table.

5 When you return to the bar, check that no cigarettes are still lit or smouldering. Stub out any that you find.

6 Empty the ashtray into a metal container or bin. Plastic will melt and burn if there is a fire.

7 Brush out any remaining ash using a small brush. A 2" paintbrush is ideal.

8 Clean the ashtray with a damp cloth or wash it if it is heavily stained.

Cleaning tables

Ideally, tables should be cleared and cleaned as soon as customers leave them. You may also be asked to clean them if a drink has been spilled.

You will need:
- a clean swab which has been soaked in sterilant
- a dry cloth
- polish, if you are dealing with wooden or glass surfaces, and a soft cloth
- a clean ashtray
- clean drip mats or coasters.

The procedure is:
1 Remove the ashtray and drip mats from the table.
2 Clean the table top and the sides with the clean swab.
3 Dry the surfaces with the dry cloth. If the surface is wood or glass, spray the polish on it and wipe with the soft cloth.
4 Replace the ashtray if it has not been used or place a new one on the table.
5 Check the drip mats. Replace any that are soiled or wet as these will not be effective, can be a source of infection and create a bad impression.
6 Check the seats of chairs are dry, especially those with fabric seats or pads. Remove damp chairs for cleaning and drying to prevent customers' clothing from becoming stained.
7 Re-arrange the chairs neatly around the table, replacing those taken from other tables, in their correct position.

Storing cleaning equipment

When you finish a cleaning operation, return all materials to their correct positions.
- Rinse or wash any equipment which has come into contact with a liquid or stains.
- After using a swab, rinse it thoroughly in warm water and place it back in the sterilising solution.
- Replace any cloths or swabs which become dirty with new linen and swabs. Change the sterilising solution if it becomes dirty.

Do this

1 Make a list of the materials and equipment available for cleaning floors. Where are they stored?

2 Discuss with your supervisor or employer what your priorities should be if breakages or spillages occur in the customer areas during a busy service session.

3 Find out:
   (a) where you can obtain clean cloths and swabs
   (b) where you should place dirty ones for washing
   (c) where they are stored during service for cleaning operations.

Maintaining service areas

Bar counter and under-counter

These areas must be kept clean, tidy and free from rubbish.

Keep the counter top clean and tidy by:
- regular swabbing of the counter top to remove stains and spillages which could damage customers' clothing and to keep the surface sterile

- clearing empty glasses and bottles
- frequently replacing ashtrays and drip mats when they become dirty
- collecting and disposing of loose material like empty packets.

Keep the under-counter clean and tidy by:
- frequent swabbing with a cloth soaked in a double-strength solution of a sterilant
- emptying containers for holding waste beer, material from ashtrays and bottles frequently following the establishment's procedures.

Back cabinet and back fitting

The back cabinet contains the shelving for storing bottles and glasses. A refrigerated cold shelf or chill cabinet is usually part of the cabinet. The top of the cabinet is usually used to store the various items of equipment such as the till, thimble measures, cutting board and knife, openers and corkscrews and accompaniments like lemon and orange slices and bottled fruit and sauces.

The back fitting may be mirrored and is usually shelved. The brackets for holding bottles on optics are fixed to either a bar or shelves.
- One section of the back cabinet and back fitting should be thoroughly cleaned each day so that all sections are cleaned once each week. There may be a job card for this operation (see below). It is normally completed before service starts.
- The shelf on top of the cabinet should be swabbed regularly during service to clear spillages and drips from optics.

PRODUCT	EQUIPMENT	CLEANING METHOD	STANDARD
UPGRADE 3K	Sponge cloth	Remove items from cupboard. 1. Make up warm solution of UPGRADE by using pre-set tap proportioner or wall pump. 2. Wall pump - 4 pushes for a wash-up sink. 3. Concentration is 1fl oz/2-3 gallons, 20-30ml/10 litre. 4. Wash with sponge cloth. 5. Rinse with hot water. 6. Allow to air dry. Replace items neatly.	No dirt or smears
Weekly CT/33		UNDERSTOCK CUPBOARDS	Diversey Limited

Job card for cleaning stock shelving (courtesy of Diversey Ltd)

Floors

The floor in the service area and other passageways must be kept clean and tidy to prevent accidents to staff.
- Clear up any spillages immediately and leave the floor as dry as possible.
- Don't place crates, boxes or other containers in the serving space or under counter flaps where staff may trip over them.

If there is an entrance to the cellar in the serving space, this should be kept closed during service or suitably guarded to prevent accidents when open.

Refrigerated units
Clean up any spillages with a swab as soon as possible and thoroughly clean equipment at the end of service.

Bottle containers and waste bins
Bottle skips, baskets and waste containers like bins will soon become contaminated with spilt beer, soiled drip mats, cigarette ash and discarded food materials. Empty and clean them at the end of each service session.

It is important to remember that the service area is the bar person's workshop where he or she prepares what is to be used for service. Without due attention to hygiene, cleanliness, and safety, it can be hazardous to both staff and customers.

Do this

1   Find out where the swabs to clean the counter top and the sinks/draining board are kept.
    (a) Are they kept in separate containers?
    (b) What strength of sterilising solution is used?
2   Ask your supervisor about the cleaning schedule for the back cabinet and fittings. Write out the cleaning schedule for each day.
3   Find out how you should clean either a refrigerated shelf or a chill cabinet. Write down the procedure you should follow and any equipment and cleaning materials you have to use.

Essential knowledge

It is important that customer and service areas are kept clean, tidy and free from rubbish to:
● prevent food and beverage preparation and service areas from becoming contaminated and causing infection or illness
● prevent accidents happening to staff and customers
● provide customers with a clean, healthy and safe environment in which to relax and enjoy their drink
● comply with the Food Safety, Food Hygiene and Health and Safety laws.

Security in the service area

As money and stock are kept in the service area, it is important that you do not allow anyone to enter the area without your employer's permission.

Right of entry
However, because licensed premises have to comply with a number of laws, certain official persons have the right of entry to the premises at any time. These include: Police, Environmental Health, Customs and Excise, Fire and Trading Standards officers.

Ask for and examine carefully their official identification. Contact your supervisor or employer immediately. Ask the person(s) to wait until your supervisor or employer arrives.

Other persons may also be on the premises as part of their work including brewery staff, delivery men and maintenance men.
● Do not leave the service area unattended while any person is on the premises including customers, workmen or officials.
● Lock the till and service area if they are to be left even for a short while.

MAINTAINING ENVIRONMENTAL CONTROL SYSTEMS

MEMORY JOGGER

What actions can you take to provide a comfortable environment for your customers?

To ensure your customers are comfortable and can enjoy their stay, you should control the environment in the bar. They should not be too hot or too cold, choked with smoke, in a draught or deafened by loud music.

Temperature

More heat will be required in the bar when the weather is cold and there are few people in it. As the bar becomes busier, you may need to reduce or switch off the heating to provide a comfortable temperature for your customers.

Be alert for obvious signs of discomfort in your customers such as fanning themselves or sitting with coats on.

Ventilation/air conditioning

As the customer areas fill up with people, the atmosphere can become very stuffy and, if a lot of customers are smoking, will become smoky.
- Switch on extractor fans to remove the smoke.
- Switch on the air conditioning system.
- Open windows.

If you open windows, check with customers sitting close to them if there are any draughts and adjust the windows as required.

Lighting

It is important for the safety of staff and customers that the service and customer areas should be adequately lit.
- Don't burn lights unnecessarily; conserve energy whenever possible.
- Adjust the lighting as required to make sure all areas are adequately lit. Replace bulbs when necessary.

Music

Many establishments play background music or have entertainment through juke boxes or video juke boxes.

When the bar is quiet, only a low volume of music is required. This can be gradually adjusted as more customers enter the bar or lounge, but the volume should never be high enough to disturb customers' conversations.

Do this

✓

1 Discuss with your supervisor what action you should take if any of the officials described on page 200 wishes to enter the service area.

2 Ask your supervisor or employer what action you should take if you have to leave the bar unattended.

3 Find out where the controls are for:
   (a) the heating in the bar and lounge
   (b) extractor fans or air conditioning
   (c) lights in the service and customer areas
   (d) piped music and any other music machines.

4 Ask your supervisor what you should do regarding the environmental control systems at closing time. Make a note of the actions you should take.

Case study

A young barman was washing glasses by hand in a sink when a glass broke. He emptied the sink and carefully collected all the pieces up. He decided to dispose of it in a bin at the rear of the premises. However, as he was walking out, he slipped on a wet part of the floor and reacted automatically by closing his hand. The broken glass he was holding broke even more and cut most of the ligaments in his hand, particularly in the area of his thumb. After several days in hospital, two operations involving micro-surgery and nine months of physiotherapy, he eventually recovered most of the use of his hand again.

1 How did the barman's actions result in his injury?

2 What procedure should he have followed and why?

What have you learned

1 While the bar is open, what two activities should you always be occupied with?

2 Why is it important that certain notices are displayed in the bar?

3 When writing out a requisition for stock to be brought up from the cellar, why is it important to draw a line under the last item?

4 When would it be wise to re-stock your supply of:
   (a) popular bottled drinks?
   (b) spirits?

5 Why is it important that you maintain a constant level of stock and accompaniments during service?

6 Give three actions you can take to prevent serving wine which has gone bad to your customers.

7 Why should you not use bottles of spirits or other drinks which come up from the cellar with the seal broken?

8 Why is it important to follow the correct storage and rotation procedures for drink stocks and accompaniments?

9 Why is it important to check glasses carefully before hand-washing?

10 Give two examples of common accidents in the bar which require an immediate response.

11 Why is it important that customer and service areas are kept clean, tidy and free from rubbish?

12 Give three reasons why you should prevent people entering the service area without your employer's permission.

Get ahead

1 Find out the approximate alcoholic strength of the following drinks:
   (a) no- and low-alcohol beers
   (b) ales, stouts and lagers
   (c) fortified wines
   (d) spirits and liqueurs
   (e) cider and perry
   (f) table wines
   (g) vermouths.

2 Make a list of the main types of alcoholic drinks offered in your establishment. Visit an off-licence and a pub run by a different brewery and make a note of substitute brands of drinks.

3 Find out how to replace corks on optics if they begin to leak.

4 Find out the names of mixed beers most frequently requested in your workplace and how to make them.

5 Ask your supervisor to show you how to operate and clean the glasswashing machine. Ask about the COSHH regulations regarding the cleaning agents used.

6 Find out what changes are made to the environmental control systems at closing time to encourage people to leave the premises.

UNIT 2NC9

Provide a table drink service

This unit covers:
ELEMENT 1:   **Take customer orders**
ELEMENT 2:   **Serve orders to table**

ELEMENT 1:	Take customer orders

What you need to do

- Make sure that all service equipment is clean and free from damage at all times.
- Deal with customers in a polite and helpful way at all times.
- Take orders for alcoholic drinks only from those people whom you are permitted to serve by law.
- Make sure that you take down customers' orders clearly and accurately to avoid misunderstandings.
- Promote certain drinks to customers at the appropriate times.
- Give customers accurate information about any drink offered by the establishment.
- Deal effectively with unexpected situations and inform the appropriate people where necessary.
- Carry out your duties in an organised and efficient manner taking account of priorities, organisational procedures and legal requirements.

What you need to know

- Why your service equipment should be clean and free from damage.
- What are the appropriate ways of dealing with customers.
- Who you may or may not serve with alcoholic drinks.
- Why it is important that you correctly identify the drinks your customers require.
- How to promote certain types of drinks.
- Why customers must be given accurate information about the drinks being served.
- How to deal effectively with unexpected situations.
- How to carry out your work in an organised and efficient manner.

INTRODUCTION

Depending on the nature and size of the establishment, tables may be situated either in front of the bar area, in a hotel or cocktail lounge, in an area set aside for meals or outside the main part of the premises.

PREPARING FOR SERVICE

There are a number of activities and checks that you should complete before you begin service to your customers. It is essential that you organise your time to complete these activities before service starts.

Check your linen

It is important that you have the appropriate linen to provide a tray service and clean up any spillages. You should have a supply of clean napkins to use on trays or salvers and clean linen glass cloths for polishing glassware as well as the normal service linen.

● Make sure that all linen is clean, in good condition and suitable to be used during service.

A cloth-covered salver/tray prevents glasses slipping and can absorb spillages. The cloth can be replaced if it becomes soiled or stained. Paper napkins or tray cloths serve the same purpose as linen, which is mainly used in a restaurant or 'luxury' setting.

Check your glassware

It is important that all the equipment that you use is clean and free from damage. This is especially true of glassware as it comes into contact with the customer's mouth.

● Check all glassware that you intend to use for lipstick and other grease smears, fingerprints, cracks or signs of chipping, especially on the rim.

Check your trays or salvers

Trays or salvers are made of various materials and used for the service of drinks in glasses and for clearing dirty glasses from tables. The trays are round and are usually found in different sizes. The smaller sizes are used to serve a small order of drinks; the larger sizes are used for large orders or for clearing tables. The rim of the tray is usually raised or lipped. All trays should be clean and polished.

Trays or salvers are usually covered with a clean linen or paper napkin or circular tray cloth if this procedure operates in your establishment.

A pen and note paper/pad

Taking orders at the table can sometimes be complicated. In order to be able to record orders accurately and supply all the drinks to the customers' requirements, you should make sure that you have a good pen and a supply of note paper or a notepad. See the section on taking orders at the table on page 209.

Essential knowledge	It is important to check all service equipment before service starts: ● to ensure that you can provide a fast and efficient service to customers ● to prevent accidents such as injuries to customers and spillages or breakages ● to create a positive impression of cleanliness and hygiene with the customer ● to comply with health and safety and food hygiene legislation.

Do this ✔	1 Find out the procedure for obtaining clean napkins and clean cloths in your establishment. Are there circular tray cloths for use with salvers? 2 Make a list of the trays and salvers used in your establishment. You should note: (a) what they are made of (b) the sizes available (c) how they are cleaned (d) where they are stored when not in use.

DEALING WITH CUSTOMERS

Three aspects of the bar or lounge waiter/waitress are very important. These are your:
● appearance
● attitude
● social and professional skills.

For more detailed information about these, read the early sections of Unit 2NC8, Unit 2NG3 and Element 1 of Unit NG1, if necessary.

Social and professional skills

In addition to those general skills given in Unit 2NC8, there are specific skills related to table service.
● Never respond in kind to a problem customer. Don't argue back, flirt or be over-familiar, or be rude to any customer.
● Show an interest in what the customer has to say. Answer politely and briefly. Excuse yourself at the first opportunity.
● You should watch what is happening at the tables so that you can respond quickly if your customers need service. However, you should avoid behaviours which can embarrass them. See the table below.

Appropriate and inappropriate behaviours

Helpful behaviour	Embarrassing behaviour
● Only giving advice when asked for it ● Suggesting appropriate drinks and guiding customers in their choice, if they are uncertain ● Suggesting suitable alternatives if customers ask for brands or products which are not available	● Hovering around tables and staring at customers ● Standing over customers to make them hurry with their order ● Being pompous or superior when giving advice to customers ● Correcting customers in front of their guests if they pronounce something wrongly or make an incorrect choice

Customer complaints and incidents

If you receive a complaint from a customer while taking an order:
● acknowledge the customer and apologise to them, if necessary
● remain calm and listen carefully without interrupting or making comment
● show them that you are taking their complaint seriously
● start to deal with the complaint or incident immediately and tell the customer what action you propose to take

Resolve any complaints or incidents that you can within your own authority, but you should always act within your organisation's procedures. Report all complaints and incidents to your supervisor and complete any records that are required.

It is important that you report all customer complaints and incidents to your supervisor as soon as possible because:

- when some incidents occur such as theft, damage to or loss of property, or injury to a customer, the establishment may have a legal responsibility
- it may be necessary to involve outside bodies like the emergency services or a solicitor
- some incidents can cause customers to become dissatisfied with your establishment which could damage its reputation when they tell other people
- the establishment can learn from customer complaints and incidents and can use them as lessons to improve their procedures and services.

THE BAR PERSON AND THE LAW

There a number of laws which apply to the sale and service of alcoholic drinks that you should be aware of. The main ones are the:

- Licensing Acts which govern the type of licence the establishment holds, who may be served and the hours of opening ('permitted hours')
- Trade Descriptions Act and other consumer protection acts which govern any descriptions of the products you sell and make it illegal for customers to be given misleading information
- Weights and Measures Acts which lay down the quantities which may be used to serve draught beer and cider, some spirits and wine by the glass
- Food Safety Act and Food Hygiene Regulations which lay down the conditions under which food and drink must be stored and served to guarantee its purity and cleanliness.

The bar person does not need to be aware of the laws in detail, but by failing to observe them may cause the employer to be prosecuted.

The main points related generally to bar work are given in detail in Unit 2NC8. The main points in relation to table service and lounge waiting are given below.

Licensing laws

When can you take orders for alcoholic drinks?
You may only take orders for alcoholic drinks during the permitted hours of opening of the establishment. These are governed by the type of licence – Full On-Licence, Restaurant Licence, Residential Licence – and whether any additional hours are allowed by the establishment holding an Extended Hours Order or a Supper or Special Hours Certificate.

- Even though you have taken an order at a table before closing time, it would be illegal for bar staff to dispense the drinks after the end of permitted hours. Take orders to the bar promptly.
- If you are working in a hotel lounge and the establishment holds a Residential Licence, you may serve residents and their guests after the end of the hours permitted by the normal Full On-Licence (usually 11.00 p.m.). Only the resident may order and pay for the drinks, not his or her guests.

Drinking-up time
At the end of the permitted hours of opening, customers are allowed time to finish up any drinks they have left. The amount allowed may be 15, 20 or 30 minutes depending on the part of the country your establishment is in and whether or not the drinks are served as part of a meal.

Who may you take orders from?
As well as limiting the times at which you may sell alcoholic drinks, the licensing laws also restrict the type of people to whom you may sell alcoholic drinks.

> **Do this**
>
> 1 Find out what type of licence your establishment has. Is it:
>   (a) a Full On-Licence?
>   (b) a Restaurant Licence?
>   (c) a Residential and Restaurant Licence?
>   What are the permitted hours?
> 2 Are there any restrictions on the type of alcoholic drinks the establishment is allowed to sell?
> 3 Find out if your establishment has any of the following:
>   (a) a Supper-hour certificate
>   (b) an Extended hours order
>   (c) a Special hours certificate.

MEMORY JOGGER

What types of customers can you not take an order for alcoholic drinks from?

You should only take orders from customers who comply with the licensing laws. You should not take orders for alcoholic drinks from:

- any person at the bar that you suspect is under 18 years of age or any person attempting to buy a drink for them
- any person in a restaurant or area put aside for table meals who you suspect is under 16 years of age
- a customer who is obviously drunk or any person attempting to buy more drink for that customer to drink on the premises
- any customer behaving in a violent or disorderly manner or who is under an exclusion order.

You should also not sell alcoholic drinks to be drunk either on or off the premises unless it is within the permitted hours of opening.

The Trade Descriptions Act

Basically, any description of the drinks offered, either written on a list or given verbally to the customer, must be accurate.
- If you are not sure of something, tell the customer you will find out.

Food Safety Act and Food Hygiene Regulations

These laws define food as any article used for food or drink for human consumption.
- Any article or equipment that is to come into contact with food or drink including glassware and trays must be clean and in good condition.

Establishment procedures

As well as acting in ways which enable you to comply with the laws and regulations outlined above, you should follow any rules or procedures regarding working practices laid down by your employer.

> **Do this**
>
> Discuss with your employer or supervisor what you should do:
> (a) if a young person between 16 and 18 years orders beer with a meal
> (b) if a customer becomes drunk on your premises
> (c) if a person who has been barred from the premises comes in for a drink or meal.

TAKING ORDERS AT THE TABLE

Taking orders from customers in a lounge area or an area where meals are served can be simple and straightforward if the table has only two or three people or quite complicated if large parties are involved.

When taking the order, three points should be kept in mind:
- each order should be recorded accurately
- you should be able to serve the drinks (in the best condition possible) without asking each customer what they ordered
- if the person is a customer in a restaurant or a resident in a hotel, a record of the order may have to be passed to the financial control point (cashier's or receptionist's desk) so that the amount can be added to the customer's bill.

The procedures involved will vary from one establishment to another depending on its size. Follow your establishment's procedures carefully.

MEMORY JOGGER

What are the three main points to remember when you are taking an order?

Writing the order

The order is normally recorded on a pad which may be either duplicate or triplicate depending on the establishment's size and procedures for stock and cash control.

Recording the order: Technique

As you should be able to serve the drinks to the customers without asking them what they ordered, develop a technique which will allow you to record orders in a way which can be used to serve the drinks later. A number of techniques are useful.

Table diagrams
This technique involves sketching a diagram of the seating arrangement and recording each drink ordered against the relevant seat.
- Identify the host on the seating arrangement as they are usually served after their guests. The host usually asks you to take the order.
- On your diagram indicate all seats even if no order is given or you may serve a drink to a customer who has not ordered.

An example of this technique is given in the diagram below.

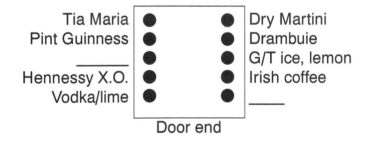

Sketching a table order

Distinctive features
This technique involves using some feature of each customer to identify them. The feature is usually some aspect of dress or jewellery. For example: red blouse – Cointreau; gold brooch – Benedictine.

Recording the order: Accompaniments and service features

Check which accompaniments your customers require with their drinks. Ask about ice, slices of lemon or orange or how the customer likes the drink to be served.

Recording the order: Cocktails

Because the recipe for some cocktails can vary, check that you are meeting the customer's requirements. For example:

● If a customer requests a dry Martini, you should check if this is simply a vermouth like Martini Extra Dry or the cocktail containing gin and vermouth. If it is the cocktail, you should ask what proportion of gin to vermouth the customer requires. Some recipes use $\frac{1}{6}$ vermouth to $\frac{5}{6}$ gin; others do not. The customer should also be asked if a lemon twist or an olive is preferred.

● Some customers may use a name for a cocktail which you are not familiar with. If you are unsure, you should ask the customer to give you the recipe. Most customers will be only too pleased to demonstrate their knowledge.

Check for accuracy

After you have recorded a large or complicated order, repeat the order back to the customer:

● to check that all the drinks have been included
● to check that all the required accompaniments have been included.

Essential knowledge	There are several reasons why you should make sure that you take down customer's orders accurately.
	● The customer will not be happy if they are given the wrong drink. Some may suffer in silence; others may complain after tasting the drink and ask for the correct drink.
	● It will not be possible to recover any part of an incorrect drink if the customer has drunk from the glass or you have added a second liquid, like a mineral or cordial, or ice and lemon.
	● Time will be lost in replacing an incorrect drink and having to readjust the till and change.
	● Having to dispose of an incorrect drink affects your employer's profit.
	● To provide a fast and efficient service to ensure customer satisfaction.

Do this ✔

1 Find out from an experienced waiter/waitress how they take down large orders. Do they use a 'shorthand' like TM for Tia Maria or DOM for Benedictine?

2 Find out how experienced staff take orders at tables. Do they take orders in a clockwise or anti-clockwise direction? What techniques do they use to remember what each customer has ordered?

PROMOTING AND SELLING DRINKS

Like a salesperson in any other type of business, you must have a positive approach to selling your products and be alert for opportunities to promote and sell drinks.

Use promotional materials

Any materials used to promote products must be accurate, helpful and clean.

● Wine and beverage lists should be up-to-date. If a product is not available, you should inform the customer when you present the list.
● Table top items like tent cards, drip mats and coasters should be clean and unmarked. Soiled items should not be re-used.

Use a positive selling approach

Positive selling requires you to take the initiative when dealing with the customer. Compare the three approaches below:

Waiter A: 'I don't suppose you will want a drink before your meal, sir?'

Waiter B: 'Do you want to order a drink before your meal, sir?'

Waiter C: (Presenting beverage list) 'May I suggest a drink before your meal, sir. I'll come back and take your order in a few minutes.'

The difference between these three approaches is:
● waiter A has a negative approach and discourages the customer from ordering
● the customer can quite easily refuse Waiter B and not order
● waiter C is using a positive selling approach. By presenting the customer with the beverage list and giving him time to look at it and, perhaps, discuss whether or not to order with his companions, Waiter C has made it more difficult for the customer to refuse to buy. This is an example of positive selling.

The main aim of the positive approach is to encourage customers to buy at times when they might not have intended to or to buy a better quality (and more expensive) product. It is not to make customers drunk.

When using a positive approach, your technique should be what is called the 'soft sell' approach. At no time should the customer feel that they are being pressured into buying. Care should also be taken not to embarrass the customer into ordering more than he wants to buy or can afford.

Promote selected drinks at appropriate times

Some types of drink are more suitable at one time than at another. Part of positive selling is to recommend drinks to your customers.

Aperitifs are taken before a meal. You can recommend/suggest:
● wine or wine-based cocktails
● sparkling wines like champagne
● sherry or chilled white port.

After a meal you can recommend/suggest:
● liqueurs or cognac
● certain cocktails, some based on brandy
● speciality coffees.

In cold weather you can recommend/suggest warming drinks like:
● hot toddies
● mulled wine or punches.

In hot weather you can recommend long, cool drinks like:
● well-chilled premium beers, such as Budweiser, Schlitz, Sol, Rolling Rock
● long mixed drinks/cocktails, such as Slings, Juleps and Pimms
● spritzers.

Promotions and special offers

Occasionally, suppliers will run promotions for a limited period on a certain brand, either when launching a new brand or trying to increase sales of a particular product.
● Make sure all promotional materials are clean and displayed in the correct position.
● Watch for 'buying signals' such as customers reading the promotional material or asking questions about the product.

● Tell your customers about any reduced prices or any offers available to them if they purchase the product.

Be alert for buying signals

You should be alert for openings to offer customers another drink.
● As you walk around the tables, you should look for customers who have almost finished their drink. A polite 'May I freshen your drink, Sir?' often brings a repeat order.
● A casual question to a customer about a drink you have served them such as 'Did you enjoy your cocktail?' or 'Was there enough tonic (soda, lime and so on) in your drink, Madam?' may also lead to a repeat order.

Do this

✔

1 Find out how drinks are promoted in your establishment. Look for:
   (a) tent cards
   (b) sections on wine lists, menu holders, menu cards
   (c) coasters, drip mats and drink decorations like stirrers.
2 Ask an experienced waiter/waitress about the buying signals they look for in customers.
3 Ask experienced staff about any positive selling techniques that they have used successfully. Make a note of any which you think you could use.
4 Find out from your supervisor/employer if the establishment has a policy for promoting certain types of drinks and what you should do to help promote them.

PROVIDING CUSTOMERS WITH ACCURATE INFORMATION

It is important that you give customers the correct information. Otherwise, customers may feel that they have been overcharged, given short measure, misled or cheated.

Be completely familiar with the beverage list and be able to provide customers with information on prices, relative strength of alcoholic drinks, ingredients of cocktails and suitable alternative drinks.

Prices

Make sure you are familiar with the price of each of the drinks you sell. If a customer questions the price you are charging for a particular drink, you should refer them to your bar manager or supervisor.

Relative strength

Make sure that you are able to advise customers on the alcoholic strength of the drinks you serve.

Note that:
● the amount of alcohol your customer consumes will depend on the size of the measure used to dispense it. For example, a double whisky dispensed with a 35 ml spirit measure is almost equal to a triple whisky served with a 25 ml measure
● there is approximately the same amount of alcohol in a glass of wine, a half pint of normal strength beer, a 25 ml measure of a spirit and a small glass of sherry or port.

If you have any doubts about the strength of an alcoholic drink, you should either check the label of the bottle or consult the bar manager or employer. Never attempt to deceive the customer or bluff them with incorrect information.

Do this ✔

1 Examine the stock of alcoholic drinks sold in your establishment. Compare the alcoholic strength of:
   (a) a bottle of ordinary beer and a lager
   (b) a bottle of dry vermouth and of sherry
   (c) a bottle of whisky and of vodka.
   Make a note of them.
2 Examine the stock of liqueurs held by your establishment. Make a list giving the name and the alcoholic strength of each type you find. Note the differences you find.

The ingredients of drinks

Most customers will be familiar with the main types of alcoholic and non-alcoholic drink. However, they may be unfamiliar with the ingredients of most liqueurs and cocktails, even though they may know their name.

Spirits and liqueurs
Try and learn about the flavour and ingredients of the less usual spirits and liqueurs. See *Get ahead* at the end of this Unit.

Cocktails and mixed drinks
Apart from spirits and liqueurs, make sure you know how cocktails are made and the ingredients of some of the more common cocktails. For further information, read Unit 2NC10. Cocktails can be served before or after meals. Many pre-dinner or aperitif cocktails are wine-based, while after-dinner cocktails are based on spirits such as brandy and whisky.

However, there are no hard and fast rules about what cocktails should be served at a particular time. The customer is always right.

Speciality coffees
You must be aware of the ingredients of the main types of speciality coffees such as Irish coffee and Calypso coffee. See Unit 2NC8 for further information.

Recommending substitutes or alternatives

It is not practical for any licensed premises to stock a complete range of every brand of alcoholic and non-alcoholic drink. Even those establishments with a well-stocked bar and cellar will not be able to provide every drink that is likely to be requested.

Substitutes
A substitute is something which is similar. If a customer requests Satzenbrau Pils and you do not stock this brand, you should suggest a suitable substitute brand. However, do not suggest that the substitute is in some way of a lesser quality by saying, 'I'm sorry, but we *only* stock Holsten Pils.'

Alternatives
An alternative is something different which serves the same purpose. If a customer requests a drink for which you have no substitute brand available, you should suggest an alternative.

The ability to offer substitutes and alternatives to your customers highlights how necessary it is that you should have a thorough knowledge of the products you sell and of other products which are available.

You should never attempt to pass off a substitute or alternative as the brand or drink a customer has requested. Always consult the customer.

Do this

1 Discuss with your head waiter or bar manager what cocktails are available to be offered to customers.
   (a) Is there a list and, if so, does it give the ingredients?
   (b) What you should do if a customer asks for details of cocktails and no list is available.
2 Find out what you could offer a customer who requests:
   (a) a brand of lager you do not stock
   (b) a brand of Scotch whisky which is not available
   (c) an orange-flavoured liqueur
   (d) a herb-flavoured liqueur.
3 Over a period of one week, make a note of any drink that you are asked for which is not available. Discuss the situation with your supervisor. What action could be taken?

Essential knowledge

It is important that you give your customers accurate information about the drinks you serve them:
   ● to comply with the Trade Descriptions Act and other consumer laws
   ● to prevent customers becoming dissatisfied, feeling cheated or misled
   ● to prevent customers consuming a larger quantity of alcohol than they wish, especially when drinking cocktails, 'light' or low-alcohol products
   ● to ensure that customers receive an efficient and high-quality service.
However you should not reveal any confidential information related to any speciality products offered by your establishment or details such as trade or cost prices of drinks or profit margins.

Do this

1 Examine any beverage list used in your establishment or any notices displayed concerning the drinks offered to your customers.
   (a) Is the list up-to-date or are some brands unavailable?
   (b) Are the prices correct?
   (c) What information is given about the quantities (measures) used to serve spirits and wine by the glass?
2 Make a copy of six entries on the establishment's price list. Try to choose different types of drink.

Case study

At the beginning of the evening session in a small city centre restaurant, the waitress noticed a small group of customers get up and leave shortly after receiving a round of drinks. Although they had booked a table, they had not ordered their meal. When she went to clear the table of glasses, she noticed that they had not finished the drinks they had been given. When she returned the glasses to the dispense bar, she noticed that several of them had a white scum on them and they were heavily smeared with a greasy film. When she drew this to the barman's attention, he shrugged and said that he hadn't noticed. Not wishing to cause any trouble, she went back to her work.

Later in the evening, a young woman screamed and stood up quickly from her table. Her lip was bleeding heavily and blood had dripped over her clothes. The cause was a glass with a chipped rim in which she had been served the house wine. She had to be taken to hospital where she received several stitches. She later sued the restaurant for negligence and received compensation.

1 *Who was at fault in these situations?*
2 *What should the waitress have done after the first incident?*
3 *How could both incidents have been avoided?*

1 State three aspects of the waiter/waitress which are important in order to satisfy customer expectations.
2 Give three examples of both helpful and embarrassing behaviour when dealing with a customer.
3 Why is it important that you should report customer complaints and incidents to your supervisor?
4 State the types of persons you should not sell alcoholic drinks to in order to comply with the law.
5 Why is it important that your service equipment should be clean and free from damage?
6 What size of tray would you use
   (a) to serve a small number of drinks?
   (b) to clear a table of a large number of glasses?
7 Give two examples of techniques you could use when taking orders to help you remember which drink each customer ordered.
8 Give two examples of methods which could be used to promote drinks to customers.
9 Give three reasons why you should give customers accurate information about the drinks you serve them.

ELEMENT 2: Serve orders to table

What you need to do

- Deal with customers without offending them and handle problem customers efficiently.
- Check all service equipment regularly and keep it clean and free from damage.
- Serve a range of drinks to meet customer requirements.
- Serve drinks only to those people you are permitted to serve by law.
- Provide accurate information in response to customer enquiries.
- Deal effectively with unexpected situations and inform the appropriate people where necessary.
- Carry out your work in an organised and efficient manner taking account of priorities, organisational procedures and legal requirements.

What you need to know

- How to deal with customers.
- Why you should keep all service equipment clean and free from damage.
- How to dispense/serve a range of drinks.
- What types of customers you are not allowed to serve alcoholic drinks to.
- Why you should provide customers with accurate information about any drinks you serve.
- How to deal effectively with unexpected situations.
- How to carry out your work in an organised and efficient manner.

DEALING WITH CUSTOMERS

The social and professional skills required when dealing with customers were mentioned in Element 1 of this Unit. Unit 2NG3 also deals in detail with working with customers. However, there are several aspects of dealing with customers while providing a table service that you should be aware of.

Offending customers

There are several ways that you can offend customers and make it unlikely that they will stay in the establishment or return again.

You should not:
- deliberately overcharge the customer by dishonestly adding up the drinks bill
- throw change down onto the table
- cadge for tips by jingling coins, giving back large amounts of small coins or leaving coins on the tray for the customer to lift off
- ignore customers by arguing, chatting or joking with other staff
- be over-familiar and talk too much to customers who wish to talk among themselves
- spend too much time with one customer or group of customers or give them preference over others
- hover around or stand close to a table where customers are talking.

Problem customers

While providing a table drink service, you will encounter several types of problem customer. Some of these and ways of dealing with them are given in the table below.

Type of customer	Actions to be taken
Grumblers	● Treat with calmness, good humour and courtesy. ● Pay particular attention to providing quick and efficient service. ● Do not respond to or agree with any criticisms that are made.
Over-familiar or flirtatious (male or female)	● Do not respond in kind as this may encourage them further. ● Provide quick service or ask a different member of staff to serve them. ● Report serious difficulties (propositions, touching) to your supervisor.
Drunks, eccentrics and trouble-makers	● Be tactful, avoid getting into conversation. ● If there are any signs of trouble, bad language or unacceptable behaviour, report them to your supervisor immediately. ● It is unlawful to serve alcohol to a drunken person or anyone behaving in a violent or disorderly manner. (See following section.)
Children running/playing	● Be tactful. Explain courteously to parents the reasons why they should keep children close to them. ● Refer continuing problems to your supervisor or a senior member of staff.

Dealing with problem customers

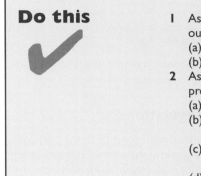

Do this

1   Ask an experienced waiter or waitress about how they address their customers. Find out:
    (a) which customers they greet formally using 'Sir' or 'Madam'
    (b) which customers they greet using their title such as 'Mr Smith' and 'Mrs Jones'.
2   Ask an experienced member of staff how they would deal with the following types of problem customer:
    (a) rude and argumentative customers
    (b) regular customers who demand immediate service when other customers are waiting
    (c) customers who constantly criticise or find fault with the drinks they have been served
    (d) a customer who orders a drink and then changes their mind after you have served it.

RELEVANT LAWS

The laws related to preparing for service and taking orders were mentioned in Element 1 of this Unit. You should also note their relevance to serving drinks at the table.

Licensing laws

Who may you serve?
The licensing laws also restrict the type of people to whom you may sell alcoholic drinks.

When you take an order at the table, not all the people who are to receive the drinks may be present. When you return to the table with the drinks, you should not serve them to any customers who you believe do not comply with the licensing laws. If you have any doubts, return the drinks to the bar and report the incident to your supervisor. You should also be alert during the service session for customers becoming drunk or argumentative and inform your supervisor so that the situation can be dealt with before any major incidents occur.

Essential knowledge	In order to make sure you do not commit an offence against the current licensing laws, you should not sell alcoholic drinks to: • any person at the bar that you suspect is under 18 years of age or any person attempting to buy a drink for them • any person in a restaurant or area put aside for table meals who you suspect is under 16 years of age • a customer who is obviously drunk or any person attempting to buy more drink for that customer to drink on the premises • any customer behaving in a violent or disorderly manner or who is under an exclusion order. You should also not sell alcoholic drinks to be drunk either on or off the premises unless it is within the permitted hours of opening. Failure to comply with the licensing laws may result in your employer (the licensee) being prosecuted, having his licence endorsed and having to pay a fine. After several prosecutions, the licence could be withdrawn and the premises would have to close.

Trade Descriptions Act

Be careful to avoid spillages when carrying a tray. If you spill drink from a glass, you may serve less than the legal measure or quantity advertised.

Serving an under-measure would also be an offence against the Weights and Measures legislation.

Food Safety Act and Food Hygiene Regulations

Any article or equipment that is to come into contact with food or drink including glassware and trays must be kept clean and in good condition. Tray coverings should be replaced and trays washed if they become contaminated by spillages during service.

Health and Safety at Work Act

This Act requires employers to provide a safe and healthy working environment for their employees as far as possible. At the same time, it is the duty of every employee to take reasonable care for the health and safety of him/herself, other members of staff and customers.
- Don't lift loads on trays which are too heavy or overload trays to such an extent that accidents are likely to happen.

Establishment procedures

As well as acting in ways which enable you to comply with the laws and regulations outlined above, you should follow any rules or procedures regarding working practices laid down by your employer.

MAINTAINING EQUIPMENT DURING SERVICE

Glassware

It is important that you check any glasses that you are given by bar staff for lipstick, fingerprints, cracks and chips from the rim and base.
- If you notice any defects in glasses, ask the bar staff to replace the drink, especially with a chipped glass as you cannot be sure when the glass was chipped and whether or not there is glass in the drink.
- Take care when collecting glasses that you use the correct techniques to avoid damaging glasses. See the section on placing and collecting glasses on page 220.

Trays and service linen

As the cleanliness of your service equipment is an important aspect of the presentation of drinks, you should:
- replace any tray coverings whenever they become wet and stained
- wash and clean trays/salvers if you have a spillage on the tray to prevent it becoming sticky and unhygienic.

Pen and note paper/order pad

- Replace note paper or a pad if it becomes wet and stained.
- Have a spare pen available in case the one you are using runs out.

Essential knowledge	It is important to check that all service equipment is clean and free from damage:

It is important to check that all service equipment is clean and free from damage:
- to offer a quick and efficient service to customers
- to be able to serve customers their drinks in a safe and hygienic manner
- to maintain a positive impression with customers about the quality of service your establishment offers
- to prevent accidents or injuries to staff or customers
- to comply with health and safety and food hygiene regulations.

OBTAINING THE DRINKS

Having obtained your customers' orders and recorded these on note paper or a pad, take the order to the issuing point for drinks in your establishment.

Ordering/dispensing mixed orders of drinks

1 Order/begin dispense of highly carbonated draught products like lagers or Guinness. The head on these drinks needs time to settle before the glass is topped up.
2 Order/dispense spirits, liqueurs, still wines and pure fruit juices next. These are not carbonated.
3 Order/pour bottled beers, soft drinks and open mixers like tonic water. These are quite highly carbonated and will lose their head or sparkle quite slowly.
4 Add ice to spirits and other drinks, top up highly carbonated draught products.
5 Order/dispense low carbonated draught products last. These lose their head quickly and you should aim to serve them with as good a head as possible.

> **MEMORY JOGGER**
>
> In what sequence should you ask for an order of drinks involving draught beers, spirits, mixers and soft drinks?

Ordering cocktails

Note that:
- if cocktails are included in a mixed order for drinks, the cocktails should be made after the other drinks have been poured. Cocktails should be served as freshly made as possible
- if you have a mixed order for cocktails, you should order the long drinks over ice to be made first and the short, cold cocktails served without ice to be made last
- glasses should not be filled to the brim. This can make them difficult to carry and serve and could stain the customer's clothing.

SERVING A RANGE OF DRINKS

Loading and carrying a tray/salver

It is important to know how to load and carry a tray or salver correctly. The tray or salver is balanced on the palm and outspread fingers of the left hand, because drinks are normally served and cleared from the right-hand side of the customer.

When loading the tray, try to keep the tray in balance.
- Do not load all the glasses and bottles on one side of the tray otherwise it will be difficult to balance.
- If you are serving in an area set apart for table meals, place the heaviest items like bottles of liqueurs and spirits close to your body or above your wrist so that you can give the tray some support.
- When loading a tray of poured drinks at the bar, place the heaviest items like pints of draught beer in the centre over the balance point and lighter items around the edges.

> **MEMORY JOGGER**
>
> What is it important to remember when loading a tray/salver and serving drinks from it?

● When distributing drinks from the tray, lift the heaviest items first. Do not unload all the drinks from one side only. Keep the tray balanced by lifting drinks from different sides alternately. See the diagram below.

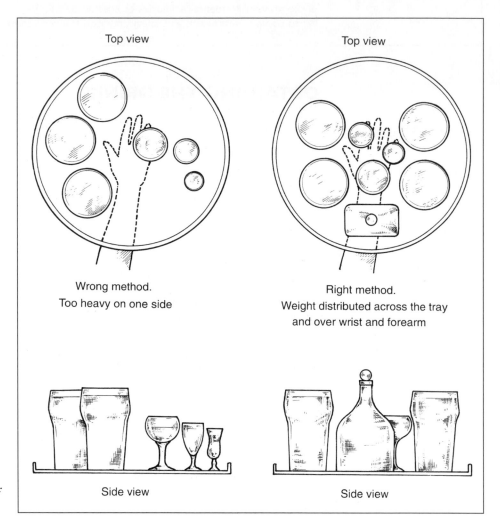

Top view

Top view

Wrong method.
Too heavy on one side

Right method.
Weight distributed across the tray
and over wrist and forearm

Side view

Side view

Right and wrong methods of loading a tray

Placing and collecting glassware

● Handle stemmed glasses by the stem using the thumb and forefinger. Straight-sided glassware should be held by the base or low down.
● Do not place or clear glasses by putting your hand over the top of the glass or by putting your fingers inside a glass.
● When clearing glasses, do not place glasses inside one another as this can lead to cracking and chipping.
● Remove glasses from tables as soon as they are empty.
● Glasses should be placed on and cleared from the table to the *right* of the customer whenever possible.

For examples of the types of glasses used for different drinks and the right and wrong ways of placing and clearing them, see Unit 2NC8 pages 170 and 197.

Serving draught beers and ciders

These are served in glasses or tankards which should either:
● bear a government stamp and a quantity marking, and/or
● have the required fill level marked by a line on the glass.

● Ales like bitter and mild are served at a temperature of 12–15.5°C.
● Lagers and ciders are served chilled at 7–10°C.
● Highly chilled beers like Budweiser are served at 3–6°C.

Cold and chilled beers should be served on a coaster as condensation forms on the outside of the glass and runs to the base of the glass.

Serving bottled beer and cider

Bottled beers and ciders should be served in a glass which holds a larger amount than the bottle capacity. A 33 cl bottle of beer, for example, should be served in a glass with a 36–38 cl capacity to allow space for the head.
● Don't use any bottle if the neck rim is chipped.
● Don't handle any bottle by the neck.
● If the drink is partly poured into a glass, place the bottle beside the glass on the table.
● Place a coaster or drip mat beneath cold or chilled beers and ciders to collect any condensation that runs to the base of the glass or bottle.

Serving wine by the glass

Wine is normally served in a tulip-shaped glass or a Paris goblet of 15–20 cl capacity. A glass marked with a line showing the correct fill height should be used if the wine is not delivered from an optic or thimble measure.

White wine is usually served at cellar temperature (about 13°C) or lightly chilled at about 10°C. Red wine is served at room temperature.

Do this

1 Observe an experienced member of staff giving an order at the dispense point. Ask them if they use any particular sequence when giving the order to the bar person.
2 Find out what method is used in your establishment when dispensing wine by the glass.

Serving spirits

These are often served with mixers or minerals, ice and other accompaniments. A Paris goblet is normally used.
● Whisky is usually served with soda water or plain water, but may also be served with dry ginger ale or lemonade. Offer ice and water if no mixer is ordered.
● White spirits like gin, vodka, white rums and tequila are served with ice and lemon or lime. Common mixers are tonic water, lemonade and cola. A larger glass like a Slim Jim is used when cola is ordered as a mixer.

Obtain your order and a supply of coasters/drip mats and:
● carry the glasses and any bottles of mixers or syphon to the table
● place a coaster/drip mat before each customer
● if possible, serve the eldest ladies first, then the youngest ladies; the eldest gentlemen, then the youngest and, finally, the host or person who ordered the drinks
● place the glasses on the table and ask the customer if he or she would like you to pour the mixer for them. If they agree, you should pour in the mixer steadily until they tell you to stop
● place the bottle on the table if there is any liquid left in it.

Brandy

Some customers may prefer to take brandy in the same way as whisky described above. In this case, it should be served in a Paris goblet.

If customers in a hotel lounge or meal area request a liqueur brandy after a meal, it should be served in a brandy balloon. Customers may request that the glass be warmed for them.

● Use hot water to heat the glass. Empty, wipe and polish the glass before pouring in the brandy.
● Name the brandy to your customer when serving it. For example, 'Your Hennessy X.O., Sir/Madam.'

Serving liqueurs

There is no standard legal measure for liqueurs and the quantity served will vary from establishment to establishment. They may be served in the normal fashion or they may be offered to customers as being served frappé (over crushed ice) or flamed.

● When using an unlined liqueur glass, you should fill it to just below the rim to avoid spillage or allow flaming.

If you are asked to serve liqueurs at the table in a meal area, bring the bottles and glasses to the table on a large salver, present the appropriate bottle and pour the correct measure into the glass in front of the customer. Handle the glass by the base or stem and place it to the right of the coffee cup, but not too close to the edge of the table.

Serving cocktails

The two most important elements of the service of cocktails are that almost all are drunk cold and they should be served as fresh as possible.

● Carry them carefully to avoid spillages or dislodging any fruit decorations or garnishes.
● Name each cocktail to the customer as you serve it.
● As condensation will develop on the glasses, they should be placed on coasters or drip mats if possible.

Serving soft drinks, minerals and juices

Not all customers will wish to take an alcoholic drink. The main types of soft drink you may be required to serve are:

● fruit squashes, such as orange or lemon barley and crushes
● natural mineral waters, such as Vichy, Evian, Ballygowan or Perrier
● manufactured minerals (often used as mixers), such as soda or tonic water, dry ginger ale, lemonade and bitter lemon
● pure fruit juices, such as orange, pineapple and tomato juice.

Presentation of soft drinks

Soft drinks should be presented well.

● They should be served in an interesting shape of glass.
● Offer ice, lemon and straws with long drinks.
● Add orange slices to colas.
● Add wedges of orange or lemon to the rim of the glasses containing fruit drinks.

As well as fruit garnishes and ice, you should decorate soft drinks with swords, stirrers and miniature umbrellas to give them a cocktail appearance.

Serving hot drinks

In winter, customers may request hot drinks like toddies made from whisky, rum or port. However, the hot drink most frequently requested after a meal is some type of speciality coffee. These consist of a base spirit, white or Demerara sugar, hot black coffee and cream floated on the surface.
- Ask the customer if they prefer their drink sweetened or unsweetened.
- Ask the customer about accompaniments such as lemon, cloves, or cinnamon with toddies and punches.
- If the customer is being served a speciality coffee in a lounge, provide him/her with a paper napkin as the cream may stick to their upper lip.

PROVIDING ACCURATE INFORMATION ON DRINKS

Occasions may arise during service when customers request information about other products offered by the establishment. The need to provide accurate information has been dealt with in Element 1 of this Unit and you were advised to watch for buying signals from customers.
- If you notice customers reading promotional literature or beverage lists, you can ask them if they would like to try a particular drink.
- If customers' attention is drawn to an attractively presented drink like a cocktail, you should inform them of the ingredients and the price and offer to have one prepared for them. Ask them if they would like to see the cocktail or beverage list if one is available.

You should also be prepared to answer questions if customers:
- query the price they have been charged for drinks
- query the amount of change they have been given
- ask if they have received the correct drink
- ask for suggestions for a different or interesting drink
- ask about the strength of cocktails, low-alcohol or 'light' drinks

It is important that any answer you give is honest and accurate. Remember, it is an offence to give a false or misleading description of any drink you offer.

Essential knowledge	It is important that you give your customers accurate information about the drinks you serve them: ● to comply with the Trade Descriptions Act and other consumer laws ● to prevent customers becoming dissatisfied, feeling cheated or misled ● to prevent customers consuming a larger quantity of alcohol than they wish, especially when drinking cocktails, 'light' or low-alcohol products ● to ensure that customers receive an efficient and high-quality service. However you should not reveal any confidential information related to any speciality products offered by your establishment or details such as trade or cost prices of drinks or profit margins.

DEALING WITH CUSTOMER COMPLAINTS OR INCIDENTS

The main points to remember when dealing with customer complaints or incidents are as follows:
- Deal with those that you can within your responsibility and report the complaint or incident and your actions to your supervisor.

- If the complaint or incident is serious or has legal implications, you should always call your supervisor immediately to deal with it.
- Any action you take to resolve a complaint or deal with an incident should be in line with your establishment's policies.

For example:

- If a customer complains about receiving an incorrect drink or flat mineral, you should offer to replace it.
- If a customer queries the price of a drink or complains of receiving incorrect change, you should offer to check the prices and change and make any corrections necessary.

However, if a customer has had property stolen, been injured, complains of short measure or that a drink has been diluted, you should call your supervisor immediately as it may be necessary to involve the emergency services or have quite serious legal implications.

Do this

Find out from your supervisor about your establishment's policies regarding dealing with customer complaints and incidents. Find out what types of incident or complaint:
(a) you have the authority to deal with
(b) you are required to draw to your supervisor's attention to immediately.

Wastages, breakages and spillages

Wastages
Details of any drink that cannot be recovered either because the customer has drunk from the glass, the drink has been mixed or because of a fault in the drink (such as a flat beer or mineral) should be recorded into a spillages or wastage book, which is usually kept at the point of dispense.

Normally, you would enter the date, the drink, the price, the reason for the wastage and your name. You should find out and follow the establishment's procedures regarding wastages.

Breakages and spillages
Clearing up breakages and spillages in customer areas has been dealt with in Unit 2NC8 (pages 196) and reporting breakages of expensive items like bottles of spirits and liqueurs in Unit 2NC6 (pages 108 and 116).

If you are delivering a tray of drinks and an accident occurs, you will have to obtain replacements for any drinks that have been spilled and clear up any breakages.

- Having to replace spilled drinks with no payment will affect the stock control procedures of the establishment as more stock will have been used than cash received.
- Replacing spilled drinks can affect the establishment's profits.

Details of breakages and spillages should be reported to your supervisor and a record kept of the cost of replacing any drinks. This may either be in the form of a receipt for the replacement drinks signed by your supervisor or entering the spillages and their cost into the wastage book. Always follow you establishment's procedures regarding spillages and breakages.

Essential knowledge	You should report all spillages and breakages to your supervisor as soon as possible because:
	<ul><li>it may be necessary for your supervisor to witness any breakages or spillages so that staff cannot be accused of theft</li><li>replacing spilled or broken stock affects the stock control procedures of the establishment and its profits</li><li>it may be possible to recover some of the cost of breakages and spillages if adequate records are kept</li><li>there may be legal implications if customers have been injured or their property or clothing damaged</li><li>replacement stock or equipment may need to be ordered.</li></ul>

Do this	Find out your establishment's policy about reporting spillages and breakages affecting:
	(a) drinks and glassware
	(b) customers' property or clothing.

CUSTOMER BILLING

When guests staying in a hotel order drinks in the lounge or bar and request to have the cost added to their bill, you should:

- obtain the customer's room number
- ask the customer politely to sign the bill – offer them the bill and a pen or pencil on the tray or salver
- take a copy of the bill to the reception area or billing office and check that the person is really a resident if you do not know them.

If a guest refuses to sign the bill, ask the head waiter or barman to initial it to verify the drink has been served.

Lounge service

In normal lounge service, you should advise the customer of the total amount and place any cash on the tray or salver. After the drink has been paid for at the bar, you should return the change and any till receipt to the customer.

- Give change neatly and correctly. Place it in the customer's hand – don't throw it down on the table.
- Don't cadge tips by leaving the change on the tray for the customer to pick up. Some unprofessional staff leave change on a wet tray to discourage customers from taking their change.

Case study	*It was the young barman's first Saturday night serving the tables in the lounge bar and he was really enjoying it. A group of his friends were in and there was a party of eight young women in, one of whom he was very keen to impress. After delivering an order to his friends, he stopped to talk to them for several minutes. An elderly customer tried several times to attract his attention, but he looked away each time. Eventually the elderly woman gave up and went to the bar herself. Later when delivering a round of draught and bottled beers, he lifted the pint glasses off the tray by putting his hand over the top of the glasses to place them. The customers looked at each other, but said nothing and left*

soon after. He hovered around the young women's table and on one occasion sat down in one of the chairs when one of them left the table.

To make up time, he loaded a large tray with the orders for three tables. On his way to deliver them, he stopped again with his friends and began to chat and make jokes. When he turned sharply to go to the first table, he collided with a customer and dropped the fully-laden tray. All the drinks were spilled and most of the glasses were broken.

At the end of the service session, the bar manager, who had been watching him most of the evening, asked him to stay behind because he wished to talk to him.

1   What do you think the bar manager said to the barman?
2   Identify as many of the mistakes the barman made as you can.
3   How should he have dealt with the spillage and breakage situation?

What have you learned?

1   Give three examples of ways in which you can offend customers.
2   State three actions you should take when dealing with over-familiar or flirtatious customers.
3   Why is it important that all your service equipment should be kept clean during service?
4   What types of customers should you not serve alcoholic drinks to?
5   What should you remember when placing and collecting glasses?
6   How should you serve spirits with mixers or minerals?
7   How should you serve liqueurs at a table in a meal area?
8   Why is it important that you give customers accurate information about any drinks that you serve them?
9   What three points should you remember when dealing with customer complaints and incidents?
10 Why should you report all spillages and breakages to your supervisor?

Get ahead

1   Try to obtain a copy of the latest Licensing Act and find out who may not be allowed to remain on the premises and what activities, such as gambling, are not allowed on licensed premises.
2   Obtain a copy of a book on spirits and liqueurs, such as *The Penguin Book of Spirits and Liqueurs* by Pamela Vandyke Price, and find out about spirits and the ingredients of the most popular liqueurs.
3   Obtain a copy of the *International Guide to Drinks* prepared by the United Kingdom Bartenders' Guild and find out the names, ingredients and methods of preparation of the most popular cocktails.
4   Find out the names of the main types of speciality coffee and which spirit or liqueur is used as the base for each one.

UNIT 2NC10

Prepare and serve cocktails

This unit covers:
ELEMENT 1: Prepare areas and equipment for serving cocktails
ELEMENT 2: Serve cocktails

ELEMENT 1: Prepare areas and equipment for serving cocktails

What you need to do

- Ensure that all work areas are clean tidy and ready for use.
- Make sure that all equipment is clean and free from damage.
- Prepare a range of ingredients and store them ready for use.
- Obtain and prepare a supply of accompaniments and store them ready for service.
- Deal effectively with unexpected situations and inform the appropriate people where necessary.
- Carry out your duties in an organised and efficient manner taking account of priorities, organisational procedures and legal requirements.

What you need to know

- What the main types of cocktails and mixed drinks are and methods of preparing them.
- What equipment you will need to assemble to prepare for service.
- What the main ingredients of cocktails are and how to prepare and store them.
- What the main accompaniments are and how to prepare and store them.
- How to deal effectively with unexpected situations.
- How to carry out your work in an organised and efficient manner.

INTRODUCTION

The first written reference to 'cocktail' as a name for a drink appeared in an American magazine in 1806. Many stories have grown around the origin of the word. Whatever the origin, cocktails are exotic drinks requiring greater skill in preparation and service than most others offered by the licensed trade.

THE MAIN TYPES OF COCKTAILS

The cocktails of the 1920s were short, iced mixed drinks based on a spirit such as gin, brandy or whisky and which usually contained two or three liquids. The ingredients were mixed together, either by shaking, stirring or building, according to a recipe.

Many of the recipes which were developed around the 1920s and 1930s have three elements: a spirit base, a sweet element and a bitter or sour element. The table on page 228 lists some traditional cocktail recipes.

Cocktail	Spirit base	Sweetening	Bitter/sour
Manhattan	$\frac{2}{3}$ rye whisky	$\frac{1}{3}$ sweet vermouth	1 dash Angostura bitters
Sidecar	$\frac{1}{2}$ brandy	$\frac{1}{4}$ Cointreau	$\frac{1}{4}$ lemon juice
Rob Roy	$\frac{1}{2}$ Scotch whisky	$\frac{1}{2}$ sweet vermouth	1 dash Angostura bitters
White Lady	$\frac{1}{2}$ gin	$\frac{1}{4}$ Cointreau	$\frac{1}{4}$ lemon

Traditional cocktail recipes

These short drinks are still what some bartenders would consider the 'true' cocktail. However, to the general public any mixed drink, whether short or long is thought of as a cocktail.

There are a large number of recipes for these drinks – over 9000 have been created – and, in some cases, the recipes differ even for cocktails of the same name. Many of the recipes have been grouped together and the main groups are given in the table below.

Group	Example
Blended drinks	Blue Hawaiian, Pina Colada
Champagne cocktails	Black Velvet, Bucks Fizz
Cobblers	Whisky Cobbler
Collins/coolers and fizzes	Tom Collins, Rum Cooler, Gin Fizz
Cups	Pimms No. 1
Daiquiris	Daiquiri, Banana Daiquiri
Flips and noggs	Egg Nogg, Brandy Flip
Frappés	Creme de Menthe Frappé
Highballs	Cuba Libre, Horse's Neck
Juleps	Mint Julep
Martinis	Dry Martini, Gibson
Pick-me-ups	Prairie Oyster
Pousse Cafe	Rainbow Cocktail
Slings	Gin Sling, Singapore Sling
Sours	Whisky Sour

The main types of cocktails and mixed drinks

Non-alcoholic cocktails

While the common idea of a cocktail is a drink based on a spirit, there are a number of non-alcoholic drinks which are also made and called cocktails or 'mocktails'. Typical of these are the Parson's Special, Pussyfoot and Shirley Temple.

Hot toddies and punches

While these are not thought of as cocktails because they are served hot, they are mixed drinks which are often popular in cold weather.

There are other ways of grouping cocktails and mixed drinks and these will be mentioned later in the section on promoting cocktails.

Methods of preparing cocktails and mixed drinks

There are four main methods of making cocktails:

- stirring
- shaking
- building
- blending.

Each of these methods will be explained in more detail in Element 2, pages 246–50.

First, however, you will need to ensure that you have all the necessary equipment, ingredients and accompaniments ready to use before service starts. We will consider these in this Element.

Do this ✔

1 Make a copy of the cocktails listed in the tables opposite. Tick off those which are offered in your establishment.
2 Find a book containing cocktail recipes. For each of the cocktails in the second table opposite, find out which spirit is used as the base.
3 Using the list you created in the first activity and a book of cocktail recipes, put next to each name whether it is shaken, stirred, built or blended.

PREPARE YOUR WORK AREA

Before each service session, it is important that the work area and all the equipment you will need is clean and in good condition.

Back bar, counter and under-counter

MEMORY JOGGER

How should you lay out your bar before service starts?

Not only is the bar the showcase for your skills and where you display your stock and equipment, it is also your work area where you will prepare and assemble all the ingredients that you will use to make cocktails. As it is a food preparation area under the terms of the Food Safety and Food Hygiene regulations, it must be kept clean and hygienic at all times.

- Clean all working surfaces with an appropriate detergent-sterilant. Move bottles from the back bar to clean beneath them.
- Wipe bottles with a damp cloth, if necessary, and polish them with a dry glass cloth.

After you have assembled and checked your equipment (pages 230–5) and prepared and stored your ingredients and accompaniments (pages 235–9), you should set out your bar in the most attractive way possible. It is also important to lay out your equipment, ingredients and accompaniments neatly to allow an efficient work flow.

- Lay out your equipment on drip trays or plastic glass mats, not on working surfaces.
- Make sure that all stainless steel or silver-plated equipment is thoroughly clean and polished with a dry cloth to remove smears. Your equipment should shine.
- Place polished steel and silver items where the bar lighting can reach them and make them shine.
- Group different types and sizes of glasses separately. Set them out in different patterns – squares, circles, diamonds, V-shapes. Place them where the bar lighting can reflect off them.
- Set out any bar snacks on the counter. Salty items like peanuts, crisps and pretzels help make the customer thirsty and more inclined to buy. Replenish and freshen as necessary.

However, before you can reach this state of preparation, you will need to perform a range of checks and activities.

A mixing glass, bar muddler spoon and strainer

ASSEMBLE AND CHECK YOUR EQUIPMENT

Before service starts, you must check that all the equipment that you will need is available and is clean and free from damage.

A mixing glass

There are several forms of mixing glass, the commonest looking like a straight-sided jug without a handle. Some may be tapered like a cone or be in the form of a large brandy balloon. The mixing glass should have a pouring lip (see the diagram).
● Check for fingerprints, smears, chips and cracks. Wash, if necessary. Polish with a clean, dry glass cloth.

Cocktail shakers

Two types of cocktail shaker are in general use:
● the Boston shaker
● the standard shaker.

Shakers may be made from stainless steel, plated silver, glass or plastic.

Boston shaker
This consists of two flat-ended cones which join together with an overlap. It is preferred by many professional cocktail-makers and is suited to making large quantities of a particular cocktail.

Standard shaker
This consists of three parts: a cone-shaped base, a top with a built-in strainer and a cap. It is generally used to make a single cocktail rather than large quantities. (See the diagram.)

● Check that all components are present.
● Clean with the appropriate detergent or cleaning agent and polish with a clean, dry glass cloth

Blender or liquidiser

There are several types which operate at various speeds. They are used in making cocktails that need fruit to be reduced to a paste or purée.
● Wash the jug thoroughly before service starts and check that all parts are operating properly. Report any faults to your supervisor.

Strainers

The most popular type of strainer is the Hawthorn. This has a coil spring around the outer edge which will allow the strainer to fit neatly when pushed into the neck of a Boston Shaker. It is also used when a cocktail is being poured from a mixing glass or blender. (See diagram opposite.) Other larger-headed strainers with two lugs which fit over the edge of the shaker are also used.
● As strainers can become sticky, soak them thoroughly before service starts, rinse and then dry them as completely as possible.

Bar or muddler spoon

This is a long spoon (which is usually made from stainless steel) with a twisted shaft and a circular, flat disc on the opposite end from the spoon. The flat muddler end is

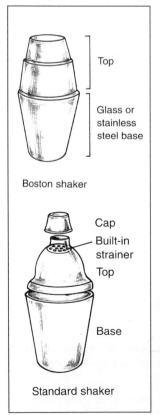

Top

Glass or stainless steel base

Boston shaker

Cap
Built-in strainer
Top

Base

Standard shaker

Boston and standard shakers

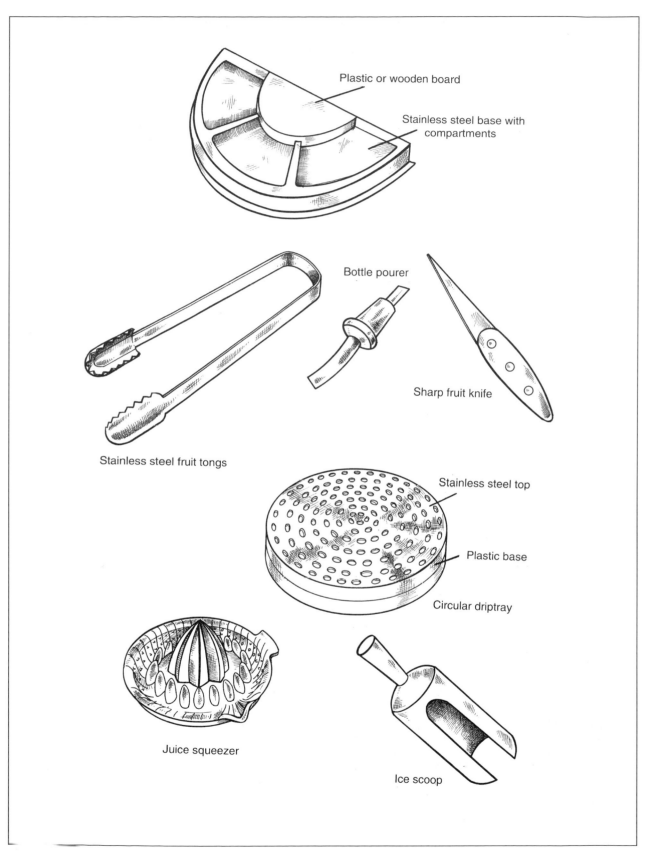

Plastic or wooden board

Stainless steel base with compartments

Bottle pourer

Sharp fruit knife

Stainless steel fruit tongs

Stainless steel top

Plastic base

Circular driptray

Juice squeezer

Ice scoop

Basic bar equipment

used to crush sugar lumps and fresh mint in certain cocktails. It is used with the mixing glass. (See diagram on page 230.)
- Clean with the appropriate cleaning agent, polish and place in or near the mixing glass.

Pourers

As legal measures from optics or thimble measures are sometimes not used in making cocktails, pourers are used on the tops of opened bottles of frequently-used drinks such as spirits, vermouth and cordials. They are usually made of either plastic or stainless steel.
- Plastic pourers are commonly used for fruit juices and cordials as the acid in the fruit can react with metal.
- Soak thoroughly and clean through with a long, thin brush to remove any syrup or sugary residues.

Cutting board and knife

A cutting board and a small sharp knife are needed to prepare oranges, lemons and other fruit. Because of the Food Hygiene laws, plastic chopping boards are now preferred to wooden boards as they are easier to sterilise. (See the diagram on page 231.)
- Wash with a detergent-sterilant. Polish stainless steel with a clean, dry glass cloth.

Fruit squeezers

There are several types and sizes of these. They include the hand-held squeezers for a single wedge, the traditional glass or stainless steel counter model (see the diagram on page 231) and the bar press strainer. Electric juice makers are becoming more common.
- Clean with an appropriate sterilant. Check that all mechanical or electrical equipment is operating correctly and report any faults.

Ice crusher, containers and scoops

As a good supply of ice of different types is required, a manual ice crusher is extremely useful. Several containers ('buckets') may be required and these should be insulated if they are to sit on the bar counter.

A stainless steel ice scoop can be used to provide a reasonable quantity of ice quickly. Ice tongs and spoons are convenient when one or two cubes are being placed in a glass.
- As ice is used in making, or as an ingredient in, most cocktails, any equipment in contact with it must be kept as clean and sterile as possible. Ensure all equipment is clean both inside and outside.

Drip trays

A number of drip trays are necessary. They can be used to store the spirit measures and shakers upside down to drain them after rinsing and as a base for pouring drinks into the glasses. Circular or rectangular stainless steel drip trays are widely used.
- Clean with an appropriate sterilant and polish with a clean, dry glass cloth.

Glassware

A good selection of glasses is an important part of the equipment needed for serving cocktails as the appearance of the drink in the glass is an essential part of the cocktail's presentation. Ideally, the bar should have a number of the following styles (for examples, see the following two diagrams):

- the classic V-shaped cocktail glass, often called a Martini glass, holding 4 fl. oz/ 12 cl
- the double cocktail glass which may be V-shaped or have a curved bowl holding 6–7 fl. oz/17.5–20 cl
- Paris goblet holding 8 fl. oz/22.5 cl, which is a good all-purpose glass
- Old Fashioned glass – a wide, short, straight-sided glass ideal for serving spirits or clear cocktails over ice
- Highball glass, a large, straight-sided tumbler, holding 8–12 fl. oz/22.5–35 cl, which is used to serve many long mixed drinks The similar shaped Slim Jim glass is also useful.
- champagne flute and saucer glasses.

Other glasses commonly found in the bar such as the 2–3 fl. oz/6–9 cl liqueur and small brandy balloons are also useful.

Champagne flute

White wine, sour or general purpose glass

Highball glass

Old Fashioned glass

Large goblet

Paris goblet

Brandy balloon

A variety of glasses suitable for serving cocktails

- It is essential that you check all glassware that you intend to use. Look carefully for lipstick and grease smears, fingerprints, cracks or chipped rims.
- Polish the glassware. Hold the base with one end of a dry glass cloth and place the glass over a bowl of hot water until the steam condenses on the glass. Polish the bowl with the other end of the cloth. Use a new dry cloth when the first one becomes too damp. Your glassware should sparkle.

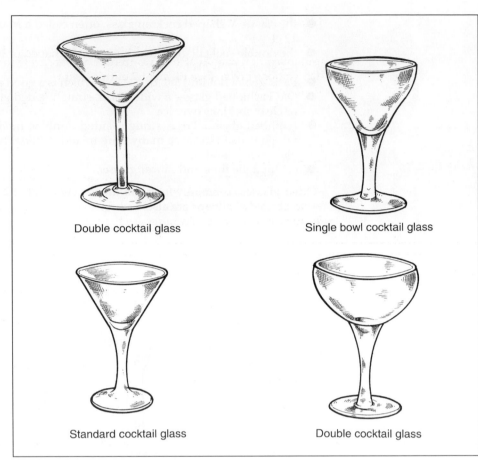

Double and single cocktail glasses (V-shaped and bowl)

Double cocktail glass   Single bowl cocktail glass

Standard cocktail glass   Double cocktail glass

Jugs

A number of small jugs for holding freshly-squeezed juices, eggs, cream and milk are required. These should be cleaned and sterilised before use with the appropriate detergent-sterilant.

Other basic equipment

Apart from the items mentioned above, you should also have:
- a 'waiter's friend' and corkscrews
- a crown cork bottle opener
- fruit tongs or fork
- small bottles to hold liquids for sprinkling
- saucers or shallow bowls
- a wine cooler
- spirit measures
- champagne stopper
- glass cloths
- coasters
- a grater
- pen/pencil and pad
- lighter or matches.

Cocktail list/menu

Any list of cocktails that are offered by your establishment should be clean and undamaged. It should also be up-to-date and accurate in relation to prices and any descriptions given. (See Element 2 of this Unit.)

● Display lists prominently either at the bar, on tables or with other food and beverage lists.

Essential knowledge	It is important to keep preparation areas and equipment clean and hygienic when preparing cocktails: ● to prevent any items of food or drink which come into contact with them from becoming contaminated and making customers ill ● to comply with the Food Safety and Food Hygiene Regulations ● to provide a high quality of service to your customers.

Do this	1 Make a list of the equipment in the section above. Tick off each item that you find in your establishment. Add any extra items that you find which are not on the list.
	2 Find out what styles of glassware are available. Try to obtain some estimate of the capacity of each type of glass either in fluid ounces (fl. oz), centilitres (cl) or millilitres (ml).
	3 Find out how the equipment used for making cocktails is cleaned.
	   (a) Which items are cleaned by hand and which by machine?
	   (b) What sterilising or cleaning agents are used? Make a list and note what equipment each agent is used for.
	4 Draw a diagram of the counter and back section of the bar. Show where the items of equipment used for making cocktails are placed ready for service.

PREPARE YOUR INGREDIENTS

Make sure that you have a sufficient supply of all the basic ingredients that you will require for preparing the cocktails on offer. Each day before service starts, you should assemble the following :

● **alcoholic and non-alcoholic drinks** Requisition any new stock of drinks you require from the cellar.

● **cream, milk and eggs** Make sure you have a fresh supply of these. They should be stored in the refrigerator in small jugs sealed with cling film.

● **sugar and salt** Make sure that caster sugar and salt are loose and dry and not caked. Replenish cube sugar, if necessary.

● **fresh fruit juices** Warm a small number of lemons, limes and oranges in a bowl of hot water. Squeeze out the juice and store in small jugs in the refrigerator.

● **fresh fruit** Some blended cocktails like Banana or Strawberry Daiquiris require fresh fruit to be used as part of the recipe. Depending on the type of cocktails you offer, you should obtain a supply of fresh fruit to meet your needs during service. Also see the section on food garnishes below.

Quick tip	**Eggs** ● Break eggs into a glass first before using them in cocktails. If an egg is not fresh, it is better to find this out before you add it to the other ingredients. ● Put egg white into a small jug and chop it with a sharp knife. This will prevent all of it pouring out as one piece and allow you to use small amounts as required. ● Use fresh eggs each day. Do not store whites or yolks overnight for use the next day. Eggs are easily contaminated and you may cause food poisoning.

Alcohol, soft drinks and bottled fruit juices

To be able to produce all 9000 or more cocktails would require a large stock of spirits, liqueurs and other ingredients to be kept behind the bar. Some would not be used very often. However, a basic stock of cocktail ingredients will allow a wide range of cocktails to be offered (see the table below).

Spirits Brandy Scotch whisky Irish whiskey Bourbon Whiskey Canadian Whisky Gin Vodka Rum (white, golden, dark) Tequila	**Bitters** Angostura Orange
	Syrups and cordials Grenadine Lime cordial Peppermint cordial Sugar syrup
Liqueurs Cointreau Curacao Crème de Menthe (green, white) Tia Maria or Kahlua Chartreuse (green, yellow) Crème de Cacao (white, brown) Southern Comfort Malibu Galliano Advocaat Pernod	**Juices** Fresh lemon and orange juice Tomato juice Pineapple juice
	Soft drinks Soda water Tonic water Ginger ale Bitter lemon Cola Lemonade Ginger beer
Sparkling wines Champagne Asti Spumante	**Sauces** Worcestershire Tabasco Tomato ketchup Vinegar
Fortified and aromatised wines Sherry (fino, cream) Port (ruby, tawny) Vermouth (dry, sweet) Campari Dubonnet	**Other ingredients** Egg white and yolk Sugar cubes Caster sugar Salt Cream

A basic bar stock for preparing cocktails

Do this ✔

Using the list of materials in the table above, tick off each item that you find in the bars of your workplace.

Pre-prepared mixes

Some cocktails like Pimms No. 1 are based on the use of pre-prepared mixes which come in a bottle. Occasionally, where fresh ingredients for the more exotic cocktails are not available, a pre-prepared mix for cocktails like Pina Colada may be used, but this is not really desirable.

Breakages or spillages

If there are any problems related to spillages from or breakages of bottles of spirits or liqueurs, you should:

- call your supervisor to witness the breakage/spillage as proof that it occurred
- complete any record that is kept in the bar of breakages or spillages
- carefully remove any broken glass following your establishment's procedures
- clean the area thoroughly and place a 'Wet Floor' sign, if necessary.

Essential knowledge	It is important that you have all the ingredients that you will require prepared and ready to use before service starts:
	● to ensure that all the cocktails advertised can be made to order
	● to enable you to provide a quick, efficient service to customers
	● to promote and maintain customer satisfaction with your establishment's products and services.

PREPARE YOUR ACCOMPANIMENTS

As well as having taste appeal, an important feature of the cocktail is that it should also have eye appeal. The presentation of the drink is extremely important.

The main aim of the use of accompaniments is to decorate the drink and improve its appearance. They can be placed either in or on the glass.

- It is important that the accompaniments either complement or contrast with the drink.
- You should not over-decorate drinks with accompaniments that contribute little or nothing to the taste.

The main accompaniments used in the preparation of cocktails and mixed drinks are:

- ice
- food garnishes
- decorative items
- salt or sugar rims.

There are standard accompaniments to some of the more famous cocktails, such as a spiral of lemon zest with a Horse's Neck, a stick of celery with a Bloody Mary and a sprig of fresh mint with a Mint Julep. It is important that you learn which are the appropriate accompaniments for the drinks that you offer and ensure that you have an adequate supply.

Ice

Ice serves three important purposes in preparing and presenting cocktails:

- it chills the liquids down to the correct serving temperature
- it improves the appearance of the liquid in the glass
- when crushed ice is used in a blended cocktail, it thickens the drink giving it more body.

Three types of ice are commonly used in making cocktails:

- ice cubes
- cracked ice
- crushed ice.

Whichever type is used, it should be clear and clean. Ice on the point of melting is of little use as it will dilute the drink. Flaked ice should not be used as it tends to melt quickly. Flaked ice which has been brought in often contains impurities.

You should always have a good supply of ice and it should be made well in advance of the time it will be required. It can be stored either in an insulated counter-top bucket, a plastic container in the fridge or in a large metal or plastic bucket under the counter.

Food garnishes

Most of these can be considered as edible decorations. They may be placed in or on the glass. They include:
● citrus fruits
● other fruits and vegetables
● herbs, spices and beans
● flaked chocolate.

Citrus fruits

Lemons, oranges and limes are the most commonly used food garnishes. Their freshly squeezed juice is an essential ingredient in many cocktails. They are used in several ways:
● cut into wedges, slices or half-slices
● zest – a small thin piece of the skin with as little of the white pith as possible. This is squeezed over the drink to extract the oils. It may or may not be placed in the drink
● twist – a long strip of zest, twisted in the centre, and often dropped into the drink
● spiral – the complete peel of the fruit cut in a spiral pattern and placed in the glass.

When preparing citrus fruits, you should remember the following points.
● Always use good-quality fruits as fresh as possible.
● Remove any sticky labels and clean the skin thoroughly before use.
● Fruit used for garnishing should be cut fairly thickly if it is to sit on the glass. Thin slices and half-slices can be placed in the drink.
● Warm fruit will give more juice than cold fruit. Soak it in hot water before squeezing.
● Prepare a small supply of lemon and orange wedges and slices on the cutting board. Store these in covered containers to keep them fresh. If they are left in the trays of the chopping board, they will soon lose their freshness.

Fruit cut into slices or twists can be kept fresh if covered with a plastic film and kept in the refrigerator. However, fruit which is kept too long will discolour a drink, causing it to be returned. Use freshly-prepared fruit whenever possible.

Quick tip

Use of substitutes
Where a cocktail recipe requires the use of fresh fruit juice, you can use a substitute if the real juice is not available.
Acceptable substitutes are:
● bottled fresh lemon juice
● bottled or packed fresh orange juice

Other fruits and vegetables

A number of other fruits and vegetables are often used as garnishes. These include:
● red Maraschino cherries
● pineapples
● olives, both black and green
● apples

- bananas
- pearl onions
- strawberries
- celery (Bloody Mary)
- cucumber peel (Pimms).

Check that you have an adequate supply of bottled and fresh fruit. Check the 'best before' or 'sell by' date on bottled fruits and vegetables. Mark the opening date on bottles to ensure that they are used before they become stale or go off.

Herbs, spices and beans
A variety of these are also used in some recipes including:
- fresh mint
- cloves
- cinnamon
- celery salt
- nutmeg
- coffee beans.

Flaked chocolate
This is broken over the top of some drinks that have cream floated on top.

Decorative items

As well as a variety of edible decorations, there should also be a variety of decorative items. These are used to:
- secure the food garnishes so that the customer does not have to put his or her fingers into the glass
- keep the food garnishes in the correct position on or in the glass
- allow the customer to stir ('swizzle') a long drink if the components begin to separate
- add to the eye appeal of the cocktail.

A supply should be kept of cocktail swords, miniature umbrellas, plastic or wire-based animals and figures, plastic swizzle sticks and wrapped straws.

Be careful not to over-decorate the cocktail. Too much decoration takes attention away from the drink itself.

Salt and sugar rims
The rim of the glass used to serve the cocktail can be given a frosted appearance by the use of salt or sugar. To give a glass a frosted rim, you should:
1 Rub the rim of the glass with a piece of cut lemon or dip it in a saucer of lightly beaten egg-white
2 Dip the rim into a saucer or dish containing fine, loose salt or caster sugar.

Salt rims are not suitable for all cocktails. They are mainly used for cocktails based on tequila, such as the Margarita.

Essential knowledge	In order to work safely when preparing to serve cocktails, you should: ● ensure that all electrical equipment is switched off and unplugged before attempting to clean it ● operate all electrical equipment safely following the manufacturer's instructions ● handle knives carefully when preparing fruit for garnishes and for use in the blender ● clean up any spillages on the bar floor immediately ● keep passageways clear while re-stocking shelves ● dispose of broken glass correctly following your establishment's procedures.

Do this ✔

1 Find out how ice is made in your establishment. How is crushed ice prepared?
2 How is prepared ice stored during service times?
3 Make a list of the food garnishes and decorative items used to prepare cocktails in your establishment.

Case study

On New Year's Day, a young barman arrived late, ten minutes before opening time, at the cocktail bar of a large hotel. The bar was completely disorganised after a staff party which had gone on until the early hours of the morning. Most of the equipment was unwashed and sticky, bottles had been left with their caps off and the fridge had been switched off and was defrosting, spreading water all over the bar floor. He decided to give priority to cleaning the equipment and had only just started when the first customer arrived as soon as the bar opened at 11.00 a.m. The customer, a resident, ordered a Prairie Oyster to help cure his hangover. As there had been no time to obtain fresh supplies of ingredients, the barman used a raw egg which had been broken onto a plate and left in the fridge overnight.

The customer drank most of his drink and then returned it complaining that it tasted and smelled unpleasant. Two days later the hotel was visited by an Environmental Health Officer after he had received a complaint from the customer who was suffering from food poisoning as a result of his drink in the cocktail bar.

1 How did the state of the bar contribute to the case of food poisoning?
2 How did the barman's priorities help to cause the problem?
3 What should his priorities have been?

What have you learned?

1 What are the three elements used in cocktails developed in the 1920s and 1930s?
2 What are the three main pieces of equipment used to make cocktails?
3 How can you polish glasses by hand?
4 (a) What is the main aim of the use of accompaniments?
  (b) What are the four main types used?
5 State the three main types of ice used for making cocktails.
6 What are the four main types of citrus fruit garnishes?
7 Give four uses of decorative items when making cocktails.

ELEMENT 2: Serve cocktails

What you need to do

● Deal with customers in a polite and helpful way at all times.
● Serve customers as soon as possible.
● Serve alcoholic drinks only to those people who you are permitted to serve by law.
● Give customers accurate information about any cocktail that you are serving.
● Promote cocktails to customers at the appropriate times.
● Make sure that you understand what the customer wants and clear up any misunderstandings.
● Prepare and serve cocktails according to the customer's demands.
● Serve cocktails in the correct glasses with suitable accompaniments.
● Deal effectively with unexpected situations within your responsibilities and inform the appropriate people where necessary.
● Carry out your duties in an organised and efficient manner taking account of priorities, organisational procedures and legal requirements.

*What you need
to know*

- What type of customers may not be served alcoholic drinks and why.
- Why legal measures must be used to serve some alcoholic drinks.
- Why customers must be given accurate information about the cocktails being served.
- How to promote cocktails to your customers.

- How to prepare and serve a range of cocktails.
- How to deal effectively with unexpected situations.
- How to carry out your work in an organised and efficient manner.

THE PREPARATION AND SERVICE OF COCKTAILS AND MIXED DRINKS

Dealing with customers and the laws governing the licensed trade have been dealt with in previous units. However, there are some aspects related to making cocktails that you should be aware of.

Before continuing with this unit, you should re-read the early sections of Unit 2NC8, Element 1 and Unit 2NC9, Element 1 to refresh your memory, if necessary.

---

*Essential
knowledge*

In order to make sure that you do not commit an offence against the current licensing laws, you should not sell alcoholic drinks to:

- any person in the bar that you suspect is under 18 years of age or any person attempting to buy drink for them
- any person in a restaurant or area put aside for taking meals who you suspect is under 16 years of age
- a customer who is obviously drunk or any person attempting to buy more drink for that customer to drink on the premises
- any customer behaving in a violent or disorderly manner or who is under an exclusion order.

You should also not sell alcoholic drinks to be drunk either on or off the premises unless it is within the permitted hours of opening of the licence.

If you do serve any of the customers described above or serve alcoholic drink outside the permitted hours, your employer (the licensee) can be prosecuted and have their licence endorsed as well as having to pay a substantial fine.

Weights and measures laws

The Weights and Measures Acts state that gin, whisky, rum and vodka must be sold in legal measures of 25 or 35 ml or in multiples, such as double or treble measures. However, there are two exceptions which are especially important to the preparation and service of cocktails and mixed drinks.

- If the drink is a mixture of three or more liquids, you do not need to use a legal measure when serving spirits.
- You do not have to use a legal measure to dispense any of the four spirits above if the customer requests a different quantity.

However, there are advantages for the beginner if legal measures are used until he or she has had sufficient practice and acquired the necessary skills and judgement.

The use of legal measures can also assist in:
- controlling the price to be charged for the cocktail
- judging the correct size of glass to be used
- maintaining stock control procedures based on the number of legal measures that can be obtained from bottles of spirits and liqueurs.

Essential knowledge	The main reasons why you should use legal measures as far as possible when preparing cocktails are:
	● because you are required by law to use legal measures for certain types of alcoholic drink
	● because the price of the cocktail may have been calculated on the basis of legal measures of the liquids used
	● to maintain stock control procedures which are based on the number of legal measures that can be obtained from a bottle of a spirit or liqueur
	● to prevent giving short- or over-measures of alcoholic drinks and over- or under-charging customers, both of which are illegal and will also make customers dissatisfied with your establishment
	● to judge the size of glass that is needed to serve the cocktail
	● because failure to comply with the relevant laws can result in the licensee being prosecuted and fined.

PROVIDING CUSTOMERS WITH ACCURATE INFORMATION

Trade Descriptions laws

The Trade Descriptions Act makes it an offence to give a false or misleading description of any drink you serve. It is important that you give customers the correct information about the measures, price, relative strength and ingredients of any cocktail that you serve them.

Measures

Where cocktails and mixed drinks are being offered for sale, any description of the drink must be written with care. If any precise measures are given in the description of the cocktail, the drink must not contain less than those precise measures. However, in reality there are no legally prescribed measures for the parts of a cocktail and there is no need to advertise the measures involved.

If legal measures are not used in preparing the cocktail or mixed drink, it is better to describe the cocktail as a 'mixture' or 'blend' of the various liquids used in the recipe.

Prices

Care should also be taken where price lists are displayed for measures of spirits and other drinks. If the price charged for a mixed drink like a Dubonnet Cocktail (containing an equal measure of gin and Dubonnet) is greater than the displayed price for a single measure of each added together, the customer could complain that he or she has been overcharged.

Because of the Trade Descriptions laws, it is extremely important that you give the customer an accurate description of any cocktail and the price.

Relative strength

Many customers are now more conscious of the amount of alcohol that they drink, especially if they are driving. You should be able to advise them of the alcoholic strength of any drink that you serve them, although this may be difficult with some cocktails where several spirits and liqueurs are combined.

● If you have any doubts about the alcoholic strength of a drink, do not try to deceive the customer. Either consult a more experienced member of staff or your supervisor.

Ingredients

Be familiar with the contents of each drink and the main ingredients. If customers request information, you should be able to give them details.
● This may not apply to cocktails which are the 'speciality of the house'. While you might give customers a general indication of the contents of a drink, the actual proportions used in such a cocktail might be regarded as a trade secret.

Essential knowledge

It is important that you give customers accurate information about any cocktail that you serve, especially about the measure, price, strength and ingredients:
● to comply with the Trade Descriptions Act and other consumer laws
● to prevent customers becoming dissatisfied and feeling cheated or misled
● to prevent customers consuming a larger amount of alcohol than they wish, especially when drinking cocktails
● to prevent customers consuming any ingredient to which they may be allergic.
● to ensure that customers receive an efficient and high quality service.

However, you should not reveal any trade secrets related to any speciality cocktail offered exclusively by your establishment. Refer any enquiries to your supervisor.

Do this

1 Examine the optics and thimble measures used in your establishment. Which legal measures are used?
2 The legal measures used usually have to be advertised on the premises. Make a copy of any notice you find which states the measures used in your establishment.

PROMOTING COCKTAILS AND MIXED DRINKS

The skilled bar person is a salesman/woman who is selling the customer a product. You should have a positive approach and be alert to any opportunities for selling.

Timing

MEMORY JOGGER

What methods can you use to promote cocktails in your establishment?

Not all cocktails and mixed drinks are suitable for the same time of day or the same occasion. Part of the skill in promoting cocktails and mixed drinks is to know which ones you should promote at the appropriate times. (See the table on the next page).
● If customers are waiting for a meal, ask them if they would like an aperitif.
● If customers cannot make up their mind, suggest an appropriate cocktail.
● If you have sold a cocktail or a mixed drink, ask the customer how it is just before they finish. This may bring a repeat order.
● When collecting glasses or replacing ashtrays, ask the customers if you can freshen their drink for them.
● If you make your cocktails with a little flair and make the process appear exciting, you may interest other customers who are watching. The bar is like the stage in a theatre.
● Interesting decoration and garnishing may also attract other customers.
● Promote cocktails that you know you make well

Pre-dinner/Aperitif cocktails
Adonis
Bamboo
Bronx
Champagne drinks
Dry Martini
Dubonnet
Gibson
Manhattan
Old Fashioned
Rob Roy
Sweet Martini

Most of the above contain vermouth,
an aperitif wine.

Long, cool drinks
Americano
Buck's Fizz
Gin Fizz
Gin Sling
John/Tom Collins
Mint Julep
Pimms No. 1
Planter's Punch
Rum Cooler

Pick-me-ups
Egg Nogg

Prairie Hen
Prairie Oyster

After-dinner cocktails
Alexander
Between-the-sheets
Crème de Menthe Frappé
Golden Cadillac
Grasshopper
Rusty Nail
Sidecar

Fun drinks
Banana Daiquiri
Cuba Libre
Harvey Wallbanger
Horse's Neck
Pina Colada
Tequila Sunrise

Exotic drinks
Bleu-Do-It
Blue Hawaiian
Mai Tai
Margarita
Pousse Cafe
Scorpion
Silk Stockings
Zombie

*Major types of cocktail and
mixed drink*

Do this

✔

Find out how and when cocktails are promoted in your establishment. Look for:
(a) tent cards
(b) wall displays/lists
(c) sections on wine list/menu card
(d) cocktail hours.

TAKING ORDERS FOR COCKTAILS AND MIXED DRINKS

When taking orders for cocktails, there are several general rules you should follow.
● Where a list of cocktails is offered, make sure the list is clean and the details and prices are accurate.
● If a particular drink is not available, you should inform the customer when you give him or her the list.

Check for accuracy

Because the recipe for some cocktails can vary, you should check that you are meeting the customer's requirement. For example:
● If a customer requests a Dry Martini, you should check if this is simply a vermouth like Martini Extra Dry or the cocktail containing gin and vermouth. If it is the cocktail, you should ask what proportion of gin to vermouth the customer requires. Some recipes use $\frac{1}{6}$ vermouth to $\frac{5}{6}$ gin; others do not. Some customers prefer a lemon twist; others prefer an olive.

● Some recipes for the White Lady add a dash of egg white, others do not.
● Check on the use of sauces like Worcestershire and Tabasco in cocktails like the Bloody Mary. Some customers may not like them to be added.
● Repeat the order to the customer to check if all the drinks have been included.

Some customers may also use a name for a cocktail which you are not familiar with. If you are unsure, you should ask the customer to give you the recipe.

Customer incidents

If a customer returns a drink as being incorrect or faulty, you should replace the drink and enter the details of the returned drink into the bar wastage book.
● Complaints about short measure or over-charging should be referred to your supervisor as soon as possible.

Also see Unit 2NG3, Element 3.

PREPARING AND SERVING A RANGE OF COCKTAILS AND MIXED DRINKS

In Element 1 of this Unit, the four main methods of making cocktails and mixed drinks were introduced briefly. These were:
● stirring
● shaking
● building
● blending.

This section deals with each of these methods in more detail. Before considering each method, you should be aware of some general rules.
● If cocktails are included in a mixed order for drinks, you should make the cocktails after you have poured the other drinks. Cocktails should be served as freshly made as possible.
● Where a mixed order of cocktails is being made, you should make the long drinks over ice before you make the short, cold cocktails served without ice. A little melted ice in a long drink is less noticeable than a warm or separated short drink.
● Remember that because a cocktail is a mixture, the parts will begin to separate if the drink is left standing too long.
● Never put a fizzy or carbonated mineral or sparkling wine into a mixing glass, shaker or blender. Any fizzy drink shaken in a shaker will explode in the same way as it would if shaken in the bottle.
● Always put the cheapest ingredients into the mixing glass, shaker or blender first. If you make a mistake, you will only lose these cheaper ingredients, not the expensive ones like the spirits and liqueurs.
● Never re-use ice or glasses. Use fresh ice and a new glass for each drink you make and serve.
● When a recipe requires ice in a drink, always put it into the glass first and pour the liquid over it. Adding ice to the liquid can cause the drink to splash out or overflow.
● Use a drip tray below the glass when you are pouring a drink. If there is a spillage, this will prevent a messy counter.
● Do not fill glasses to the brim. This can make them difficult to carry and serve and could stain the customer's clothing.
● Lift stemmed glasses by the stem and tall glasses by the base. Do not put your fingers on the bowl or near to the rim where the customer will drink from.

MEMORY JOGGER

What are the general rules related to preparing and serving cocktails?

If you wish to obtain information on health and safety and food hygiene legislation you should contact:
- the Environmental Health Office of your local council
- the safety officer if you are employed in a large establishment
- the regional office of the Health and Safety Executive (Agency) or the HSE Information Centre in Sheffield.

Measures and proportions in cocktail recipes

Some cocktail recipes are written as proportions such as $\frac{1}{3}$ gin, $\frac{1}{3}$ Cointreau, $\frac{1}{3}$ lemon. Others are more vague and mention a 'measure' of a spirit and a '$\frac{1}{2}$ measure' of some other ingredient. Occasionally, a measure like a fluid ounce (fl. oz) is used. When preparing any of the following drinks, you should establish what measures are used in the establishment for the cocktails offered. The measures used will:
- affect the price to be charged
- affect the size of the glass you need to use.

The traditional and current legal measures and their imperial and metric equivalents are given in the table below.

Measures	Imperial equivalents	Metric equivalents
Traditional		
$\frac{1}{4}$ gill (4-out)	1.25 fl. oz	3.552 cl
$\frac{1}{5}$ gill (5-out)	1.00 fl. oz	2.841 cl
$\frac{1}{6}$ gill (6-out)	0.83 fl. oz	2.368 cl
Current		
25 ml	0.88 fl. oz	2.500 cl
35 ml	1.20 fl. oz	3.500 cl

Note
As there are no legal measures required for making cocktails if they contain a mixture of three or more liquids, some establishments may still use traditional measures when preparing cocktails although a mixture of imperial and metric measures in a bar is not permitted in most circumstances.

Traditional and current spirit measures

Do this

1 What questions would you ask a customer who had ordered:
   (a) a Dry Martini?
   (b) a Bloody Mary?
   (c) a Nutcracker?
2 Find out the method of pricing cocktails in your workplace. What measure does the establishment use?

Making stirred cocktails

Stirred cocktails are made in a mixing glass using a bar spoon or muddler. Stirring is used when the cocktail to be made is clear such as a Dry Martini.

Assemble your equipment
You will need:
- a mixing glass
- a bar spoon
- a strainer.

Procedure

1   Assemble your ingredients, prepare the garnishes, add plenty of ice to the mixing glass to cool it down from bar temperature. Glasses should be chilled with ice at the same time.
2   Holding the strainer across the top of the mixing glass, pour off any excess water from the ice.
3   Add the cocktail ingredients to the mixing glass and use the bar spoon to stir them around vigorously with the ice to mix and cool the liquids. Do not stir the mixture for too long or the ice will melt and weaken the cocktail.
4   Remove the spoon and hold the strainer across the top of the mixing glass. Tilt and strain the drink into an appropriate size of glass. (See the diagram below). Add the appropriate accompaniments.
5   Throw away the ice and clean all the equipment used as soon as possible.

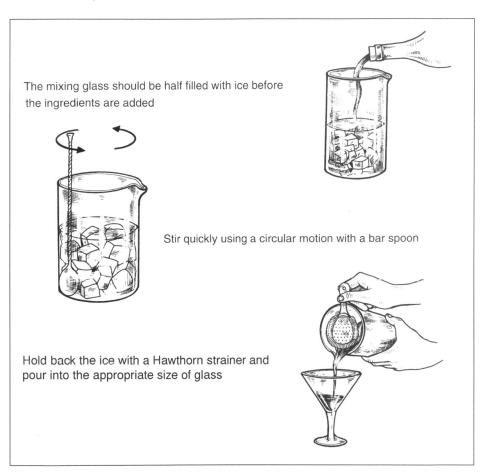

The mixing glass should be half filled with ice before the ingredients are added

Stir quickly using a circular motion with a bar spoon

Hold back the ice with a Hawthorn strainer and pour into the appropriate size of glass

Steps in mixing a stirred cocktail

Popular stirred cocktails

Examples of popular stirred cocktails are the Dry Martini, Manhattan, Rob Roy and Bamboo.

Making shaken cocktails

Shaking is used when the ingredients would not naturally mix together and could not easily be mixed by stirring. Some ingredients like syrups are thick and heavy; other ingredients like spirits tend to be thinner and lighter. Shaking is the most efficient method of combining such ingredients quickly as well as other ingredients like fruit juices, egg white and cream. Shaking is also used when the ingredients are not clear but opaque.

Assemble your equipment
You will need either a Boston shaker and Hawthorn strainer, or a standard shaker.

Procedure
1 Assemble your ingredients, prepare the garnishes and place plenty of ice in the shaker until it is approximately half full. Let the shaker cool down and then strain off the excess water. Use the Hawthorn strainer with the Boston shaker.
2 Add the cocktail ingredients to the ice and place the top of the shaker on securely.
3 Hold both the top and bottom of the shaker firmly using both hands for the Boston and either one or both hands for the standard shaker.
4 Shake quickly using short, sharp movements to mix the ingredients completely through the ice. Don't 'rock the baby to sleep'.
5 Strain the cocktail into an appropriately-sized glass and add the appropriate accompaniments.
6 Throw away the ice and wash the shaker and strainer thoroughly. Leave them to drain on a drip tray. (See the diagram below).

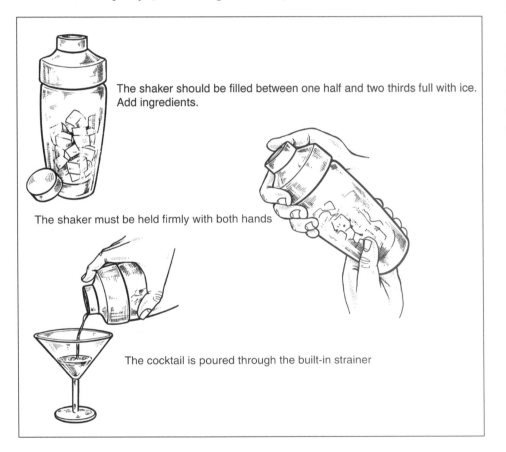

The shaker should be filled between one half and two thirds full with ice. Add ingredients.

The shaker must be held firmly with both hands

The cocktail is poured through the built-in strainer

Steps in shaking a cocktail

Popular shaken cocktails
Examples are the Alexander, Sidecar, White Lady and Between-the-Sheets.

Making built or poured cocktails and mixed drinks

Built cocktails and mixed drinks differ from the other three types in that they are made in the glass in which they are served. In some cases they are left unmixed, as in the Pousse Cafe, or they are stirred in the glass with a bar spoon or swizzle stick.

Popular built cocktails and mixed drinks
Examples are the Pousse Cafe, Harvey Wallbanger, Mint Julep and Horse's Neck.

Making blended cocktails and mixed drinks

MEMORY JOGGER

What are the general rules when working with a bar blender?

A blender or liquidiser is most commonly used when fresh fruits are required in a drink. Crushed ice is used, rather than cubed ice to add thickness and texture to the drink. Because the blender is an electrical appliance care should be taken when using it in the bar. See the table below.

Do	Don't
● Check the switch is in the OFF position before plugging it in to the power supply.	● Put your hand or any object into the blender while it is operating.
● Site the blender as far away from any water as possible.	● Leave leads trailing through wet areas or across passage-ways.
● Make sure the jug is firmly placed on the base before switching on.	● Remove the jug from the base before switching off as this will damage the machine.
● Make sure the lid is fitted securely to prevent liquids splashing out of the jug.	● Overfill the jug as it will not work properly or efficiently.
● Blend only for the recommended time.	● Push your hand into the blender while drying it as the blades are very sharp.

Using the bar blender

Assemble your equipment
You will need:
● a blender or liquidiser
● either a Hawthorn strainer or a strainer designed for the jug of the blender.

Procedure
1   Cut any solid ingredients into small chunks, assemble the other ingredients and have a good supply of crushed ice available. Prepare any garnishes.
2   Add all the ingredients to the jug of the blender and place the top firmly on the jug.
3   Place the jug onto the base and switch on for the recommended time.
4   Strain or pour the cocktail into an appropriately-sized glass. Add the appropriate accompaniments
5   Throw away the ice and any remnants.
6   Clean the jug by half filling it with warm (not boiling) water and switching it on for 20–30 seconds. Empty out the water and rinse with clean warm water. (See the diagram on the next page.)

Popular blended cocktails
These include Pina Colada, Banana Daiquiri, Silk Stockings and Scorpion.

Essential knowledge

The four main methods of preparing cocktails are:
● mixing using a mixing glass, bar spoon and strainer
● shaking with either a Boston or standard shaker
● building or pouring in the glass
● blending using a bar blender or liquidiser.

Do this

✔

Find out the recipes for the 16 alcoholic cocktails mentioned above and the four popular non-alcoholic cocktails listed below. Give details of the recipe for one of each and record the appropriate accompaniments.

Use the scoop to add the correct quantity of crushed ice to the blender

Chop any fruit into small chunks for most efficient blending

Pour straight into the glass or strain through a Hawthorn strainer

Steps in making a blended cocktail

Non-alcoholic cocktails

Because some customers may not wish to drink and drive, but still appreciate an interesting drink, you should also offer a range of non-alcoholic cocktails. These can also be promoted to young people who may not legally be sold alcoholic drinks, or as 'pick-me-ups' on the 'morning after'.

Popular non-alcoholic cocktails
These include the Parson's Special, Florida Cocktail, Shirley Temple and Pussyfoot.

Case study

When a young silver service waitress reported for duty, she was told to go and work in the cocktail lounge because they were short-handed. The bar manager told her to take orders at the table and come to the bar to have the drinks dispensed. Her evening started badly and didn't get any better. She served a couple two short cocktails. When she asked for payment after delivering the drinks, they ordered a repeat and said that they would pay for both rounds together. When she returned to the table with the second order, she found that the customers had left without paying. Later, a group of young people decided to have a joke with her and ordered a round of cocktails but deliberately mixed up the names. When she attempted to order them, the bar staff laughed at her and told her to go back and take the order properly.

Finally, when a customer who had to drive enquired about the alcoholic strength of a Zombie, she attempted to bluff him and said that it was just the same as a normal drink. A second customer at the next table leaned over and contradicted her and told her cus-

tomer that it was extremely alcoholic and at least the equivalent of a treble measure of spirits or more. The customer, a Trading Standards officer, complained angrily to the bar manager. The waitress was told to leave the lounge and was sent home.

1   *Who was mainly at fault for the situations that occurred?*
2   *What should the waitress have done before starting to take orders?*
3   *How could she have prevented the 'walk out' happening?*
4   *What law did she fail to comply with?*

What have you learned?

1   State what types of customer may not be sold alcoholic drinks and why they should not be served.
2   Why should you use legal measures to dispense some alcoholic drinks?
3   (a) Why is it important that you give customers accurate information about any drinks that you serve them?
     (b) Are there any exceptions?
4   Where can you obtain information about health and safety and food hygiene legislation?
5   Give two methods that you could use to promote cocktails.
6   What should you check when taking orders for cocktails and mixed drinks?
7   Why should you put the cheapest ingredients of the cocktail into the mixing glass, shaker or blender before the more expensive liquids?
8   In what order should you make a mixed order of cocktails? Why?
9   Why should you not put fizzy or carbonated drinks in a shaker?
10 Give two examples of each of the following types of cocktails:
     (a) stirred
     (b) shaken
     (c) built
     (d) blended
     (e) non-alcoholic.

Get ahead

1   Learning to make the 16 cocktails given above will give you the opportunity to acquire the basic techniques of making cocktails and mixed drinks. However, you should try to obtain a copy of a reliable cocktail book such as the *International Guide to Drinks* compiled by the United Kingdom Bartenders' Guild to find out the recipes for many well-known cocktails.
2   One popular method of promoting cocktails is to use colour themes and produce a range of cocktails all of the same colour. For example, green cocktails can be produced by using a liqueur like green Chartreuse, Midori or Crème de Menthe.
     Find out what liquids you could use to produce a range of cocktails that are all blue, pink or red, yellow, brown and orange.
3   Professional bartenders' associations like the United Kingdom Bartenders' Guild and the Bartenders' Association of Ireland often have cocktail-making competitions. Contact one of the professional associations and get information about any events being held locally.

Store, prepare and maintain cask conditioned beers

This unit covers:
ELEMENT 1: Store and prepare cask conditioned beer ready for service
ELEMENT 2: Maintain cask conditioned beer

ELEMENT 1: Store and prepare cask conditioned beer ready for service

---

What you need to do

- Handle casks safely and correctly during delivery and storage.
- Position casks correctly prior to preparing them for service.
- Make sure that casks are free from damage and that all equipment is clean and free from damage.
- Prepare casks for service using the correct procedures and equipment.
- Store casks correctly after preparation until they are put into service.
- Keep the storage area clean and tidy and maintain the correct storage conditions for the beer.
- Check that the beer is of the correct quality before putting the cask into service.
- Deal effectively with unexpected situations within your responsibilities and inform the appropriate people where necessary.
- Carry out your duties in an organised and efficient manner taking account of priorities, organisational procedures and legal requirements.

What you need to know

- What is cask conditioned beer.
- What the main cask sizes are and the main components of wooden and metal casks.
- Why you must handle casks carefully and correctly when they are delivered to the cellar and either stored or placed in position.
- Why the storage area must be kept clean and the storage conditions correctly maintained.
- How to prepare casks for service.
- How and why you should check that the beer is of the correct quality for service.
- How to deal effectively with unexpected situations.
- How to carry out your work in an organised and efficient manner.

Do this ✔

As you read through this unit you will meet some unfamiliar technical terms, many of which have alternatives which are used in different parts of the country.

Use a small notebook and, when you find an unfamiliar or technical word or phrase, make a note of it, write an explanation of it and add any alternatives that are given. For example, an entry might read:

Stillage – equipment used to hold a cask in position in either a cellar or a bar.

Alternative names: stillion, horsing, thrawl, gantry (gauntry)

CONDITIONING IN THE CASK

Cask conditioned beer, also known as 'real ale' or 'traditional ale', differs from keg beers because conditioning takes place in the cask.

Care should be taken not to confuse conditioning with 'condition' in the beer.
- *Conditioning* describes the changes (biological, chemical and physical) which occur during secondary fermentation and while the beer matures in the cask in the pub cellar.
- *Condition* in the beer refers to the amount of carbon dioxide in the beer which gives it sparkle and head.

THE STRUCTURE OF CASKS

Casks are traditionally made of wood, usually from oak. As wooden casks are difficult to clean and expensive to make and maintain, they have been largely replaced by metal casks.

Both wooden and metal casks have two openings:
- a bung hole on the body of the cask
- a tap hole on the narrow end section.

When casks are filled at the brewery, the tap hole is sealed with a 'keystone', a circular piece of hardwood or plastic which has a smaller circle cut into it. This smaller circle does not go completely through the keystone.

Older types of wooden cask occasionally have only a cork as a keystone. Modern types have a metal ring, called the 'keystone bush' around the tap hole to hold a wooden or plastic keystone.

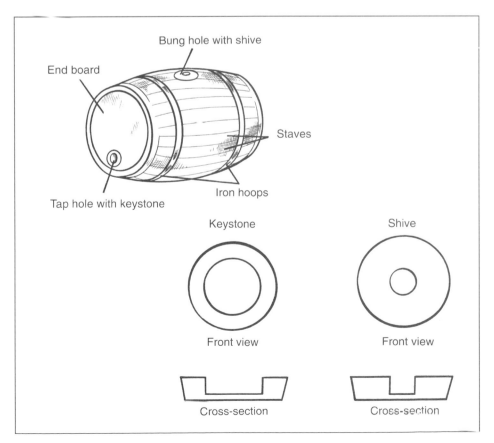

The structure of wooden casks

253

After filling, the bunghole is sealed with another circular piece of wood or plastic called a 'shive'. The shive has a hole drilled in it which also does not penetrate completely through (see the diagram on page 253). Some shives have small plugs made of wood, cork or plastic (known as a 'tit' or 'tut') set into them.

CASK SIZES

Traditional cask sizes are based on the 36-gallon barrel and are known by various names:

Traditional sizes	Names
4.5 gallons (36 pints)	Pin
9 gallons (72 pints)	Firkin or 'Nine'
18 gallons (144 pints)	Kilderkin, Kil, Kiln or 'Eighteen'
27 gallons (216 pints)	Half-hogshead
36 gallons (288 pints)	Barrel or 'Thirty-six'
54 gallons (432 pints)	Hogshead

Some breweries are now using metric sizes:

Metric sizes	Imperial equivalents
25 litres	about 5.5 gallons
50 litres	about 11 gallons
100 litres	about 22 gallons
150 litres	about 33 gallons

CASK TAPS

Traditionally, cask taps were always made from brass, sometimes plated with chrome. As brass contains lead, which can be harmful to health, these taps have been gradually replaced by those made from stainless steel or heavy duty plastic.

The commonest types found in the cellar for connection to the beer lines are:
- screw, or straight-ended
- turndown
- double-ended (to feed two lines).

When cask conditioned beer is to be served from casks mounted on the bar, a 'racking tap' is used. The taps used to dispense beer into beer lines are fitted with a hop filter to prevent sediment from entering the lines. The beer line is attached to a tail piece and connected by means of a threaded nut to the tap. (See the diagram on the next page.)

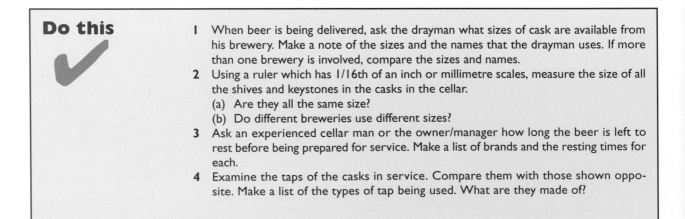

Do this

1 When beer is being delivered, ask the drayman what sizes of cask are available from his brewery. Make a note of the sizes and the names that the drayman uses. If more than one brewery is involved, compare the sizes and names.
2 Using a ruler which has 1/16th of an inch or millimetre scales, measure the size of all the shives and keystones in the casks in the cellar.
　(a) Are they all the same size?
　(b) Do different breweries use different sizes?
3 Ask an experienced cellar man or the owner/manager how long the beer is left to rest before being prepared for service. Make a list of brands and the resting times for each.
4 Examine the taps of the casks in service. Compare them with those shown opposite. Make a list of the types of tap being used. What are they made of?

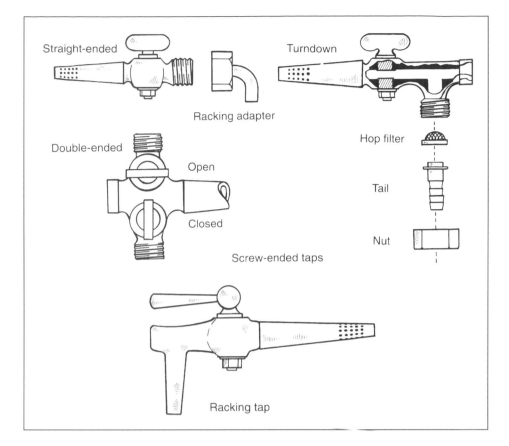

Common types of cask tap (courtesy of CAMRA Ltd)

RECEIVING AND STORING CASKS

Cellar hygiene and safety

This subject has been dealt with in detail in Unit 2NC7. Re-read the relevant sections to refresh your memory, if necessary.

The main point related to cask conditioned beers, not covered in that unit, is that beer lines not in use should be filled with water and regularly flushed to keep them in good condition.

Receiving casks

It is sometimes difficult to establish how long a beer has been in its cask as some brewers mark their casks with batch numbers, also called 'gyle' numbers, or with letters. Other brewers use a date label but this can refer to either:
● the date the beer was racked into the cask, or
● the date of shipment from the brewery.

When taking delivery of casks, do the following.
● Check with the drayman if the date labels refer to racking or shipment to obtain some estimate, if possible, of how long the beer has been in the cask. Use them in chronological order. Always use the lowest number or earliest date first.
● Chalk the delivery date on the casks so that you will at least know how long they have been in the cellar and be able to rotate your stock correctly on the 'first in, first out' principle.
● Handle casks carefully. Remember:
  – A 100-litre cask of beer will weigh over 100 kg (220 lb), more than enough to cause severe bruising or more serious injury if you mishandle it.

MEMORY JOGGER

What details should you check concerning the dating of casks when they are delivered?

255

     – A fall of only a few inches is enough to break the stave of a wooden cask or break the seal around the end boards. The resulting spillage will be very difficult to stop, leading to considerable wastage as well as an expensive repair for the brewery.

     – If the casks are too large to be carried flat to the storage area, they should be rolled there to mix the finings thoroughly with the beer.

Essential knowledge

When moving casks in the cellar or placing them into position for service, it is important that you use safe handling and lifting techniques.
- Check that the route you are to take is clear of obstructions and that you have adequate space for movement.
- Test the load to see if it is within your capacity to lift and carry.
- Wear heavy gloves and check whether there are any sharp areas like splits in the wood or damage to the rim of metal casks.
- Keep your feet apart to maintain your balance.
- Bend at the knees, keep your back straight and use your leg muscles to lift and take the strain of the load.
- Hold the load close to your body and avoid twisting when carrying it or placing it down.
- Bend at the knees, keeping the back straight when placing the load. Be careful about trapping fingers and toes.

If you have any doubts about your ability to lift or carry a particular load, don't attempt to move it without asking someone to help or use a mechanical hoist if one is available.

Storing casks

If there is enough stillage space in the cellar, casks should be placed in the serving position when they are delivered. If this is not possible, you should either store them on their side with the shive at the top or in an upright position if vertical stillaging is used.

- Wedge horizontally-stored casks with blocks to prevent them being disturbed or rolling about the cellar.
- If a cask is found to be leaking, wedge the cask with the leaking section uppermost and mark it as an ullage. Inform your supervisor so that the value of the contents of the cask can be claimed back from the brewery.

Storage conditions

In order to bring cask conditioned beers to maturity and to maintain them in good quality for service, you must pay careful attention to the cellar environment; in particular, to the temperature, humidity, ventilation and lighting in the cellar.

Re-read the sections on maintaining the cellar environment in Unit 2NC7 to refresh your memory, if necessary.

POSITIONING CASKS READY FOR SERVICE

The ideal situation is to place casks in their serving position when they are delivered. If there is not sufficient space to do this, casks should be set in position several days before being prepared for service.

Horizontal forms of stillage

The stillage (also called the stillion, horsing, thrawl/thrawll or the gantry/gauntry) is the name given to the equipment used to mount the casks into their service position.

The commonest form of stillage is to have two horizontal beams raised between 12 and 18 inches (300–450 mm) above the cellar floor. On the rear beam, wooden or metal 'saddles' are permanently fixed. (See the diagram below.)

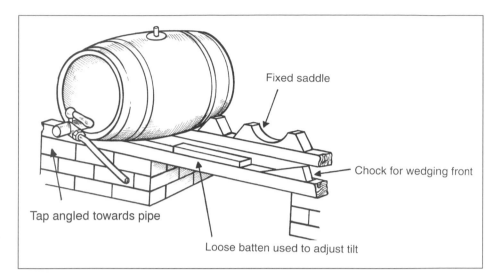

Fixed saddle

Chock for wedging front

Tap angled towards pipe

Loose batten used to adjust tilt

A traditional two-beam stillage system (courtesy of CAMRA Ltd)

Another common form of stillage is a concrete or brick shelf around the cellar wall. Wooden or steel saddles are firmly fixed to the shelf.

A number of self- and automatic-tilting devices are available as well as a number of stillage systems with mechanical tilting mechanisms. (See the diagram below.)

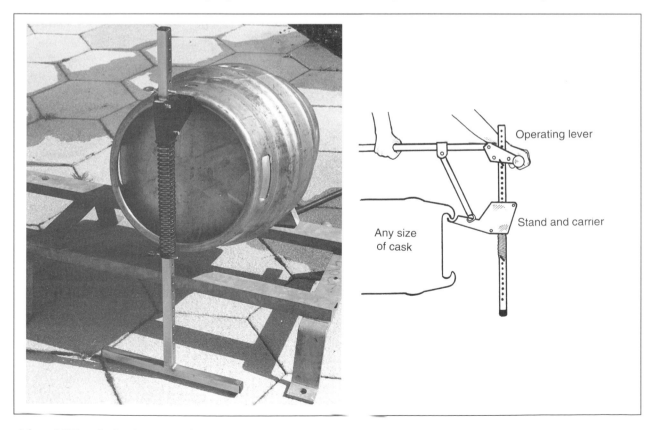

Operating lever

Stand and carrier

Any size of cask

A barrel tilting device (courtesy of Vegacourt Ltd)

Chocking with wooden wedges

The traditional method of positioning casks outside the cellar on, for example, bar counters or tables at beer festivals was to use wooden wedges (also known as scotches, chocks and blocks).

● The cask is supported at three points: two at the front; one at the rear. (See the diagram below.)
● The longest side of the wedge is placed in contact with the surface on which the cask is mounted (bar, table).
● There should always be finger clearance between the cask and the surface.
● After the cask has been chocked ('scotched'), it should be left undisturbed for as long as possible.

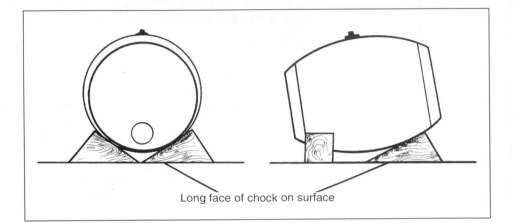

Positioning a cask with wooden chocks (courtesy of CAMRA Ltd)

Long face of chock on surface

Chocking with wooden wedges is no longer considered suitable for permanent stillage in the cellar.

Vertical forms of stillage

Putting casks in a horizontal form of stillage requires a fairly large amount of space and the weight of a large cask often makes it difficult for one person alone to handle. When vertical forms are used:

● casks are stored on their end faces with the keystone plug facing upwards
● the casks can be slightly tilted by using a thin piece of wood under one part of the base to encourage the sediment to gather up in one place.

The main advantage of this system is that casks can be placed anywhere in the cellar and used without having to be moved to new positions.

Cask hygiene

When the cask is in position on the stillage, inspect the keystone and shive for signs of dirt or mould growth. Regardless of how clean these look, they should both be scrubbed with a detergent-sterilant.

Remember that when you are preparing the cask for service (see *Venting and tapping* in the next section) parts of the keystone and shive are driven into the cask. If the parts driven into the cask are not cleaned, you may transfer infection into the cask and spoil the beer.

Each year almost 750 000 people have to take time off work because of injuries caused by the mis-handling of loads. It is important that you learn and use safe lifting techniques:
● to prevent injuries to yourself and other staff, such as back injuries, hernias, sprains, strains and crushed fingers and toes
● to prevent unnecessary damage to stock and equipment
● to comply with the employee's responsibilities under the Health and Safety and the Manual Handling Operations legislation.

Do this

1 Examine the casks in the cellar. Make a list of the brands available and the date labels or gyle marks on each cask. Try to identify which brewery uses a particular type of label.
2 Observe a delivery of casks from a brewery.
  (a) Ask the drayman if the date on the label refers to:
    – the date of racking, or
    – the date of dispatch from the brewery.
  (b) Examine the date labels. Do they all have the same date or are they mixed dates?
  (c) Ask about the effects of the Manual Handling regulations on delivering casks.
3 Observe how casks are stored on delivery. Note any of the following points:
  (a) The casks are placed on the stillions by the draymen.
  (b) The new casks are stored behind older ones and chocked into position.
  (c) Casks are stored in either a horizontal or vertical position.
4 Draw a rough sketch of the type of stillion used in the cellar. Note the use of any of the following:
  (a) two-tier systems
  (b) automatic or manual tilting mechanisms
  (c) the use of wood or steel in their construction.

PREPARING CASKS FOR SERVICE

When the cask is in position, three operations must be performed to prepare it for service. These are:
● venting or spiling
● tapping
● connecting the beer line.

Before you proceed with these operations, you need to consider when you should perform the operations and the equipment you will require.

Timing
The instructions from the brewery supplying the beer should be followed as closely as possible. Some breweries recommend that casks be vented on delivery, but this can only be done if casks are in their service position on the stillage.

Generally, casks should be vented two to three days before being used. However, low condition beers may only require a few hours after venting and tapping before being ready to serve.

Equipment
You should make sure that you have got all the equipment you will need for each operation before beginning it.

Venting and tapping casks in a horizontal position

Venting or spiling

Assemble your equipment.
You will need:
- a hardened steel punch or spiling tool
- a soft spile or venting peg (see the diagram below)
- a wooden or rubber mallet
- a hand-towel
- a protective apron or suitable waterproof clothing.

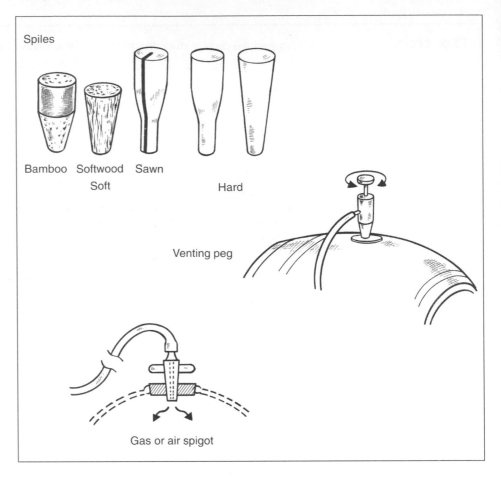

Spiles

Bamboo Softwood Sawn
       Soft

Hard

Venting peg

Gas or air spigot

Methods of preparing casks for service (courtesy of CAMRA Ltd)

Procedure

1 Pierce the shive
- Make sure the shive is clean.
- Place the end of the spiling tool or punch into the hole in the shive.
- Cover your hand and the spiling tool with a bar towel to prevent beer being sprayed around the cellar if the pressure in the cask is very high.
- Strike the head of the spiling tool sharply and cleanly with the mallet to pierce the shive.

2 Insert the soft spile
- Hold the soft spile in your free hand close to the shive.
- When the spiling tool is withdrawn, place the soft spile immediately in the shive and hold it firmly in place.
- Tap in the soft spile with the mallet until it is firmly held in the shive.

3 Clean the equipment

- If there has been any spillage, you should clean this up immediately with an appropriate detergent.
- The spiling tool should be cleaned and placed in storage.

The length of time the soft spile needs to be in place will vary with the amount of condition in the beer. High condition beers will require a longer venting period than low condition beers.

Quick tip

It is important to check from time-to-time that the soft spile is not saturated with yeast or that the spile hole is not blocked with hops which prevents proper venting.

- Remove the soft spile carefully twice each day while venting to check the spile is working efficiently.
- If you have a good stock of soft spiles, fit a new spile each time you check.

---

4 Insert the hard spile

Test when the soft spile needs to be replaced by a hard spile by wiping the froth from the top of the soft spile. If bubbles start to form on or around the soft spile, do not replace it. If no bubbles form after a short time, remove the soft spile and tap in a hard spile.

The hard spile is used to seal the cask and keep the rest of the carbon dioxide sealed in the cask, which is necessary to keep the beer in good condition.

Some low condition beers do not require soft spiles as there is very little secondary fermentation. These beers should have a hard spile fitted when venting to preserve their condition.

Tapping

The time to insert the tap into a cask depends on the nature of the beer. Generally, you should follow the brewery's instructions. There are three possibilities. Casks can be tapped:

- when the cask is vented
- one or two days before being used
- several hours before being required for service.

Ideally, casks should be tapped at least several hours before being required for service to allow for any sediment disturbed by the process to settle.

Assemble your equipment

You will need:

- two taps (which have been sterilised) in case one leaks
- a spare keystone of the same size as that in the cask to be tapped in case the keystone splits
- a heavy wooden or rubber mallet
- a clean bucket, preferably with a lid.

Preparation

1. Make sure the keystone is clean.
2. Make sure that the tap is clean and working smoothly.
3. Check the position of the beer line to which the cask is to be connected so that the tap end can be correctly angled. For example, the tap end can be faced to the right if the pipe comes from that direction.
4. Place the bucket directly beneath the keystone.
5. Remove the hard spile.

Procedure

1. Take the tap in one hand with the threaded end facing the direction where it will meet the beer line.
2. Place the other end of the tap against the keystone. It should be held square to

---

MEMORY JOGGER

What checks should you make before inserting a tap into a cask?

the keystone and in the centre of the cut out.

3   With the mallet in the other hand give one or two gentle 'feeler' strokes and then drive the tap home with one sharp blow.

4   Once the tap is driven home, do not hit it again or the keystone plug might split.

5   Close the tap if it was opened and replace the hard spile in the shive.

6   Check for leaks in and around the keystone and in the tap.

Do this ✔

1   Examine the soft spiles if these are used in the cellar. What are they made of?

2   Make a list of the brands of cask conditioned beers offered for sale in your establishment. Find out what is the recommended timing for venting the different brands before service. Write the timing next to each brand.

3   Find out how long before being used that casks are tapped. Is it the same for each brand? Using the brand list you made for **2** above, write in the time before service that each brand is tapped.

Venting and tapping casks in a vertical position

Where beer is to be dispensed from a cask in the vertical position, a different procedure is required. The beer is extracted by means of a cask syphon system which consists of a body section and an extraction tube or 'lance' (see the diagram below for the components of the system). Both venting and tapping are done through the keystone plug. The shive is not used.

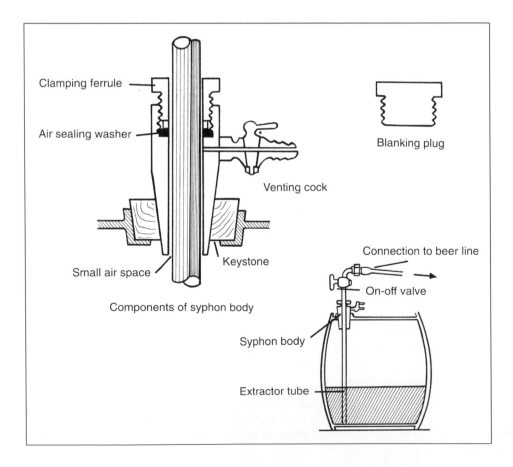

Components of a vertical system (courtesy of CAMRA Ltd)

Tapping
1 Make sure the keystone plug is clean.
2 Fit a blanking plug to the top of a clean and sterilised body section.
3 Drive the body section into the keystone with a single sharp blow.

Venting
Venting is done by means of a venting cock on the body section. Open the venting cock very slowly.

If the beer is lively, a tube can be fitted to the venting cock and run to a container to catch the liquid forced out.

CONNECTING THE BEER LINE

Before connecting the beer line to the tap, it is important to check the beer in the cask for quality and to remove any loose sediment that may have lodged in the tap after the tapping operation.

When casks are in a horizontal position, you should open the tap and draw off the beer into a straight-sided glass. Keep drawing off about half a pint at a time up to three pints or until the beer is bright and clear. Smell and taste the beer to check that all is well. If the beer does not clear, leave it to settle before repeating this procedure.

Casks in a horizontal position

Assemble your equipment

You will need:
● a washer
● a hop filter
● a tail piece
● a nut to match the thread on the tap end
● a spanner to match the nut.

Procedure
1 **Check the beer line**
   It is important to check that the cask to be connected is the same brand as the cask being replaced. All beer lines should be marked with the appropriate beer name.
2 **Assemble the tap fittings**
   ● Into the threaded tap end insert a washer, a hop filter (often combined with the washer in one piece) and the tail piece. On some fittings the tail piece may already be fitted into the line.
   ● Slip the nut over the beer line, if this is necessary.
   ● Connect the beer line to the tail piece, if necessary, and move the nut up to the threads on the tap end.
   ● Tighten the nut until it is hand tight. Open the cask tap. If no leaks appear with the nut hand tight, it should not be necessary to tighten it with a spanner.
   ● If the tap leaks, tighten the nut with the spanner.
3 **Remove the hard spile**
   To draw up beer through the line, you must remove the hard spile slowly and gently before the cask is put into service.

Connecting casks to gas or air systems

Because the beer in casks is exposed to air when the hard spile is removed, it can lose condition or become sour within two to three days of being put in service. To extend the service life of beer, a number of systems have been developed. These include top pressure, blanket pressure, air pressure and air filtration.

All these systems require the hard spile to be replaced with a spigot. After venting the cask, you should remove the soft spile and replace it with a gas spigot which should be screwed tightly into the vent hole in the shive.

● Make sure the gas pressure release valve (if fitted) in the spigot is screwed into the closed position.
● Make sure the gas non-return valve is in position before the pipe carrying the carbon dioxide, nitrogen, or air is connected.

Casks in a vertical position

When the cask is in a vertical position, it is more difficult to extract a sample for checking before putting a cask into service. Use a long glass tube or pipette to extract several samples of beer. Pour these into a straight-sided glass to check for clarity, odour and taste.

Assemble your equipment

You will need:

● an extraction tube (also called a syphon tube, extractor or 'lance') which has been cleaned and sterilised, a clamping seal or ferrule, and possibly an air sealing washer
● a new washer
● a hop filter
● a tail piece (sometimes)
● a nut which matches the syphon thread
● a spanner.

Procedure

1 Remove the blanking plug from the head of the body section.
2 Place the clamping ferrule on the extractor tube. Make sure the air sealing washer in the syphon body is in good condition.
3 Insert the extractor tube to the required depth. Remember the beer will clear downwards from the top. You can adjust the depth as required.
4 Tighten the clamping ferrule.
5 Connect the beer line as described above for casks in a horizontal position. Open the valve at the head of the extractor.
6 The venting cock should be opened when the cask is in service.

Once these operations have been completed, the beer is ready for service to your customers. However, it is always advisable to draw off some beer from the beer engine in the bar to ensure that any sediment drawn into the line from a cask you are replacing is cleared from it before service to customers is resumed.

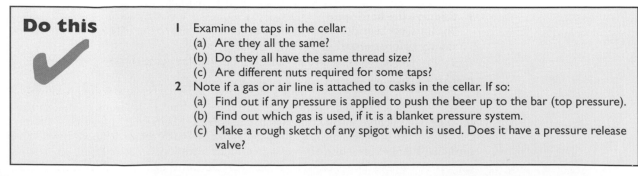

Do this

1 Examine the taps in the cellar.
  (a) Are they all the same?
  (b) Do they all have the same thread size?
  (c) Are different nuts required for some taps?
2 Note if a gas or air line is attached to casks in the cellar. If so:
  (a) Find out if any pressure is applied to push the beer up to the bar (top pressure).
  (b) Find out which gas is used, if it is a blanket pressure system.
  (c) Make a rough sketch of any spigot which is used. Does it have a pressure release valve?

Essential knowledge

The main reasons why you must handle casks correctly when delivered and in storage are because:
- the weight of a full cask is sufficient to cause serious injury if it should fall on a person or if a person is struck by one out of control
- wooden casks, in particular, can be easily damaged if they are dropped even a few inches. Collision with other casks and walls can also damage a cask
- damage to casks can cause them to 'weep' and leak into the cellar. Spoilage organisms in the air may also enter the cask and infect the beer making it sour
- casks should be used on a 'first in, first out' basis and newly delivered casks stored apart from casks previously delivered
- newly delivered casks should be chocked in the correct position with the bung hole upwards so that they may be rested and reach the correct temperature as soon as possible
- ideally, casks should be stored in their serving position on the stillage close to the beer line to which they will be connected in order to ensure a smooth changeover when a cask is replaced.

Case study

During a busy service session, the best bitter ran out. At the same time a new delivery was being brought into the cellar. The barman rushed down and told the draymen to place a new 150-litre cask onto the stillage. He pulled out the tap from the old barrel with the line still attached and attempted to drive it into the keystone of the new barrel. Because of the problem caused by the attached beer line, he had to strike a second hard blow to drive it home. He split the wooden keystone and the cask began to empty out onto the cellar floor. He began to panic and, as the draymen had left, he attempted to lift the barrel into an upright position to stop the leakage. While trying to lift the front of the cask, he slipped and the cask fell, trapping and crushing the fingers on his right hand. He escaped shortly afterwards when the cask had almost completely emptied and he was at last able to move it.

1 *The barman made a number of basic mistakes, especially in relation to health, safety and hygiene, as well as with normal operating procedures for preparing casks for service. Identify as many as you can.*
2 *Taking each step in sequence, outline what procedures he should have followed.*

What have you learned

1 Explain the difference between the terms 'conditioning' and 'condition' in relation to beer.
2 What names are given to the two openings in a cask and the plugs used to seal them?
3 What are the traditional names given to casks containing 18, 36 and 54 gallons? How are the contents of casks frequently expressed at present?
4 What problems can arise with date labels on casks? What can you do to make sure they are used in the correct order?
5 How should you store casks in a horizontal position?
6 Before you vent or tap a cask it is important to check that the shive and keystone are clean. Why?
7 What three operations have to be performed to bring a cask in position on the stillage into service?
8 When should you replace the soft spile with a hard spile?
9 State the main reasons why you should handle casks correctly during delivery and storage.

ELEMENT 2:   Maintain cask conditioned beer

What you need to do

- Check the level of beer in casks in service observing the relevant Food Hygiene regulations and establishment procedures.
- Tilt casks when the beer level falls to the appropriate point.
- Seal casks during service breaks using the appropriate equipment.
- Seal empty casks and store them ready for collection.

- Maintain the correct storage conditions in the cellar.
- Deal effectively with unexpected situations within your responsibilities and inform the appropriate people where necessary.
- Carry out your duties in an organised and efficient manner taking account of priorities, organisational procedures and legal requirements.

What you need to know

- Why the level of beer in casks in service should be checked regularly and how to check the level.
- How to tilt casks in service correctly when required.
- Why casks should be sealed between service sessions.

- How to seal empty casks and store them ready for collection.
- How to deal effectively with unexpected situations.
- How to carry out your work in an organised and efficient manner.

INTRODUCTION

When casks are in service they must be checked frequently to ensure that the quality and efficiency of service is maintained. Basically, four operations are involved:
- checking the level of beer in the cask
- tilting the cask (also known as 'stooping')
- spiling between service sessions
- maintaining the cellar to prevent problems arising with the beer.

When casks are empty, they must be sealed and removed from the stillage and stored ready for collection.

CHECKING THE LEVEL OF BEER

The level of beer in each cask should be checked between each service. This is normally done using a dipstick inserted through the shive.

Dipsticks are usually in the form of a four-sided rod or a strip with four cask sizes engraved on them. Separate dipsticks are required for each type of cask used in the cellar – wooden, metal or steel-lined.

Casks in a horizontal position

The best time to check the level of beer in the cask is immediately at the end of each service session. If a cask requires tilting, this operation is best done several hours before the cask is used again.

Remove the dipstick from its storage location. If it has not been kept in a sterilising solution, it must be sterilised before use to prevent the beer becoming infected.

Procedure
1. Remove the hard spile or gas spigot from the shive. Remember to disconnect the gas supply where top or blanket pressure systems are in use.
2. Make sure the dipstick is dry and insert it vertically into the hole in the shive until it reaches the bottom of the cask. Try to avoid any unnecessary movement

of the dipstick when it is in the cask as this will disturb the sediment.

3 Lift the dipstick cleanly from the cask and note the level of beer in the cask. Where several casks are in service, the level can be chalked on the cask or other record kept.

4 Clean and dry the dipstick after measuring each cask to avoid transferring infection from one cask to another.

5 When the level of beer in each cask in service has been measured, the dipstick should be either cleaned and placed in storage or placed into a trough of sterilising solution.

Casks in a vertical position

Whether or not you will need to use a dipstick where the syphon system is used will depend on how the extractor is inserted.

● If the extractor is only partially inserted, it is possible to check the level of beer in the cask by loosening the clamping ferrule and raising the extractor until air is drawn through the top holes.

● If the extractor is fully inserted, removing the extractor completely from the cask will give an indication of the level of beer in the cask.

Precise measurement of the amount left in the cask requires the use of a dipstick which is designed to measure the various sizes of cask in a vertical position.

Procedure: Using a dipstick

1 Close the valve at the top of the extractor to prevent the beer running back and disturbing the sediment.

2 Undo the clamping ferrule and withdraw the extractor tube from the cask. Make sure it is kept clean while out of the cask.

3 Insert the dipstick through the hole in the syphon body until it reaches the bottom of the cask avoiding any unnecessary movement.

4 Withdraw the dipstick cleanly from the cask and note the level.

5 After using the dipstick, put the extractor back into the syphon body, re-tighten the clamping ferrule and very slowly open the valve to re-fill the extractor tube without disturbing the sediment.

You should observe the same hygiene rules given above when using a dipstick with casks in a horizontal position.

Leaking casks

If a cask in a horizontal position is found to be leaking ('weeping'), it should be taken out of service and sealed as described below. It should then be taken to the collection area and chocked with the leaking part uppermost. The cask should then be marked as an ullage and your employer informed so that the value of its contents can be reclaimed from the brewery.

Tilting the cask

The ideal situation would be to set casks in their final serving position from the start so that no tilting is necessary. This is not always possible:

● because of the amount of sediment in the beer, and/or

● because the cask will leak from the shive if it is completely tilted.

However, withdrawing two or three pints from the cask can prevent this type of leakage.

Timing

Casks should be tilted to their final serving position when they are between one-third and two-thirds full. This allows any sediment disturbed to settle back evenly.

The best time to tilt casks is after service ends at night. This allows up to 12 hours for any sediment disturbed to settle and the beer to fall bright.

Final tilt angle

The cask should be tilted to the point where the curve at the tap end of the cask is horizontal (see the diagram below). This should give the cask a fall of approximately three inches from the back to the front.

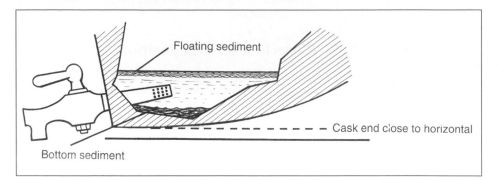

Final tilt angle (courtesy of CAMRA Ltd)

Procedure for tilting the cask

There are several different methods of tilting depending on how the cask is mounted on the stillage. Whichever method is used, the whole procedure should be done very gently to prevent the beer sloshing backwards and forwards in the cask and disturbing the sediment. When tilting, you should observe the following general rules.

- Tilt the cask slowly in a single, uninterrupted movement until it reaches the final tilt angle.
- Do not over-tilt the cask. Over-tilting can:
  - disturb the sediment if you have to drop the cask back again
  - cause the sediment to collect around the tap and be drawn into the beer line
  - angle the tap end towards the surface of the beer where it can draw in the floating sediment ('top break') as the beer runs out.
- Before tilting the cask, make sure it is firmly held at the opposite point from which you are raising or lowering the cask.

When tilting a cask which is mounted on chocks in the bar, you should:
1 check the front chocks are securely in position
2 lean over the cask from the front
3 hold the back rim with one hand and lift gently
4 slide the rear chock forward with your free hand until the cask is in the correct position.

If the cask is tilted correctly then the maximum amount of beer can be extracted without too much wastage. Any faults with the equipment used to tilt casks should be reported to your supervisor immediately.

Spiling between service sessions

If a cask is in a vertical position you should close the venting cock at the end of each service session. When a cask is in the horizontal position and where no pressure system is used, you should tap in the hard spile at the end of each service session. The cask must be sealed to prevent all the carbon dioxide escaping from the beer, leaving it flat. Sealing the cask between service sessions also reduces the exposure of the beer to spoilage organisms.

- The hard spile should be removed when service is resumed. Do not leave the hard spile resting loosely in the shive as it can be drawn back into the hole when beer is drawn from the cask.

- Where a carbon dioxide top pressure system is used, you should turn off the gas supply to the cask when it is not in service to prevent the beer absorbing too much gas and becoming difficult to serve.
- When a cask is not in frequent use in the bar, it is best to leave the hard spile in and only remove it when a drink is to be drawn from the cask.

Do this ✔

1 Locate where the dipsticks are stored in the cellar. Note the following points:
   (a) Are they the rod or strip type?
   (b) What are they made of?
2 If the dipstick is used for measuring more than one size of cask, make a note of the height of the beer (inches/millimetres) in the various sizes of cask when one gallon is left. For example:

   Pin   86mm
   Firkin   69mm
   Barrel   45mm

3 Find out how casks are tilted in the cellar. Write out a set of instructions for yourself for tilting a cask.
4 If casks are tilted by mechanical means, make a rough sketch of the mechanism involved.

Essential knowledge

The main reasons why you should frequently check the level of cask conditioned beer are:
- to recognise when it is necessary to tilt the cask to its final serving position
- to prevent the level of beer in the cask falling below the level (approximately one-third full) at which the sediment will be highly disturbed by tilting
- to alert the bar staff if a cask is being used too slowly because they are using its pump infrequently
- to prevent wastage by not using the beer quickly enough or by drawing sediment through the beer line if the level falls too low
- to avoid wasting beer which becomes cloudy with sediment when pulled through the pipe either because the level in the cask is too low or the cask is over-tilted.

REPLACING A CASK

Because of the floating sediment ('top break') and bottom sediment ('bottom break'), it is not possible to completely empty a cask. Ideally, the cask should be taken out of service and replaced before any sediment is drawn through the beer line.

Procedure
1 Turn off the cask tap or the valve on the extractor tube.
2 Unscrew the nut connecting the beer line to the tap or extractor.
3 Disconnect the pipe from the tail piece in the tap or extractor, if necessary.
4 Drain the beer from the line into a bucket below the tap. Follow the establishment's procedure in disposing of this beer.
5 Test the beer in the new cask for clarity, smell and taste.
6 Connect up the beer line to the new cask (as described above).
7 Open the cask tap or valve on the extractor tube.
8 Remove hard spile, open venting cock or switch on gas supply.
9 Draw the beer up through the beer engine in the bar to expel air from the line until the beer flows properly.

PREPARING A CASK FOR COLLECTION

When a cask is empty, it should be sealed immediately. The lees or 'bottoms' should be left in the cask.

Procedure

1 Drive the hard spile tight into the shive.
2 Remove the tap or extractor and syphon body from the keystone and seal the hole immediately with a cork bung.
   Sealing the cask reduces the possibility that it will become fouled and makes it easier to clean and sterilise.
3 Remove empty casks from the stillage as soon as possible to leave space for new casks to be positioned.

If there is not a separate area to store empty casks, they should be placed in an upright position and marked as empty so that they can easily be identified.

MEMORY JOGGER

How should you seal empty or ullage casks ready for collection? Why?

MAINTAINING STORAGE CONDITIONS

It is important that the conditions in the cellar are kept as close as possible to the ideal. It requires regular attention to the cellar conditions to provide cask conditioned beers with the care necessary for them to be served properly to the customer.

Develop a routine which allows you to control the most important aspects of the cellar environment:
● temperature
● humidity
● ventilation
● lighting.

Temperature

It is important to bring the beer down to cellar temperature as soon as it is delivered. It is equally as important to maintain the beer at a constant temperature (13–14°C) while it is in service.
● If the beer gets too cold, it may develop a 'chill haze' which can be permanent.
● If the beer gets too hot, even for a short period, the finings will not work properly and the beer will become cloudy.
● If the temperature is allowed to vary up and down rapidly, this will disturb the beer and it can become cloudy.

Some form of cooling may be required in the summer months. There are several methods of providing cooling in the cellar. Apart from the methods described in previous units, there are also:
● in-cask cooling coils which fit into the cask through the bung (shive) hole
● cooling jackets connected to a beer-line cooler which circulates cold water.

Humidity

It is important that the level of humidity (dampness) in the cellar should be kept as low as possible to prevent moulds and bacteria from developing and infecting the beer.

Ventilation

Poor ventilation is the main cause of high humidity and the growth of cellar mould. Effective regular ventilation must be provided to control the atmosphere in the cellar and keep it free from contamination. If the cellar air is not fresh and clean, bacteria, spores from moulds, yeast and off-flavours can develop in the beer.

Lighting

The level of lighting in the cellar should be sufficient to enable you to carry out routine work safely and to light up all areas of the cellar so that dirt will not build up unnoticed.

Do this

1 Find out the procedure for removing empty casks. Note:
 (a) How are they sealed?
 (b) Where are they stored?
 (c) In what position (horizontal/vertical) are they stored?
 (d) Are they marked in any way?
2 Find out from the drayman or brewery what the ideal storage temperature is for their beers. Make a list of the brands and the ideal cellar temperature for each.
3 Describe any method of controlling the cellar temperature that you find in your workplace.
4 Draw a rough sketch of the cellar and mark any doors, ventilation flaps, windows, air vents or air bricks that you find.

Case study

The licensee of an establishment, who prided himself on selling real ale in the best condition possible, was surprised when customers began to return drinks and to complain about their beer being cloudy and having an off-taste. The problems seemed to occur especially just after opening in the morning when a particular barman was on duty. The licensee made a point of going down to the cellar one morning when the barman was working there. He saw him using a funnel to return several buckets of waste beer from the previous night into one of the casks. The barman then went on to each of the other casks and began to take readings with the dipstick. Each time he stirred the cask. When he began to tilt the casks, he let several of them drop down suddenly before adjusting the chocks.
1 *How was the barman responsible for the poor condition of the beer?*
2 *How should he have performed his duties?*
3 *How was he in breach of Food Safety and Food Hygiene Regulations?*

What have you learned

1 When is the best time to check the level of beer in casks? Why?
2 Why is it important to avoid any unnecessary movement of the dipstick when measuring the beer remaining in a cask?
3 When is the best time to tilt casks? Why?
4 What problems are likely to occur if you over-tilt a cask?
5 Why is it important to spile a cask between service sessions?
6 If a carbon dioxide gas pressure system is used, why should you switch off the gas between service sessions?
7 State the main reasons why you should check the level of cask conditioned beers frequently?
8 Why is it important to seal an empty cask?
9 Why is it important to try to maintain cask conditioned beer at a constant temperature in the cellar?

Get ahead

1 Find out about how beer is made. Look in a good reference book like an encyclopaedia or find a book about beer-making in your local library.

2 Find out about the conditioning process for cask conditioned beer. Try and get information from one of your establishment's suppliers about racking, priming, fining, secondary fermentation and maturing.

3 Make a list of the tools and equipment used for working with casks in the cellar. Find out the names of suppliers for major items like taps, mallets, dipsticks and so on from your supervisor.

4 Sometimes casks are connected to gas or air systems. Try to obtain a copy of a publication like *Cellarmanship*, published by CAMRA, and find out more about these systems.

Index

Page references in italics indicate illustrations